KU-539-865

ROGER CROSS

The Yorkshire Ripper

Grafton

An Imprint of HarperCollins*Publishers*

Grafton
An Imprint of HarperCollins*Publishers*
77–85 Fulham Palace Road,
Hammersmith, London W6 8JB

A Grafton Original 1981
9 8 7 6 5 4

Copyright © Roger Cross 1981

The Author asserts the moral right to
be identified as the author of this work

A catalogue record for this book
is available from the British Library

ISBN 0 586 05526 6

Set in Times

Printed in Great Britain by
HarperCollinsManufacturing Glasgow

All rights reserved. No part of this publication may be
reproduced, stored in a retrieval system, or transmitted,
in any form or by any means, electronic, mechanical,
photocopying, recording or otherwise, without the prior
permission of the publishers.

This book is sold subject to the condition that it shall not,
by way of trade or otherwise, be lent, re-sold, hired out or
otherwise circulated without the publisher's prior consent
in any form of binding or cover other than that in which it
is published and without a similar condition including this
condition being imposed on the subsequent purchaser.

Acknowledgements

My thanks, particularly, to Jonathan Margolis; also to: Jill Armstrong, Trevor Atkins, Mick Bateson, Michael Bilton, Bill Bridge, Michael Brown, Paul Calverley, Lorna Cross, John Edwards, Clive Entwistle, John Fisher, Terry Fletcher, Derek Foster, Bruce Greer, George Hill, Malcolm Hoddie, Tom Hopkinson, Derek Hudson, David Kerr, Angus King, Esther Leach, Jack Windsor Lewis, Chris Oakley, Sue Pape, David Parry, Stephen Shaw, Ian Smith, Gavin Summers, Jeremy Thompson, Jack Tordoff, Stanley Vaughan, Alan Whitehouse, and to every policeman kind enough to discuss the case over the five years, officially and unofficially.

Photographs: West Yorkshire police and Yorkshire Post Newspapers Ltd; photograph of the Sutcliffe house by Jack Tordoff.

Contents

1: Distant Voices 7

2: Growing Pains 41

3: So Sweet, So Clear 73

4: Near, but Far 89

5: Over-Controlled 107

6: 'Nice Talking to You, George' 119

7: Different Voices 177

8: Lost Weekend 199

9: Retrospective 231

Epilogue: Better Let Him Sleep? 241

CHAPTER 1

Distant Voices

When Sgt. Robert Ring used to patrol the sprawling Wybourne council estate he set some sort of record for spotting disqualified drivers. He never forgot a face. Ten minutes before 11 p.m. on the second day of the New Year (1981) Ring, a policeman in Sheffield for 26 years, sat in a South Yorkshire Police Chevette 'Panda' car and studied the V8 Rover 3500 in the drive of Light Trades House, headquarters of BISPA (British Iron and Steel Producers Association), off Melbourne Avenue, leafy and dark, perfect for 'business'.

P.C. Robert Hydes was 31, a father of two, although still only a probationer with the force. He had been in less than a year since deciding to leave his job in the engineering industry. It would be good experience for him to go and speak to the young lady in the car and see what her game was. They strolled up to the Rover and tapped on the driver's window. The man with the jet-black beard and wavy, almost crinkly hair, seemed nervous, agitated. His name, he claimed, was Peter Williams, and this was his girlfriend.

By the time that first weekend of the year was over P.C. Hydes and Sgt. Ring were the most famous coppers in the world. The girl in the passenger seat of the Rover was just glad to be alive.

For most Yorkshiremen, Airedale starts, or perhaps ends, in the northern fringes of Bradford, brushing the extremities of the wool city, winding away to the north west, onwards and upwards towards Lancashire – one of Yorkshire's Dales in the sense that it is called a dale, and the brown and busy river Aire flows at its heart. But Airedale is different from the Wharfdales and the Swaledales, the Nidderdales and Langstrothdales. Climbing out of the centre of Bradford the road levels and for a mile or so you are in Asia. The buildings are still soot-stained, but the woodwork of the shops and houses is brightly painted. The streets leading off Manningham Lane take you to Lumb Lane and Oak Lane, the heart of Bradford's immigrant community – the country people and peasants who jetted from the East to a new life in the bosom of Empire.

Bradfordians and the discerning from surrounding towns have discovered you can buy almost anything in this busy segment of the city; silks, spices and renowned Indian and Pakistani foodstuffs at the myriad small, often modest, eating places; Bharjis and Bhounas, Biryanis and Kebabs, served on formica-topped tables by dark faces with the broadest of Yorkshire accents. In the same area you can also buy sex. Yet Manningham Lane, dismissed contemptuously and unfairly by the ignorant as nothing more than an offensive red-light blight on the city, soon changes. The imposing stone houses, Victorian and Edwardian, have had the soot blasted away by the time the road begins to descend gently towards Shipley. The river Aire is to the right in the bottom of the valley. Before you reach the park gates on the left, the stone villas, once the homes of businessmen, now house offices for dentists, solicitors, management consultants, and some have become hotels. Continuing along, past the park, with its massive and intricate stone gateways, the streets to the left climb away up the hill. Emm Lane is the first past the park, a steep climb towards Heaton. Almost symbolic. A lot of desirable houses in Heaton, and when you get up there, fine views across the Aire valley.

Manningham Lane becomes the A650 and Shipley becomes Bingley, the road first twisting over the river. To the left, the golf course; Bingley rugby club pitches are to the right, almost up to the river. The hill beyond is covered in homes, a lot of them council houses.

As quickly as Shipley becomes Bingley, Bingley becomes Keighley. From here it's left, or west, for Colne and Nelson and Burnley, Lancashire; right, or north, for Skipton, the market town thronged by tourists' cars from spring to autumn, where shopkeeper Fred Manby in the High Street still displays some of his wares on the pavement – buckets, brooms, shovels and inside, guns, cartridges, sink plugs, candles, even wood-burning stoves, for those who can afford atavism. Skipton, self-proclaimed gateway to the dales. But Keighley is really in the dales, and Bingley, and Shipley, all in the same dale as Skipton – Airedale. Less than a dozen miles separate Keighley from Skipton, but it might as well be a hundred. It's the difference between Satanic mills and Horse and Hound.

Anna Patricia Rogulskyj lives in Keighley. The door of her stone-fronted terraced house in Highfield Lane is secured by a network of wires, strings and alarms. She's intensely suspicious of strangers at the door and prefers to remain barricaded behind it with her five cherished cats. On her head are three half-inch-deep dents. She will not go to the hairdressers, because the dents in her head upset them, so she cuts her own hair. Known in the town's pubs as 'Irish Annie' she's nervous and often under sedation, yet she still manages to look smart and well-groomed when she does go out. She says she drifts off into her own world a lot of the time, and cries a lot. She no longer works and her social worker often has to do her shopping for her.

On Monday 7 July 1975, the *Yorkshire Post* carried a brief, three-paragraph story on its back local-news page. The headline said 'Woman in hospital after alley attack', and the article read, 'Policewomen were waiting at the bedside of an injured woman in Leeds General Infirmary at the weekend. Mrs Anna Patricia Rogulskyj, 34, believed to be divorced, of Highfield Lane, Keighley, was found with head injuries in an alley near to the Ritz Cinema, Alice Street, Keighley, about 2 a.m. on Saturday morning. She has regained consciousness but is still very ill, and the policewoman will remain at her bedside until she can give an account of what happened.' Even now Anna Rogulskyj finds it hard to describe exactly what happened on the night of 4 July. Irish-born, of Polish extraction, she and her husband had been apart for two years.

On Friday 4 July Mrs Rogulskyj decided to go into Bradford for a night out. She caught the bus from Keighley to Bradford and by midnight was in Bibby's Club, not far from Manningham Lane. Two Jamaicans eventually gave her a lift back to Keighley, where they dropped her outside her home before 1 a.m.

She had expected to find her boyfriend there, but he had left, so she put on her favourite Elvis Presley record. She quickly worked herself into a temper and decided to walk across town to the man's house and try to sort the matter out. She knocked on the door and then knocked again. Then she hammered on the door, beating her fists and shouting at the top of her voice. But there was no answer. In a fury she pulled off one of her shoes and smashed the heel against a nearby ground-floor window, but still there was no reply.

The sound of crashing glass had cooled her quick temper and she decided to make her way back to Highfield Lane. Soon afterwards, at 2.20 a.m., her low moans were heard and she was found lying on her back, fully clothed, in an alley behind the Ritz cinema, not far from where she lived. Her handbag was nearby but nothing appeared to have been stolen from it.

She was rushed to the casualty department at Airedale hospital where it was quickly realized that she had received three severe blows to the back of her head. When doctors removed her clothing they discovered strange slash marks on her stomach. Her attacker had exposed her abdomen before inflicting the wounds and then pulled the clothing back into position. Her head injuries were so severe that she was transferred to Leeds General Infirmary and underwent a 12-hour operation. At one point she received the last rites.

The police in Keighley were confused as the attack appeared to have no motive. Robbery was ruled out and there was no evidence of any sexual interference. Mrs Rogulskyj's boyfriend and the youth who found her clutching her head on the ground in the alley were soon traced, closely questioned, but quickly eliminated as potential attackers. Mrs Rogulskyj was unable to remember anything after breaking the window at her boyfriend's house with her shoe and setting off for home. She recalls nothing of the attack reliably, but is sadly aware of its consequences.

The legacy of that night for the tall, grey-blonde Mrs Rogulskyj is a life spent largely behind pulled curtains in a housecoat with her cats. On the rare occasions she leaves her home, she prefers to walk in the middle of the streets because she is scared of the shadows, and terrified of people approaching her from behind. Above the fireplace in the small terraced house, which she has tried unsuccessfully to sell, is an incongruous jumble of pictures. Portraits of Christ hang alongside television faces such as American actor David Soul and BBC North TV presenter Khalid Aziz. The house has since been bought out of the £15,000 Mrs Rogulskyj received from the Criminal Injuries Board. She is obsessed with the fear that she may be attacked again. The terror of that night has been compounded for her by the subsequent linking at the height of the Ripper scare of her assault with the mass-killer. 'There are nuns and priests in my family, yet my name has been associated with those other girls,' she points out.

Recollections have become blurred for Mrs Rogulskyj, but one strange memory takes her back to November 1974, just a year after she and her Ukrainian-born husband had parted.

She used to go to her local corner shop most days, but she remembers one period particularly well, because the owner used to tell her about a man who had insisted repeatedly on leaving a message for her: Would she go out with him for an evening for a few drinks and a meal? Eventually, she agreed and he drove her into Bradford to a restaurant in the city centre – she can't remember which – but she does know the waitresses all wore long black skirts or dresses.

The stranger was friendly, and courteous, but he seemed to know a lot about her, even though she had never seen him before in her life. He said his name was Michael Gill and that he lived with his grandmother, who was old and ill, and he also had cats. They finished their meal and he drove her back to Keighley. And no, he wouldn't come in for a coffee because he had to get home to put his grandmother to bed. He didn't even give Mrs Rogulskyj a kiss on the cheek, and she never saw him again.

Six years later, after a man had been arrested in Sheffield in connection with the Yorkshire Ripper inquiry, detectives on the case were to return and question her further. 'They asked me if I had ever met a man called "Peter Logan", "Trevor", or "Gill",' she said later.

Back in 1975 satisfactory explanations for the strange attack were not easily arrived at. Detectives at Keighley suspected that the blows to the back of Mrs Rogulskyj's head had perhaps come from a Cuban-heeled boot. Could the three lacerations across her stomach be the work of the West Indian boyfriend? Mrs Rogulskyj had drunk a lot at a Shabeen, a West Indian drinking club, earlier that night, and the police were told that such injuries were sometimes inflicted upon girlfriends who had been unfaithful.

Twelve miles south of Keighley, between Bradford and Huddersfield, is Halifax, a place of even darker Satanic mills than Keighley, clinging grimly to a cleft in the foothills of the Pennines. Five weeks and six days after Mrs Rogulskyj was left for dead, 46-year-old Mrs Olive Smelt prepared for her Friday night out. It was to be the same pattern as usual: meet her girlfriends in Halifax and have a few drinks; before going home, call at the fish and chip shop for the family's supper. Husband Harry would stay in and put his young son Stephen, who was nine, to bed and watch the television with 15-year-old daughter Julie. Mrs Smelt, who worked as an office cleaner for a firm of Halifax solicitors, met her friends and had some drinks. Just before closing time in a town-centre pub they met two men they knew, who said they would give the women a lift home. They pulled up in a lay-by in Boothtown Road,

Boothtown, just a short walk from Mrs Smelt's home in Woodside Mount.

She set off walking quickly, worried in case the fish and chip shop closed before she was able to get the supper. As she took a short cut through an alleyway (by now it was 15 minutes before midnight) a man walked up behind her and started to overtake her. She was to say later that he was aged about 30, 5′ 10″ tall, slightly built and had dark hair with some beard, or growth, on his face.

The man had only just spoken the words 'Weather's letting us down, isn't it?' when Mrs Smelt received a crashing blow to the back of the head and then another as she fell to the ground. She dragged herself along the pavement desperately shouting for help, and a few minutes later frantic neighbours were knocking on the door of Mr Smelt's home in nearby Woodside Mount. Soon after his wife was helped into their house she was rushed to Halifax Infirmary and then to Leeds Infirmary, where she spent ten days.

A policeman who saw the X-rays of her skull said it looked like a smashed eggshell. Although her clothing had been disarranged it was not until doctors removed her skirt and underclothes that they were able to discover two slash marks, each between 6″ and 8″ long, on Mrs Smelt's back, just at the top of her buttocks. The wounds were similar to the ones inflicted on Anna Rogulskyj and again the victim's handbag was found nearby with nothing apparently taken from it.

Two pointless attacks on women late at night, but which at that stage were not linked by the police. It was to be more than three years before police confirmed that their assailant could be the Yorkshire Ripper, but there were common denominators other than the fractured skull the two women received.

Mrs Smelt was to suffer from severe depression and memory loss. Far from being glad to be alive, for many months she wished she was dead. She was to be plagued by gossip, fear and family problems.

'Sometimes I would just sit in the house in the evenings and get very depressed. I felt life was pointless and would feel like screaming out, except I used to tell myself that they would put me away if I did that. For months I completely lost interest in everything. It was hard for my husband, because there was no doubt for a while the police seemed to suspect him for the attack. I suppose it's only natural, but our sex life deteriorated. My two daughters would persuade me to go out and buy clothes, but I only went because I wanted to please them. But then they used to laugh at me because I would never go anywhere to wear them. Before the attack I used to enjoy housework and cooking, but afterwards I just did it to keep me going, to avoid sitting and thinking. There was a time when I could not be near a man, or even look at one without feeling funny. I just could not stand men, and I know it sounds horrible but sometimes I would look at my own husband sitting there. My mind used to play all sorts of tricks.'

Mrs Smelt later deliberately took a job tidying the bedrooms in a men's hospital near her home in an attempt to cure herself. She and her 54-year-old husband, a civil servant, then had the added burden of their eldest daughter, Linda, suffering a nervous breakdown which doctors attributed to her mother's attack. Son Stephen, now 15, still locks the door when he leaves his mother for school. She tried briefly to go out with her friends again on a Friday night, taking a taxi home for safety, but gave it up after two attempts.

'I just felt I had to go to bed at 10 o'clock, and even if I went out with my husband I got the feeling of wanting to be at home. I would have to leave him in the middle, I couldn't stand crowds any more and had this over-whelming feeling of tiredness. Our sex life suffered and there was a lot of bitterness and rows. The gossips even had it that I was a prostitute and everywhere I went I felt I was being stared at. It got to the stage where I wondered how I was ever going to walk down the street again, and that's when I began to wonder if I would have been better off dead,' says Mrs Smelt. She knows the scars to her head and back, and even two lacerations above the eyes, caused by an unidentified sharp instrument, have mended but fears the other scars will never quite knit together completely.

For years there had existed a rivalry between the police of Leeds, with their big-city problems and big-city ways, and the County force. The old County force, the West Riding, became the West Yorkshire Police in 1968 when it amalgamated with smaller town forces such as Dewsbury, Wakefield and Huddersfield. Yet it was still the County force with its county ways. They weren't always the same as those of Leeds, but then neither always were the problems. Rivalry, indeed, there was, and not always too friendly. Yet as neighbours they survived with only the occasional sneer from the city about the amount of paperwork the county seemed to indulge in, and a few knowing winks and nudges from the other direction about the sometimes questionable tactics of the city boys.

But there were, and are, differences. Solving a murder or a robbery in one of the densely packed back-street areas in Leeds wasn't quite the same as sudden death or a theft in Selby or Skipton. Then the Mandarins of Whitehall passed down their judgement. From 1 April 1974 – All Fools Day

– the two forces were to be one, and would incorporate Bradford also.

Four lines in the Government's 5,000-word White Paper on local government reorganization dealt with the biggest upheaval Britain's police service had ever faced. It amounted to the second cannibalization of established forces in six years, affecting the second and third largest in the land – Lancashire and West Yorkshire. The Lancashire force was to be fragmented almost beyond recognition, shrinking from a strength of 7,000 to less than 3,000, while West Yorkshire was to be basically divided in two. The southern part of the old West Yorkshire area was with Sheffield to form the new South Yorkshire Metropolitan Police while what was left was to merge with Leeds and Bradford to produce the West Yorkshire Metropolitan Police.

Many officers in both forces felt that if the changes had to be made then the whole lot should have been merged to form one force 7,500 strong, a number of them objecting to being placed in the same category as the fire and ambulance services in the context of local government. One officer, writing to the *Yorkshire Post,* forecast at least five years of re-adjustment. He added, 'The role of the police is ever-changing in our complex society, and it is essential for police to concentrate their energy and resources on devising measures to meet the changing patterns in crime and public order which confront them. When something happens to disturb this concentration then it is to be regretted.'

But the decision was taken and the preparations had to be made, from the appointment of a new Chief Constable (the old West Yorkshire's Mr Ronald Gregory beating the old Leeds City's Mr James Angus for the top job) to which force buttons to use, which helmet badges (5,000 new ones at 20p a time), and where the Headquarters were to be. The Headquarters were, and are, at the old County head-quarters in Wakefield, and Chief Constable Mr Ronald Gregory's force is now the West Yorkshire Metropolitan Police.

April 1974 was still eleven months before Anna Rogulskyj was attacked. The new force faced a stern test within a week of being born when an old lady was killed in her Coronation Street-type corner-shop in the heart of the steeply terraced streets of Beeston to the west of the M1 motorway as it drives into the heart of South Leeds. This was very much a city-type murder.

Detective Chief Supt. Dennis Hoban was put in charge of the inquiry. Mr Hoban was that rare animal in the police service, an immensely likeable yet totally ruthless man. Once head of the Leeds City C.I.D., he was renowned as a 'thief-taker' and not one to disregard his instincts as far as solving crime was concerned. His obsessive tenacity, coupled with a friendly disposition, made him feared and liked in almost equal proportions by villains as well as by his own officers. Eighteen months after the contentious amalgamation of forces, he found himself at the side of a foggy, wet playing field in Chapeltown, Leeds, gazing at the body of a very dead blonde woman when he should have been at home having his breakfast.

She was lying face upwards on a sloping grass embankment of the Prince Philip Playing Fields, off Scott Hall Road, her marble-white body obscenely exposed. Her jacket and blouse had been torn open and her bra pushed up exposing her breasts. Her trousers had been dragged down around her knees, although her pants were still in position.

There were six buttons on the grass close to the body,

five of which had apparently been ripped off her blouse, and one off her jacket. Her handbag strap was looped around her left wrist as if she had been holding it when she fell. She had received at least one massive blow to the head and had been severely stabbed about the body. Mr Hoban noticed congealed blood around her throat.

The pathologist, Professor David Gee, Head of the Department of Forensic Medicine at Leeds University, told him later in the day that the woman had in fact been dealt two blows to her head with a hammer-type instrument, one of the lacerations penetrating the full thickness of the skull, and had received 14 stab wounds in the chest and stomach, and one in the neck. Professor Gee thought the stab wounds were from a knife with a blade that was not less than 3″ long, about ¾″ broad, and sharp on only one side. He thought the head injuries had been inflicted while she was standing and the stab wounds as she was prostrate on the grass. Wilomena McCann, 28, a mother of four, was just 100 yards from the front door of her home.

Home for Wilma, as the fiery Scot preferred to be called, was a council house in nearby Scott Hall Avenue, where her almost perpetual drunkenness was reflected in the increasingly deplorable living conditions that had evolved for her and her four young children in the months prior to her death. She had convictions for drunkenness, theft and disorderly conduct, and police suspected that she acted as a prostitute. Twenty-eight-year-old Wilma had travelled to Leeds from her native Inverness in 1970 with hope. She and her husband Gerald McCann had decided to make a new start in Yorkshire but this proved to be a false hope. Wilma, who had once worked as a still-room assistant at the luxury Gleneagles Hotel, near Perth, adjoining the famous golf course, had chosen Leeds because six of her brothers were living in the same area.

Joiner Gerald McCann decided to leave Wilma and their four children when he tired of their perpetual rows and recriminations, mainly about Wilma's love of the night-life and wilful insistence on having her own boyfriends. He felt that, despite all her other faults, his strawberry-blonde wife at least looked after the children well. But he was wrong. Throughout the summer and autumn of 1975, Wilma's neglect of her children and their home increased in almost direct proportion to the amount she drank, and by October there was hardly a night when she didn't fluff up her hair and put on her lipstick and set off for the bright lights in Leeds. Being a good-time girl, as the police insist on incongruously labelling the Wilma McCanns, might not have been all that good, but it was better than sitting at home and staring at the television until the white spot appeared, all the while wondering where the money for the rent was going to come from.

For Wilma the night of 29 October was no exception. By 7.30 p.m. she had got out of her house-coat and into a pink blouse, white flared trousers, and dark blue bolero jacket. She said goodnight to the children: Sonje, nine, Richard, seven, Donna, six and Angela who was five. Her instructions to Sonje were clear; the oldest was to make sure the youngest didn't get out of bed after mummy had gone to work. Then Wilma was gone, out of the back door as always (no need for the neighbours to know she was going out every night), and past the nearby Prince Philip Playing Fields towards the pubs and the clubs. This was what Wilma looked forward to each day, the freedom to go where she liked, dance with whom she liked, drink with whom she liked and take lifts from whom she liked. If there was to be a bit of a kiss and a cuddle on the way home, so what, life was too short to worry much about tomorrow.

Wilma had agreed to a divorce from Gerry on the grounds of her adultery, which she readily admitted, but had never bothered turning up at the numerous appointments he had made for them with a solicitor. He had found himself a girlfriend and often used to visit the children during their playtime at school. Wilma had told him that she didn't need his financial support, and she could see to the children's needs. After all, hadn't she got at least thirty boyfriends?

By 8.30 p.m. she had had a couple of warming whiskies, washed down by glasses of beer in the Regent pub in Kirkgate, down by the market; then on to the Scotsman, then the White Swan. The week-day 10.30 p.m. closing time in Leeds, unlike most of the surrounding areas where it is 11 p.m., never suited Wilma but, what the hell, there was always the Room at the Top nightclub on her way back home towards Chapeltown.

Clutching a plastic tray of chips with curry sauce poured over the top, Wilma headed north and homewards. This would be like all the other nights; after all she could always step out into the path of a passing lorry, wave it down and if necessary almost bully the driver into giving her a lift.

Wilma was never short of a word or a phrase, particularly when she had had a drink, and if the mood were to take her and the lorry driver was going to Scotland, well, why not, it'd be a chance to see the relatives, and one of the neighbours would look after the kids for a couple of days. One lorry driver, making his way towards the M62 motorway, did stop when Wilma stepped into the road and flagged him down, but when he wound down his window and was greeted by an almost incoherent mixture of instructions and abuse, delivered in a thick Scottish accent, he said 'Sorry' and passed on, leaving Wilma at the side of the road. But then a car stopped.

Soon after 5 a.m. one of Wilma's neighbours' daughters was shocked to see the two eldest McCann children, with their school-coats over their pyjamas, clinging to each other for warmth in the fog at a bus stop in Scott Hall Road. They were confused and frightened and were looking for their mummy. They had searched the surrounding streets and decided to wait at the bus stop in case she was to come home from work that way.

Just over an hour later, at 7.41 a.m., milkman Mr Alan Routledge saw what he thought was an abandoned Guy – after all it was Bonfire Night the following week – near the edge of the Prince Philip Playing Fields. Or could it be a pile of rags? He started to move towards it when his younger brother Paul's ten-year-old voice echoed through the fog. 'It's a body.' A woman; was she blonde? It was hard to tell; her head was covered and matted in blood. Why should she be lying on her back facing the sky?

Dennis Hoban wondered about that. The woman had been hit on the head from behind and the blow had probably killed her, but whoever had done this had gone to the trouble of turning her over and lifting her clothing in order to inflict those terrible-looking wounds. The purse was missing from the dead woman's handbag, a white purse with a top clasp bearing the word 'Mumiy' which Sonje had written, and an unknown amount of cash. Was it a violent robbery, a punter who hadn't wanted to pay, or could there be some other explanation?

Professor Gee, based at Leeds for sixteen years, and a recognised expert on poisons, took his time with the post-mortem, as usual. Prof. Gee's report to Mr Hoban was to confirm that Wilma had indeed been the worse for drink. Blood samples showed she had consumed 12–14 measures of spirits in the few hours prior to her death (183 mgs. of alcohol per 100 ml. of blood). Mr Hoban was interested to learn that while no semen had been found on the vaginal swabs a positive semen reaction had occurred on the back of her trousers and pants.

As ever, for those left behind, the pain was unrelenting. The lines of anguish and heartache on the face of Mrs Betty Newlands, Wilma's mother, went deeper as the months and years passed, and as her daughter's unsmiling visage leapt at her from the television screens and newspaper pages. She was to say at her home in Inverness, much later, 'Wilma was not a prostitute and I hope and pray every day that the Ripper is caught, brought to trial and Wilma's name cleared. I can't get the horrible business out of my mind. I would not like any other mother to go through what I have experienced. That is another reason I hope this man is caught and brought to justice.'

Ten weeks later, on the afternoon of 9 January 1976, a prostitute was found stabbed to death in Leeds. Barbara Booth, 24, and her curly-haired three-year-old son Alan, were found in pools of blood on the living-room floor of their home in Greenhow Crescent, Burley. A blackened meal of curry and rice was still on the cooker and a visibly shaken Dennis Hoban described the scene inside the terraced house as 'bloody'. Mrs Booth, fair-haired and pretty, advertised in a contact magazine and as well as selling sex specialized in photographic modelling, particularly in the afternoons. The man she lived with, West Indian Mr Alan Ruddick, who worked as a disc jockey, had found the door to their house jammed when he arrived from a visit to a club. As he leant against the door and tried to ease it open he was horrified to see Mrs Booth, whom he called Babs, behind the door. He recalled, 'I bent down and said, "Oh, Babs, what is wrong with you?" She was warm and I rubbed her hands and begged her to speak to me. But she just lay there, her eyes wide open. Across the room was my little boy and I ran to him. He was lying in a twisted position with his face towards the fire so I rubbed his hands and turned him over and there was this horrible hole in his neck. The television was on, and the lights, and Babs had been cooking a meal but it had burnt.'

Dennis Hoban, never one to mince his words or prevaricate, and famous for giving straight answers to straight questions at press conferences (a rare quality) did not shirk the obvious question. He was prepared to link Mrs Booth's death with that of Wilma McCann, mainly, he said, because they were both prostitutes, and also because of the intense savagery of the attacks. 'The killer might have a fixation about prostitutes and could well strike again. Other women could be in danger – not ordinary women in the street, but probably women who follow this way of life. Any street-girls, models on the seamier side of Leeds, and the prostitutes who may know or suspect a client that may be this way inclined and violently opposed to their way of life, should come forward and see us,' was his plea.

Two days after the killing the *Yorkshire Post* story carried a headline across four columns saying ' "Love Diary" check after Jack-the-Ripper Killings.' Yet within hours the possibility of a latter-day Ripper legend seemed to evaporate with the news that a 19-year-old student had been arrested in Bradford in connection with the stabbing to death of an 85-year-old widow and a 16-year-old youth a few miles apart between Bingley and Eastburn in the Aire valley. Unbeknown to Mr Hoban, he had also confessed to killing Mrs Booth and her young son. The following June, Mark Andrew Rowntree, adopted son of a wealthy Guiseley family, pleaded not guilty at Leeds Crown Court to four charges of murder but guilty to manslaughter in each case, on grounds of diminished responsibility, and was committed to Broadmoor for an unlimited period. But by then Mr Hoban had a fresh set of problems.

The previous year, 1975, had been quite hectic for Mr Hoban, who had been awarded the Queen's commendation for bravery. Years before he had established a reputation within the old Leeds City Force as something of a 'whizz-kid', rising through the ranks more rapidly than anyone previously. But his finest hour had come at the beginning of 1975. A bomb had been planted in the gents' toilets of a city-centre store and after it had been evacuated, and the surrounding streets closed off, Mr Hoban coolly defused it himself, even though army bomb-disposal officers were at that moment racing down the A1 from Catterick Camp. He said he had done it because he didn't think the soldiers would arrive in time, pointing out that he had been 'on a course, you know, after all'. He said the award from the Queen would go nicely with the two medals for bravery and an inscribed watch from Scarborough police his own father, Patrick, had been awarded many years earlier.

But the watch was of no use to son Dennis as he nosed his dark blue Daimler Jaguar, one of the first gas-powered cars in Leeds, into the city's breakfast-time traffic just two weeks after the Booth killings, and headed north again towards Chapeltown.

Emily Monica Jackson, aged 42, lived with her husband and three children in Back Green, Churwell, on the fringes of Morley, a fiercely independent town west of Leeds, with a dour and renowned Rugby Union team. Due to local-government reorganization, while still independent and proud, Morley found itself technically part of Greater Leeds. It can number among its sons Herbert Asquith, a former Home Secretary, and Donald Nappy, later Neilson, who became better known as the 'Black Panther', the kidnapper and murderer of heiress Leslie Whittle and three sub-postmasters.

Emily Jackson's husband, Sydney, was the roofing expert in Churwell, and in the first few weeks of 1976 had been kept busy with the damage caused by high winds. The couple had lived in the village for seven years, having moved from Holbeck in Leeds, and Sydney Jackson was known as a hard worker who did a good job.

Some people may have thought it a bit odd that he never drove the blue Commer van with the ladder on top which carried his equipment, but instead was always chauffeured by wife Emily. She was friendly enough, always pleasant, although they never seemed to go into the village pubs, the Commercial, the Fleece, and the New Inn, known graphically as the 'Top Hole', 'Middle Hole' and 'Bottom Hole' from their positions on Churwell Hill as it climbed towards Morley out of Leeds. The Jacksons did like a drink, almost nightly, but in pubs very different from the ones found in Churwell.

One of their favourite haunts was the Gaiety, the miserable, sprawling, modern-style drinking house set down incongruously at the side of the Roundhay Road, Leeds, surrounded by worn-out terraces of houses; on the fringes of Harehills, a mile from the Chapeltown area, but a favourite haunt of prostitutes. They gather in the doorway at lunch-times casting weary eyes over the collection of businessmen and labourers, even journalists, who pack into the dimly lit bar to gather round the postage-stamp-sized dance-floor for the daily strippers. They are there again in the evening when the clientele is mainly West Indian, and the music disco-loud.

The Jacksons' married life had not been without difficulties and, at one point, Emily had left her husband for an 18-month period. In 1971 they had been desolate when their eldest son Derek, then 14, had fallen headlong through a bedroom window and died on the pavement below. In a way it had brought the couple closer together than they had ever been, but it hardened their resolve to live for the day and not worry too much about what the future held. In an attempt to push the tragedy to the back of their minds they started drinking heavily and visiting pubs most nights of the week. They certainly did not try to keep that secret, but one other aspect of their nocturnal travels was totally unknown to friends and neighbours.

Mr Jackson was to say that one of their marital problems had been his wife's insatiable sexual appetite, which he had found difficult to cope with. She had had her share of boyfriends, but Mr Jackson had accepted the situation philosophically, and in recent times always travelled with her into Leeds at night in the blue Commer van, which Emily used as a mobile love-nest when necessary. Just before Christmas they had been under some financial pressure and the strong-willed Emily had announced to her husband that she was going to start taking money from men she might pick up on their evening drinking expeditions. Tuesday 20 January 1976 was to be no different. Mr Jackson had been busy dealing with repair work created by the high winds, but by the time the early-evening television news came on, and the children had had their teas, the Jacksons were ready.

Emily was always careful with her make-up and her brown hair was regularly trimmed, and for this particular trip she changed into a skirt, a close-fitting blue and white striped sweater, over which she pulled a white cardigan, and sling-back shoes. Finally, a blue, green and red checked overcoat to keep her warm until the van heater started to do its job. Emily was 5′ 6″ tall and slightly overweight, but she knew she would be busy that evening. She always was. They shouted goodbye to the children, Christopher and Angela, at 6 p.m. and 15 minutes later Mrs Jackson was parking the Commer van in the car park at the side of the Gaiety.

They went inside the pub where Mr Jackson bought them some drinks; it was to be closing time before he re-emerged. Within minutes of their arrival at the Gaiety Mrs Jackson had finished her glass of lager and left her husband standing near the bar. She said she was going to have a look round and see who she could see.

Forty-five minutes later, at 7 p.m., a prostitute sitting on the wall outside the pub saw Emily Jackson and the two exchanged a few pleasantries before the elder woman saw a green hard-topped Land Rover parked a short way down the road. Mrs Jackson left the girl and walked quickly towards the vehicle. After she had got in, it drove away along Gledhow Road. The other prostitute remembered how the passenger door seemed to have been patched with grey or silver paint and that it had a small aerial on the front nearside wing near the windscreen.

A description of the driver was even more detailed. He had been a fattish man aged about 50, with mousey-coloured, ear-length hair, an unshaped full beard with gingery blonde-coloured sideburns, and a round nose which appeared squashed. His eyes had been closed, making it seem as if he was going to sleep. His face may have been scarred and his left hand was deformed with a noticeable scar, as if it had been burned, stretching from the knuckles on the back of the hand to the wrist. The scar was of normal skin colour but appeared stretched and wrinkled. The man looked as if he could have come straight from a building site, with dusty clothing, a dark blue anorak-type jacket, dark blue overall-style trousers, and possibly black boots or wellingtons with thick soles. At 10.30 p.m. closing time, Sydney Jackson stepped out of the warm and noisy pub into the car park and found the van, but no sign of Emily. He waited a few more minutes, thinking she might be in another bar with one of her 'boyfriends', and then decided to take a taxi home.

The van was to stay there all night. The following morning, at 8.10 a.m., as the Jackson household stirred itself for another day, a workman took a short cut through a narrow passageway which would take him from Manor Street along the side of some disused buildings and into Roundhay Road, just 800 yards from the Gaiety. Something caught his eye as he passed the end of a short cul-de-sac running between two derelict buildings. It was a bulky object, with what seemed to be a coat partially covering it.

The attack on Emily Jackson had been so ferocious and pitiless that Dennis Hoban was to say later, in an off-the-record moment, that he had been almost paralyzed with numbness at what had waited for him in that miserable cul-de-sac. Emily Jackson had been left laying on her back with her legs apart. She was still wearing her tights and pants, but her bra had been pulled up to expose her breasts. Her handbag was nearby but nothing appeared to have been taken. Mr Hoban thought immediately of Wilma McCann: 'I knew at that moment that we were dealing with an extraordinary man,' he said.

Like Wilma, Mrs Jackson had received two devastating blows to the head with a hammer-type instrument; then her killer had inflicted 51 stab wounds to her lower neck, upper chest and lower abdomen. Mr Hoban was shaken to be told that the numerous stab wounds in her back appeared to have been caused by an X-shaped instrument, something similar to a Phillips screwdriver. The wounds suggested that the weapon had been between $\frac{1}{8}''$ and $\frac{3}{16}''$ diameter, while the shape of the depressed fractures of the skull meant the weapon was a blunt object, circular in outline and approximately $1\frac{1}{2}''$ diameter. A further indignity for the dead woman had been the killer's need to stamp on her. A heavy-ribbed wellington boot impression was found on her right thigh and identified as having been made by a Dunlop Warwick, probably a size 7, but no larger than a size 8.

A similar bootprint was found in nearby sand. As forensic experts bent down to examine closely the extent of Mrs Jackson's terrible injuries and the ground immediately around her, the only reminder of the previous night 'on the town', as she used to call her trips into Leeds, was the faint smell of once strong but cheap perfume.

The post mortem examination was to show that while semen was present on a vaginal swab, it was thought to be from sexual activity prior to the attack. Blood and urine samples were devoid of alcohol.

Soon after 9 a.m., just an hour after the body had been discovered, a distraught Mr Sydney Jackson knocked on the door of his next-door neighbour but one and asked if she would look after the two children when they came home from school if he was not there. He said Emily had had an accident, but was too upset to say what sort. It was almost midnight before the police took him home and the following morning he sat in his armchair with tears pouring down his cheeks and said, 'I know what people are saying, but I didn't do it. There's nothing I want to say to the man who did do it, there's nothing I can say, but if he's done it once, he'll do it again. I just pray they catch him.' The children had gone to his sister in another part of Leeds and were still unaware that their mother had been killed. They were soon to know the awful truth. Mr Hoban seemed to have no doubts about who had killed her. He felt the Jackson and McCann deaths were the work of one man, and revealed that the police had again examined the file on the unsolved murder of a Mrs Mary Judge, aged 43, who had been found battered to death six years previously on waste land across the road from Leeds parish church.

It had been eleven weeks and five days since the McCann killing, yet four months were to pass before Mr Hoban was to give evidence at the inquest on the strawberry-blonde Scot. 'There is little doubt in my mind,' he said, 'that both offences relating to Mrs McCann and Mrs Jackson were committed by the same person – some psychopath with a deep hatred for this type of girl.' As he spoke, a coloured girl from Saint Kitts sat in her terraced home off Roundhay Road, a few strides away from the Gaiety, and nursed her shaven head. She had been released from hospital just two days earlier.

A week before, on Saturday 8 May, 20-year-old Marcella Claxton had been to a late-night drinking party at a friend's house in Chapeltown. She had set off to walk the short distance to her home the following morning after 4 a.m. A large white car pulled up alongside her and, although she wasn't 'doing business', Marcella asked the driver for a lift. Instead of driving to her home the man went to Soldiers Field, an open recreation area, just off Roundhay Road.

The man's excursion into Roundhay was not surprising, even though he clearly showed a preference for the seedier inner-city areas. For while most of Roundhay is considered one of the best, if not the best, residential areas of Leeds, it borders both Chapeltown and a district more run down than Chapeltown – Harehills. Roundhay has hundreds of splendid stone Victorian mansions in large grounds and luxurious blocks of flats overlooking one of the best parks

in England, Roundhay Park. Roundhay is where the rich
and cultured live, and is often regarded as one step above
equally expensive areas on the northern fringes of the city.
But it has its shabby sections, so the favourable Leeds
postal area, Leeds 8, does not necessarily indicate a good
address. Roundhay also has acres of pleasant but
unremarkable 'thirties semi-detached development. But
for this man's purposes, it was the open spaces and quiet
of the Roundhay Park area that were attractive. He offered
Marcella £5 to get out of the car and take her clothes off
for sexual intercourse on the grass, but she said she did not
want to do it. She said she left the car and went behind a
nearby tree to urinate. The man, who had a beard and a
moustache, got out of the car at the same time and seemed
to drop something. Marcella said, 'I hope that isn't a
knife', and he replied that it was his wallet. She had almost
finished by the tree when the man walked towards her and
the next thing she felt was a blow at the back of the head,
and then another. As she lay on the wet grass and saw the
blood on her hand where she had touched her head, she
noticed the man standing nearby. His hair and his beard
were black and crinkly and she was aware of his hand
moving rhythmically in front of his trousers. He went to
the white car with the red upholstery but soon returned; he
appeared to be wiping himself, and threw some tissues on
the ground near Marcella. He pushed a £5 note into her
hand and told her not to call the police before getting into
his car and driving away.

'He had been, you know, masturbating himself, the
bastard,' she recalls. Marcella, whose clothing was by now
covered in blood, managed to half-walk, half-crawl to a
nearby telephone box and call for an ambulance. The
gaping wound in the back of her head needed 52 stitches
and a seven-day stay in hospital. For many months

afterwards she was to hate the sight of men and could hardly bear to be in the same room as a man. She would not go out and even now does not go anywhere unless she has to. Depression and giddy spells still plague her, and when Marcella tried to hold down a job in the pressing department of a local factory she was soon forced to give it up. Even the birth of her baby son, Adrian, at the beginning of 1981, while the front pages of the newspapers were full of the arrest of a Bradford lorry driver found in a car with another coloured girl in Sheffield, gave her little hope for the future. She sees no sense in her friends' claims that she is 'lucky to be alive', pointing out that in reality she often wishes she had died that night on Soldiers Field. Her dark brown eyes fill with tears as she twists her hands nervously and stares at the floor of her home in Gathorne Terrace, recalling that terrible night. 'After I had dialled 999 and was sat on the floor of the telephone box, a man in a white car kept driving past. He seemed to be staring and looking for me. It was the man who hurt me.'

Baby Adrian screams for his feed and Marcella Claxton holds him to her, almost crushing him against her she presses her face against his. Five years have done nothing to ease the ache.

In the summer of 1976 Dennis Hoban had to leave his beloved Leeds, the streets and pubs he knew so well, to work from the West Yorkshire Police Headquarters, at Wakefield, ten miles away, as Deputy Head of the Force C.I.D. to Assistant Chief Constable (Crime) Mr George Oldfield. In the bar of the Town Hall Tavern, and the Victoria, at the back of the Town Hall and its Law Courts, where he often took a drink with colleagues and journalists just before afternoon closing time, Mr Hoban made no secret of his feelings. While recognizing the accolade he had been accorded by the Chief Constable he did not relish the prospect of being 'desk-bound'.

He was succeeded as head of the Leeds C.I.D. by his deputy and long-time close friend, Det. Chief Supt. Jim Hobson. Mr Hobson lived in Wetherby, a small country town north of Leeds, with his wife and daughter, who had studied to become a teacher. He had stepped into Dennis Hoban's shoes, and on the morning of Sunday 6 February 1977 he was to follow in his footsteps.

Twenty-eight-year-old Irene Richardson was, like Wilma McCann, someone who had found herself in search of a few of life's luckier breaks, yet her circumstances conspired to make Wilma seem almost fortunate by comparison. At the beginning of 1977 Irene was faced with the bleak prospect of both her daughters, aged four and five, living with foster parents; no proper accommodation; and because of her lack of money, found herself hanging around the street corners of Chapeltown looking for customers. On 22 January, a Saturday, she should have been at Leeds register office to marry her boyfriend, Stephen Bray, but neither had turned up because neither had admitted to the other to being already married.

On the night of Saturday 5 February, she left her rooming-house in Cowper Street, Chapeltown, at 11.30 p.m., saying she was going into town, to Tiffany's Club, where Stephen Bray had worked as a doorman before leaving for Ireland.

Tiffany's was a 'no denims' supper disco, so Irene Richardson had brushed her shoulder-length brown hair and made a real effort to look good. The brown cardigan, blue and white checked blouse, yellow jacket and skirt did not quite match, but Irene was hungry and she needed a drink.

At 7.30 a.m. the following morning, accountant Mr John Bolton jogged across Soldiers Field and saw a woman on the ground at the rear of the sports pavilion. He asked her, 'What's the matter?'

If there is such a thing as a scale of horror in a policeman's mind the sight that awaited Jim Hobson and pathologist Professor Gee when the woman's coat was removed from her body was as terrible as possible, and equally strange. Irene Richardson had received a massive fracture of the skull from three blows to the head with a hammer-type instrument. She was lying face down with her hands under her stomach, and her head, with the brown hair so carefully brushed now matted with blood, turned to the left. Her bra was still in position but her skirt had been pulled up and her tights pulled off the right leg and down. She had been menstruating and one of the two pairs of pants she had been wearing had been removed and pushed inside the tights, while the other pair were still in place. The coat she had been wearing was draped over her buttocks and legs in such a way that only her feet were showing. When it was removed it was discovered that her calf-length brown boots, which had been removed from her feet, had been placed neatly over her thighs. She had been stabbed in the neck and throat and had three stab wounds to the stomach, all savage, downward strokes, so severe they had caused her intestines to spill out.

Blood and urine samples were taken but no alcohol was found to be present and Professor Gee estimated the time of death to be about midnight – only half an hour or so after she had left her rooming house. Professor Gee told Mr Hobson that the fracture of the skull appeared to have been caused by a hammer $1\frac{1}{2}''$ in diameter. One of the blows had been so severe a circular piece of skull had actually penetrated the brain. A vaginal swab indicated the presence of semen, but this was estimated to have been from sexual activity at some point during the 24 hours prior to death.

Near the body, West Yorkshire scene of crime experts discovered and recorded tyre marks which indicated a medium-sized saloon or van had been used by the killer. From the almost perfect 'prints' in the soft ground of Soldiers Field checks with tyre manufacturers established that the vehicle had been fitted with two India Autoway tyres and a Pneumant on the rear offside, all of them cross-ply. Mr Hobson's elation at this genuine break in the hunt was quickly tempered by the daunting statistics produced by his men.

With the co-operation of vehicle and tyre manufacturers they had drawn up a list of vehicles with a rear track width of between 4' 1½" and 4' 2½", the dimensions obtained at Soldiers Field. The list was a depressing 26 vehicles long, ranging from the Datsun 1300 to the Morris Minors (all of certain years) and taking in Ford Corsairs registered between 1962 and 1970. Bearing in mind that the tyres were likely to wear out and be changed within a matter of months, Mr Hobson asked for and received the co-operation of the press in not disclosing the nature of the police 'clue'. Without the benefits of computerization, he had to arrange with local vehicle taxation offices for his men to move in at night to check by hand all the vehicles in West Yorkshire which fell within those categories on the list – a staggering 100,000 cars.

Any excitement Mr Hobson may have felt about the police being close to a breakthrough was tinged with the knowledge that if the track width that they were working on was out by as little as ¼", more or less, dozens of other vehicles would come within the framework of their inquiry. If the owner of the car, even if they found the right one, changed only one or two tyres, then the whole exercise would be totally nullified. Within days of the discovery of Irene Richardson's death, Jim Hobson had asked to see the files on other potentially relevant attacks, and had been particularly interested in the case of Marcella Claxton, who had travelled to Soldiers Field but survived nine months earlier.

He also rang Det. Chief Supt. Wilfred Brooks, the head of Lancashire C.I.D., who was based in Preston. Were there any similarities between the killings in Yorkshire and the death of a 26-year-old prostitute in Preston, in November, 15 months earlier, just three weeks after Wilma McCann had died?

Mrs Mildred Atkinson had set off to collect the Sunday papers on 23 November 1975, and noticed a garage-door flapping in the wind as she walked along Berwick Road, Preston. As the door blew open she saw a body lying face down in the garage, with a coat over its head, and blood on the ground beside it. Mrs Atkinson thought it might have been a drunk who had banged his head. Joan Harrison may have been 26 but she often looked 20 years older, her chronic alcoholism having taken its toll. She was known to have close associations with other alcoholics, drug addicts and prostitutes in the Preston area, and although she had previous convictions for theft, but not for prostitution, it was known that she had felt the need to resort to taking money for sex to feed her drinking habit. Joan was also hooked on the morphine present in cough mixtures, which she had been known to consume at the rate of eight bottles a day, and she had been described at her last appearance at Preston Magistrates Court in 1974 as a 'complete wreck of a human being'.

Throughout most of Thursday 20 November, she had been at St Mary's Hostel for the homeless, with occasional visits to a number of nearby pubs for a drink. When she returned after closing time in the afternoon she had been extremely drunk and was allowed to go to bed in the home. Shortly after 4 o'clock a man at the hostel had intercourse with her, but it was to be 10 o'clock before she had sobered up enough to return to her own home. She left angrily ten minutes later when the man she was living with refused to give her more money for drink, and was seen walking towards Preston town centre along Church Street at 10.20 p.m. She was wearing a light green three-quarter-length coat with an imitation fur collar, a turquoise blue jumper with a bright yellow tank-top over it, dark brown trousers, and brown suede calf-length boots.

Mrs Atkinson's emergency call that Sunday morning had brought the police within minutes to the garage in Berwick Road. She had been half right. The body was that of a drunk, but a woman not a man. Joan Harrison was lying face down and covered with her coat. She had been moved a few feet from where the initial attack had taken place. Her trousers had been pulled down and one leg was out of her pants and tights and one boot had been taken off. There was one laceration to the back of her head, which appeared to have been caused by a hammer-type instrument, and extensive injuries to her head, face, body and legs, which pathologist Dr John Benstead thought had been caused by violent kicking and stamping. On Joan Harrison's left breast were bite marks which seemed to indicate clearly a gap in the upper front teeth of her attacker. There were no stab wounds. Her handbag and purse were missing and robbery and sex appeared to be the motivation for the attack.

Swabs from the vagina and anus indicated semen had been deposited by a secretor of the rare blood group B. The blood group of the man at the hostel who had had sexual intercourse with the dead woman the previous day was discovered to be group A. Mr Brooks and Mr Hobson parted with open minds after their meeting, and because of the sexual assault and apparent robbery, both elements missing from the Yorkshire attacks, did not at the time link Joan Harrison's death with these. Her purse had been hidden in a bush in a local park, and the handbag was found on a refuse tip seven months later, 400 yards from the place where she died. A key ring, some rings, and a man's wrist watch were missing.

Mr Hobson's men continued the laborious and painstaking job of sifting through vehicle registration details in the middle of the night. He even had teams of officers scrambling round on their hands and knees in pub car parks and at the side of the road in Chapeltown. They had to perform this task without the owners' knowledge, as one changed tyre could upset the sought-after combination.

Mr Hobson also took what he now recognizes to have been an extremely hazardous decision – to put policewomen volunteers on the streets posing as prostitutes. They were monitored by other officers at all times and never got into a car, simply talking to any driver who pulled up at the kerb asking if one of the women was 'doing business'. They couldn't be left for too long a period in the same stretch as the fact that they never got in with any of the would-be customers would quickly become noticeable. They possessed short-wave radios and nearby officers were able to take down the description of the car and the men who pulled up alongside them.

Says Mr Hobson, 'It was only for a short period, but when I think about it now, and knowing what we know now, it makes me shiver. Those girls were very brave to volunteer and put themselves at risk.' The police were never to release details of the injuries to any of the victims, other than the broadest generalizations, but the severe nature of the wounds inflicted on Irene Richardson's stomach were to percolate through to pressmen, and the headlines became bigger and blacker with words like 'Maniac' and 'Triple-Killer' prominent. The legend had firmly taken root, and the word most frequently aimed at the public consciousness was 'Ripper', with all its connotations of Victorian melodrama and horror, of disembowelled prostitutes in foggy back streets. And this was just the beginning.

CHAPTER 2

Growing Pains

Bingley has seen better days; it is a slightly run-down mill-town in a rural setting, closer in spirit to Bradford than nearby Ilkley, which is very much a middle-class preserve. The better-off inhabitants of Bingley are likely to live near the pretty village of Eldwick; they might even say they live in Eldwick. To look at, Bingley today is a pleasant-enough place, with little indication of the worrying level of unemployment in the area. The town's working life is dominated by the ultra-modern Bradford and Bingley Building Society office, one of many proud temples to Yorkshire thrift to be found in old West Riding cities and towns, and the Damart thermal underwear factory, which may with a little licence be seen as a symbol of the other Yorkshire virtue of commonsense. These thriving industries are not enough, though, and men have to be bussed daily in large numbers into the Magnet Joinery factory in Keighley, a few miles away. Bingley has its famous sons; Harvey Smith, the horseman, John Braine, the novelist, actor Rodney Bewes and the concert pianist, John Briggs are acknowledged in the town as Bingley people. But Bingley now has a notorious son.

When John Sutcliffe looked at the bundle of blankets his bride of just over a year clutched to her side, he had to bend closer to see what was inside – a small, red face with tightly closed eyes and black hair.

This one would have to grow a bit to play centre forward

for Bradford City, or open the bowling for Yorkshire. But John's wife, Kathleen, was content. Their first-born was a son, and John would be able to teach him all those sports he was so daft about. It was 2 June 1946 and, thank God, the war was long since over. John Sutcliffe was 24, three years younger than his wife, and they had married the year before.

It had been a long war, but Sutcliffe had seen the Mediterranean, even if the circumstances had been less than perfect. He had been based in Gibraltar with the Royal Navy, but by the end of the war was a petty officer-cook on a minesweeper sailing out of Aberdeen. He was young and fit, apart from an annoying skin complaint he had picked up in Gibraltar which could have been caused by the heat.

Back in Bingley, where both he and Kathleen (family name Coonan) had been born, a new life was beckoning. It was good to return to familiar pubs and the cricket and the football he loved so much and played so well. He was a man's man, something of an extrovert, interested in amateur dramatics as well as sport.

He got a job as a baker with the Co-op in Bingley, and found a house – just a two-up, two-down stone terraced cottage in Heaton Row, off busy Ferncliffe, but a home, a start. The skin rashes were a nuisance, though. They were aggravated by the heat in the bakery, said the doctor, and John Sutcliffe was forced to leave and seek employment in one of Bingley's textile mills at the side of the river Aire. Not as hot, but hellish noisy.

As he and Kathleen examined the small bundle she held in the Shipley and Bingley Maternity Hospital, they were happy. The baby was a boy and there was nothing wrong with him; ten fingers and ten toes, and everything in the right place. He was a scrawny little thing, just 5 lb in weight, yet they'd soon put that right when they got him home. And they knew what they were going to call him. Peter. Peter William. There were to be other children over the next 15 years, three girls and three boys altogether, but Peter was always to be special to Kathleen Sutcliffe. The first-born, the oldest, but also the smallest, the weakest, the one who rarely left her side in the first few years, almost like a puppy.

Even when he was to start at the local St Joseph's R.C. school nursery in September 1948, and then when he moved up into the junior section when he was five, he never wanted to be at school. He couldn't wait to get home to his mother. In fact John was to complain to Kathleen that she was over-protective towards Peter, that she should encourage him to be more independent. But Kathleen took no notice. Peter was shy and he was quiet and he wasn't very big. If he wanted to stay inside with her most of the time, reading his comics and not losing out in those rough games that boys play, well that was all right with her.

Kathleen was from a slightly different background to her husband – working-class, just the same, but upper working-class, if there was such a thing. When she had taken up with John Sutcliffe some members of her family hadn't been too impressed, regarding him and his home as a bit rough and ready.

In some ways the young Peter seemed in awe of his father, so aggressively masculine. But Peter had a friend in his mother, as did all the Sutcliffe children. She seemed to have love to spare, although none of them had any doubt about who was the favourite, not that it seemed to bother them. As sister Maureen was to point out years later about Peter's wedding day, Kathleen hardly took her eyes off her eldest son all day, and afterwards, at the reception, simply sat and gazed at him and his new wife, eyes wide with happiness. Yet back during his first two or three years at school, John Sutcliffe had been so concerned about Peter that he would sometimes make sure he was passing St Joseph's at afternoon playtime.

He recalls: 'Peter was always a little on what you might call the weak side; he took a long time to develop. In fact I don't think he started walking until he was about 15 months old, although he seemed quite normal otherwise. He learned to talk quickly and was mobile enough crawling around the floor. But he virtually learned to walk holding on to his mother's skirts and it was something he did until he was about three or four. Every time she moved he grabbed her and walked around the house with her. He walked everywhere with her. When he got to school he always seemed detached from the other children. I used to call in the afternoon to see how he was. There was a little corner in the schoolyard where he used to stand with his back in the angle of the buttress and he stayed there the whole of the playhour unless one of us called to see him. Then he'd come across and talk. He never seemed to get very much involved with the other children; he was never physically strong enough to cope with the usual sort of pushing and pulling that goes on among kids. He never took part in sport, and he was a very quiet kid. He'd rather sit in the house and read, anything that had words in it in fact. He was well into his teens before he started to make friends but he never caused any trouble at home. Their mother idolized all the children and I suppose he got that little bit of special attention because of his liking for staying around the house. The others, as they grew up and were a few years older, were off, but not Peter. He was always on his mum's side as well as being at her side.'

Any hopes John Sutcliffe had that Peter's transfer to the 'big school', nearby Cottingley Manor Secondary School, might help the boy become more outgoing and confident received a jolt when Peter was 12. Unbeknown to his parents he had been the subject of bullying at school from soon after his arrival, an attractive target through his lack of height and weight and almost timid nature. The outcome of over 12 months' bullying was for Peter Sutcliffe to devise his own antidote, an elaborate subterfuge which fooled the bullies as well as his parents.

After breakfast he would make a point of shouting a noisy 'I'm off, mam', before banging the door as if he'd gone through it. Instead he would tiptoe quietly upstairs and instal himself in the loft of their home in Manor Road, Cottingley, on the outskirts of Bingley, where they had moved a few years earlier.

There he had his comics and a torch and he would stay until lunchtime before sneaking down the stairs and repeating the procedure, banging the door and shouting 'Hello, mam.' The deceit was to last for almost two weeks before the school got in touch with John and Kathleen Sutcliffe, who were angry and sad that their son had felt the need to go to such lengths. John Sutcliffe went to the school and made it clear to the headmaster that he expected the culprits to be identified and deterred and, indeed, Peter did not find the need to play truant again. But not fighting the other boys, not chasing the girls, was in Bingley, as almost anywhere else, enough to set Peter Sutcliffe apart. He was regarded as 'different'.

One of the girls in his class at Cottingley Manor, who had started with him at St Joseph's nursery the same day when they were toddlers, was always struck by his shyness. Mrs Kathleen Arangie, who still lives in Bingley, says that even as children it was recognized how close Peter Sutcliffe had been to his mother. 'He was very shy and not like the rest of the boys in our class; in fact you only had to look at him and he would colour up and turn away. He never seemed interested in girls and if you turned around you would probably find him with a half-smile on his face, but he would quickly turn away if he thought you were looking at him,' she remembers.

With the indignity of the bullying still fresh in his mind as he ended his teenage years, Peter Sutcliffe decided to prepare himself for possible further problems. He started body-building, which surprised his father, a surprise which was to turn to something close to amazement later when Peter developed the strongest grip in the family, easily beating his two-years-younger brother Michael, a much rougher diamond than Peter, at arm wrestling.

So puberty did its work, and even though the girls in his class recall little other than his shyness from those years, his evolving personality is remembered clearly by one of the boys. In fact the face that Peter Sutcliffe never allowed the girls to see is the one class-mate Peter Burton, who is stll living in Bingley, remembers best – the Peter Sutcliffe who would boast of never refusing a 'dare'.

'He would do anything. He never seemed to care about getting caught or punished. Peter was caught climbing onto the school roof a few times looking for lost balls, which was forbidden, and as he got older, he tried to be the class clown in the classroom. He always seemed to be trying to get a laugh, to make the rest of us laugh. Yet he never seemed to be bothered about having a girlfriend or what passed as a girlfriend, like the rest of us did. I know he always thought the world of his mother, who was a marvellous woman, very protective towards the children. But Peter was the only one who seemed to return that affection in any major way. He was the one you used to see going to the shop with her basket. He was always happy to run errands for her. He was always more likely to argue with his father than his mother.'

With their growing family John and Kathleen Sutcliffe decided that they needed somewhere with more room, so he went to see the local council housing department. They were both pleased when they were offered a four-bedroomed semi-detached house in Cornwall Road, a steep climb on foot out of Bingley town centre but with an excellent view south across the valley. On a sunny day you could see the river Aire sparkling down there if you looked closely between the flat-topped houses. For Peter there were new friends to be made, and although he and his father never seemed to get on particularly well together he did try his hand at cricket and football, but only in the street or in the nearby fields with the boys and two or three girls who formed what could loosely be termed their gang.

When he was fifteen and ready to leave Cottingley Manor Secondary School in the summer of 1961 Peter Sutcliffe's academic achievement was the norm for the children of the working-classes in Bingley, and most other towns in the industrial North – almost total academic anonymity. Periods of enthusiasm and even evidence of ability at mathematics and English were few and far between, although his liking for art had never wavered. He didn't know what he wanted to do and didn't much care, the magic age of 16 looming and the prospect of a provisional motor-cycle licence occupying most of his thoughts.

Mr Michael Mahoney remembers Peter Sutcliffe as one of his pupils at Cottingley Manor not because he was in any way distinguished, but because he was part of the first class he ever taught on entering the profession. 'I always had the impression that, as with nearly all children of that age, he wanted to be part of the group, because all the other boys were mad about soccer and other sport; even though he was not, he would join them on their terms. The only area he showed any real interest in was practical lessons such as art and craft. He had some artistic ability, although he was not outstanding. Peter's trouble was he was always very hesitant to draw attention to himself, always the last person to speak up in class. He would never say anything during discussions unless he was asked a point, and then he would make it very obvious that he wished you had not singled him out. He was the sort of boy a teacher could easily overlook,' remembers Mr Mahoney. What didn't go without notice, though, was that Peter Sutcliffe had left school without sitting any of the examinations. But you don't need exams to ride a motor cycle, and in 1962 you didn't even need to wear a crash helmet when you rode it.

Peter's father had become firmly established at the wool mill down by the river in the heart of Bingley and had become a production line inspector, following the lines to see they were weaving the correct patterns. The boy didn't, however, save the money for his first second-hand motor bike from the wages he regarded as a pittance. No sooner had he started working under the same mill roof as his father than he seemed to have left to become an apprentice fitter with engineers and millwrights Brierley and Fairbank at their Central Works in Church Street, Bingley, in August 1961, just a few weeks after leaving school. By the following May he had decided the long road of apprentice-ship was not for him either. You could be dead before you were qualified to call yourself an engineer.

John and Kathleen went away for a short holiday with another couple, and their son, Keith Wilson, now a bricklayer and still living in Bingley, went to stay at Cornwall Road to keep Peter company. 'His conversation seemed to revolve only around motor bikes. He was motor-bike mad. Girls didn't seem to come into his thinking at all when I knew him.' So keen was the young Sutcliffe on motor bikes he even kept a Norton 600 engine beneath his bed. Billy Emery, a friend before and after he left school, often used to stay at Cornwall Road and sleep in the same bed as Peter. The Sutcliffe household was always a happy, warm place for him, particularly the welcome he received from Peter's mother. 'I used to enjoy going there, and sometimes would call seven nights a week. They seemed like a happy family and Mr Sutcliffe was a good baker. If there was a birthday he would bake the cake.' As they discovered the joys of drinking, before and after they reached the legal age of 18, the boys would regularly visit pubs in Bingley and sometimes go into Bradford.

Disconcertingly for Mr Emery, motor bikes, not girls, were Peter's main topic of conversation. 'I only went for a ride with him a few times on the back of his bike but he drove like a maniac. Peter never seemed to have any girlfriends, nor did he seem bothered about them. He was dead keen on keeping fit and had some chest expanders. We used to have some competitions with them but Peter could always beat me and his brother, Mick. He was good at mending the motor bikes and if anything went wrong with mine he would put it right. If it needed a spare part he would think nothing of going down to the garage and buying it for me.'

Peter may not have endeared himself to his father by his almost total disregard for sport, but a note of admiration overtakes John Sutcliffe as he recalls the first welcome signs of manliness in his son. The body-building exercises seemed to have been successful.

'Peter wasn't very big but he could throw those bikes around like a TT rider. It was as if he had found something at last that he was good at. He had two or three bikes, but as soon as he was old enough to have a car he got one. He seems to have had one ever since. He started going out more with the other boys of his own age, although he didn't make a lot of lasting friendships, and he never seemed to bother with girls at all,' says his father.

The burgeoning admiration was not totally mutual. Peter never came to terms with the amount of time his father spent with his cricket and football, his bowls and his amateur dramatics. But Peter kept an eye on his mother. Running errands was no trouble now, particularly on the back of a BSA Bantam, just like a despatch rider.

He had gone from being an apprentice engineer to working as a labourer, grinding cotton and synthetics into powder for the moulding trade, but a month before his eighteenth birthday he changed jobs yet again. Something completely different, he told a sceptical mother and father. 'I have thousands of people below me where I work now,' he added to his giggling sisters.

The house in Cornwall Road was a noisy, busy place, with the children and their friends and various neighbours constantly in and out. But after Peter had got the job as a gravedigger he seemed to become even more detached from his sisters' girlfriends, none of whom he had ever made feel particularly welcome in Cornwall Road. They remember him as a smart, even sharp dresser, but a man who rarely spoke; when he did it was about death and things appertaining to his job at the cemetery. When the house was full he preferred to stay in his bedroom and the girls and their friends were never allowed into his room. One increasingly regular caller at the house at that time was a woman from nearby Ferncliffe Road, who had the Sutcliffe children nudging and sniggering in the cruel way that children do at the funny signs she used to make with her hands and fingers. Mrs Wendy Broughton was a deaf mute whose visits became more regular; often she would call at the Sutcliffes' when Kathleen was out working. Was this fuel for the estate gossips? If the gossip reached Peter it didn't seem to bother him then, although he was to be mightily angry 12 years later about his father's friendship with Mrs Broughton.

Bingley cemetery is known locally as the coldest place in the town, yet in its pretty setting, overlooked by a local beauty spot, the Druid's Altar, and adjoining the playing fields of Bingley Grammar School, it is an attractive rather than a depressing sort of cemetery. But not the sort of place most Bingley lads would choose to work.

When Peter Sutcliffe started working there in 1964 he didn't think much to the £7 for a 44 hour week, but enjoyed what he assured his parents was a 'healthy outdoor job'. He was 18 now and had a car and a bit of money in his pocket, and they were good lads at the cemetery. They liked a drink and they liked a laugh.

Didn't Peter always have a morbid sense of humour, they say now. Gary Jackson worked there at the time and remembers the larks as he and Peter waited for the girls to come out of the nearby Bingley Girls Grammar School. There were two in particular who used to come over to see what was happening and Peter used to clown about and jump from grave to grave. And when they were digging fresh graves, they would come across a collapsed coffin that had been underground for years. There would be skeletons but it never bothered them. There was extra money to be earned when undertakers brought bodies to the chapel of rest and asked such as Peter and Gary to wash the bodies down. Five shillings, not bad money in those days, one of the perks of the job.

One of Peter's jokes was to get to work early, ahead of the others, and go and lie down on a slab with a shroud over himself. When the others came in he would start moving and moaning to give them a fright. Peter had a neatly trimmed beard in those days and his workmates nicknamed him 'Jesus'. Laurie Ashton, now a welder, was a colleague at the cemetery. 'Peter used to enjoy the job so much he would work overtime in the morning and at nights for some extra money. He certainly had a morbid interest in death and all things connected with it, although I suppose most people would regard anyone working in a cemetery as being morbid.

'We had been out boozing with another pal, Eric Robinson, one night and had certainly had a few drinks when Peter mentioned he had the key to the morgue. He said there were two "ripe ones" in there and suggested we should go and have a look at them, and seemed quite disappointed when we turned down his offer. Once he was re-opening a grave at the cemetery and I saw him chasing some grammar-school girls with an old skull. I thought that was a bit much but Peter was very amused. He came back laughing all over his face about it. Most of the time Peter was quiet and in some ways strange. It always seemed odd to me, for example, that on very hot days when we were digging graves everyone would take their shirts off and work stripped to the waist, but not Peter. He would just take his jacket off. He seemed very self-conscious and shy. If any of the lads wanted to go to the toilet they would go behind a gravestone, but not Peter. I always thought he was good looking but he never seemed able to chat up the girls. I often used to sleep with them at Peter's house, where there was always something going off, but not Peter.'

Friend Eric Robinson, now a window cleaner, who says he also worked at Bingley Cemetery with Peter Sutcliffe, remembers clearly after one funeral, when the artificial grass was still round the opening in the ground, Peter jumping into the grave and removing the lid from the coffin as if he was looking for something, and then shouting to nobody in particular, 'There's nowt here.' Not long afterwards, in the Royal Standard pub in Manningham Lane, Bradford, they were having a drink and Peter suddenly took his hand out of his pocket and opened his fist to reveal a selection of five or six rings. 'He had offered them to his sister Maureen who was about to get married, but she had recoiled in horror when he had told her they were from the fingers of bodies at the cemetery,' recalls Mr Robinson.

'Peter, of course, thought it was hilarious. On the other hand he was very backward at coming forward with girls other than his sisters. If we were in a pub and a couple of girls came in who Peter liked the look of he would mention it, but he never seemed to have it in him to go and talk to them. I got the impression that he thought that chatting girls up was somehow distasteful. I often wonder if it was anything to do with the fact that when we were back at the Sutcliffes' house at night his father on occasions would quite openly flatter the girls and pretend to fondle them – that is, his sisters' friends. He would reckon to mess about with them. There was no harm done, but it seemed to make Peter uncomfortable. He always seemed much closer to his mother, who was a very pleasant, kind woman.'

Peter Sutcliffe spent a lot of time in pubs and Eric Robinson was always struck by his attention to detail. 'His eyes would be everywhere and he didn't seem to miss anything. In fact he would notice things that you didn't.

Like if a girl was with a bloke and not taking any notice of him. He would draw it to our attention.' It was in the Royal Standard that younger brother Michael remembers Peter deciding to liven up the proceedings one evening. 'Late on in the evening we slipped into the toilet and Peter let off a smoke bomb. The fire brigade came and it caused a bit of a panic at the time, but it was his sort of joke,' says Michael Sutcliffe. 'Anything that he could make funny then he would make funny. If you were down in the dumps he would try and bring you straight out of it. He once shot ten starlings on the clothes line at home and they hung there with their claws. He called it "dead man's grip"; it was the sort of thing that amused Peter.'

Sutcliffe continued to regale his friends with increasingly bizarre stories of his experiences in Bingley cemetery. He told Keith Sugden how he had been digging a grave when he had come across some slabs of stone at a lower level. He claimed he had jumped in and landed on a body that had not been buried long. Mr Sugden remembers vividly the apparent delight Sutcliffe had derived from telling the story, of how he had landed on the chest of the body and it had sat upright, green and slimy with no eyeballs.

Mr Sugden regarded it as far-fetched, one of Peter's black comedies, but says there was no doubting the pleasure he got from relating the tale. For part of the time he was particularly friendly with Peter Sutcliffe, Mr Sugden lived in a flat in a house in Shipley he shared with other young people, male and female. Sutcliffe stayed there regularly and at one time spent more time living in the flat than he did at home in Cornwall Road. It was a lively time and most weekends there was drinking and other pleasures to be had. The men outnumbered the women, but the girls didn't complain, says Keith Sugden. 'I was involved with one particularly, but the others were not spoken for. In fact they were the sort of girls who made it a point of honour to spread their favours around. But Peter never bothered with any of them, even though there was unlimited opportunity. In fact he seemed very happy when I split up with my girlfriend. I well remember one morning when the two of us sort of staggered down to the kitchen for some breakfast after a heavy night drinking, although I must admit I was in a worse state than Peter. Very fragile. One of the girls had heard us coming and was laying naked on the table with her legs open. She said, ''Right, who wants me for breakfast?'' It sounds sordid, I know, but it was quite funny at the time. Peter was disgusted of course, and was not interested.'

When Mr Sugden became involved with another steady girlfriend, who was later to become his wife, he was aware of Sutcliffe's displeasure. The bearded gravedigger made it perfectly clear that he thought they were better off as a twosome. They often went out as a threesome but Mr Sugden believes Sutcliffe tried to create a split between him and girlfriend Doreen, and on one occasion went out of his way to create a situation she would find offensive.

He had arranged to collect the couple at Doreen's home, but when he arrived he had two other girls in the car with him. Mr Sugden believed they had been selected for their tart-like qualities. Mrs Doreen Sugden remembers the evening well. 'I didn't like the look of the girls at all, and when we got to the pub in Shipley Peter went out of his way to tell me they were on the game. His strategy worked, because I said I was upset and wanted to go home.' Mr Sugden adds that Sutcliffe had regularly boasted that he could always get what he described as 'scrubbers'. That night in Shipley, Doreen insisted on being run home, and all five of them got in Sutcliffe's car. When they arrived at her house, Sutcliffe whispered to Sugden that he should come to Cornwall Road a little later, when he had said goodnight to Doreen.

'I have to confess that I went and the girls were still there. It was obvious that one of them was intended for me and Peter suggested that I should sleep with this girl in the living-room while he took the other to his bedroom. But all of a sudden Peter's girl seemed turned off him and insisted on going home. We drove them to Keighley where they lived and that was that. It was a strange night.'

Yet Sutcliffe had a few more surprises for his friends. Mr Sugden says that some time later, a few months after he and Doreen had married and his contact with Sutcliffe had become almost non-existent, they had met in the Ferrands Arms in Bingley. Peter had mysteriously asked him if he would come into the toilet with him and when they were there had calmly unzipped his flies and asked Mr Sugden to look at his penis. 'It did look a mess and it certainly seemed as though he had contracted venereal disease. I told him the best thing he could do was to go to St Luke's hospital in Bradford and get it sorted out. I was staggered really, because apart from the two girls that night in the car with Doreen, I had never seen Peter Sutcliffe bother with girls. I never even saw him try and chat one up, and if they did come to him he would just nod and say "yes" or "no". It was as if, when we were friends, he was quite happy trailing after me.'

The only time Mr Sugden saw Sutcliffe show any sign of violence was on one occasion in the flat when a youth seemed to be forcing his attention on an unwilling sixteen-year-old girl. 'Peter told him to stop but he wouldn't, so he simply went over to him and knocked him down. Peter wasn't very big but he was very strong.'

Before they drifted apart Sutcliffe had asked Doreen if she could arrange for one of her friends to go out with

him. 'I asked some of them but they all said the same –
they thought Peter was weird. Once after Keith and me had
had a row Peter came to my house and invited me out for a
drink. He became really mad when I refused and said
something about "didn't I realize Keith only wanted me
for one thing". You know, sex. His eyes went all funny,
really wild. It was as if this was another attempt by Peter to
keep Keith and me apart. Some nights, Keith would come
to our house and sit and play the guitar and Peter would
just sit staring at him. There was a time when I used to
think that Peter was in love with Keith. Although I now
realize he simply admired him. Me and my sisters used to
tease Peter at the time saying "Where's your boyfriend
tonight, then?" – meaning Keith.'

Doreen Sugden was living in Cornwall Road when her
younger sisters Colleen and Jacqueline had been friendly
with Sutcliffe's sisters. Colleen, now Mrs Young,
remembers staying at the Sutcliffes' for the night when she
was 10 and Peter was almost 19. She had been standing at
the top of the staircase and completely unexpectedly felt
herself being lifted up bodily and thrown down to the
bottom, where she picked herself up, luckily uninjured,
and looked towards the top of the stairs.

'Peter was standing there, staring down at me with those
funny dark eyes. He had that silly, sickly, giggly grin on his
face that was so familiar. He never said a word. When I
used to stay at the Sutcliffes' house at night we would lock
the door of the bedroom. That house in Cornwall Road
came to life at midnight and on one occasion I opened my
eyes and saw Peter going through his sister Maureen's
handbag. He didn't say anything and Maureen told him to
get out, but he gave her such a look. It was his eyes that
were so strange, they look through you rather than at you.'

Mrs Young says that after the Jacqueline Hill murder in

November 1980 she had watched the dead girl's mother branding the killer as a coward on television and had said to her sister, 'I bet it could be one of the Sutcliffes.' That sister, Mrs Jacqueline Ibbitson, offered the thought, 'The strange thing about Peter Sutcliffe was always that none of the men who knew him could ever see anything wrong about him, but the girls all thought he was weird. In fact none of the girls in Bingley that I ever knew would ever have anything to do with him.'

But the unpredictable graph of fate was to witness the crossing of two lines which then entwined and clung to each other in a mysterious way – mysterious to all but two. The girls of Bingley may not have felt able to respond warmly to the eldest Sutcliffe boy, the one with the beard and the black, demanding eyes, the one who worked in the graveyard and made jokes about corpses, but as he sat in the back room of the Royal Standard in Manningham Lane that night in 1966, and listened to the music of the weekly disco, he did something his friends had never witnessed before. He deliberately chose to talk to a girl.

Sonia Szurma really shouldn't have been at the Royal Standard at all that night. Her father would have been displeased if he had known the disco was actually in a pub. Bodhan Szurma was a careful man, almost obsessive where his daughters were concerned. They may have been in Bradford, in England's northern parts, but there were the values of the old country to maintain. He and his wife Maria, a Ukrainian, had arrived from Czechoslovakia at a transit camp near York in 1947. Polish-born, according to Home Office records, he had been a physical-training teacher and university lecturer in the old country. Here he was in a completely new land, with new ways and a new language to learn. He could of course play chess, with its international language, but it wasn't going to be easy.

The council-owned semi-detached in Tanton Crescent, Bradford, was an improvement on the temporary house in Earl Street, since demolished, and there was a garden to grow flowers and vegetables. It wouldn't be that bad; no reason why Czech couldn't be spoken in the house. After all, an Englishman's home, even an émigré's home, is his castle.

The job as a yarn-tester in a nearby factory was not too difficult, and there was the Ukrainian Association to help. At Tanton Crescent Marianne was born first and then, on 10 August 1950, Oksana. Mr and Mrs Szurma's gesture towards the old country and the old ways and names was subjected to a rethink four years later, with the prospect of school looming, and Oksana became Sonia.

The house in Tanton Crescent was to be a haven for serious matters like books and music, current affairs, and reminiscences about the places they had left behind; not a place for the frivolous aspects of life, like playing tennis in the street, bringing friends home from school, or even television – definitely not television. Marianne went to London when she was sixteen and went on to become a licentiate of the Royal Academy of Music, specializing in piano performance. She is a piano teacher today and lives in Alperton, Middlesex.

Sonia, whom neighbours remember sitting knitting on the front step with mother, talking in Czech, was artistic and musical also, and her father had high hopes for her as she approached her final examinations at Grange Grammar School. Sonia had attained six C.S.E.s when she was seventeen, and it was said among her schoolmates that her father had not been pleased with her performance. One can only guess as to whether he had been pleased a few months earlier when the young man in black leather motor-cycle gear and a Mexican-style moustache and beard had appeared in Tanton Crescent and was shyly introduced as Peter from Bingley.

But Peter wasn't the same as the other boys. That first night in the Royal Standard he hadn't been bothered about dancing, but had sat and talked. He was a bit of a humorist, a bit of a joker with words, yet somehow shy, his dark eyes watching her intently as she told him about herself. She wasn't like the other girls, either; certainly not the ones in Bingley. They spoke with accents different from Sonia's, for this girl had inherited some of her parents' way of speech. He didn't seem to mind, and there was none of the silly talk that the few other boys she had made any contact with seemed to indulge in; and none of those straying hands, urgently fumbling to squeeze and caress where they shouldn't. He was a gentleman, Peter; he knew how to treat a woman. Father would be pleased about that, surely.

1966 was not just to be the year John Sutcliffe cheered excitedly in front of the television set in Cornwall Road as England at last won the World Cup; or when his eldest son Peter made an announcement 'This is Sonia' that was to shake yet please his parents. (She was the first girlfriend he had ever taken home, and the last.) It was also to be the year when Peter made another friend, Trevor, destined to be his best friend, yet fourteen years later to agonize over his rôle.

John Sutcliffe well remembers the day he met Sonia. 'Peter took us all by surprise. He just walked in one Sunday evening with this dark-haired, lovely girl. He said, "Dad, this is Sonia", and we said our hellos. They came in and sat down and had a meal with us, the first of many. She was the very first girl he had ever brought home and I was impressed. Sonia was very quiet, she's always been very quiet, a beautiful girl, but very, very quiet.'

But he doesn't remember Trevor Birdsall; there's no reason why he should. Trevor was eighteen, a local youth from Bingley, and met Peter in a pub, their common ground. They were to spend many hundreds of hours either in pubs or driving to or from them in Peter Sutcliffe's succession of cars over the subsequent years. They shared a liking for hand-pulled Tetley's beer. And they shared a terrible secret.

When they first became friendly Peter told Trevor Birdsall about his girlfriend Sonia, and how she was going to be a teacher. Bodhan Szurma's attitude to her studies did not falter despite Sonia's less than satisfactory performance with her C.S.E. examinations in the summer of 1967.

It was decided that an 'O'-level course at the local technical college in Bradford would be necessary if she were ever to go to teacher-training college. Peter's career structure was less clearly defined, and in the same year, at the age of 21, he was surprised to find himself an ex-grave-digger. Yet he shouldn't have been. There had been too many mornings when an extra hour in bed after the previous late night had tested the patience of his boss at the cemetery to the limit. 'Peter was a good, hard worker but a bad time-keeper. I had to sack him because he could never get to work on time,' remembers Mr Douglas McTavish, who still lives at Bingley cemetery and coincidentally is now a drinking friend of Sutcliffe's father in Bingley Working Men's Club.

But Peter was not deterred. One of the things that impressed his father about his eldest son was his ability regularly to find work, his concern at not being a parasite on society. Peter's motivation was not to seek job satisfaction. His reward came with the few pounds in his pocket. As long as there was enough to put a couple of gallons of petrol in the car and to buy a drink of an evening then that was O.K.

By the end of 1969, van driver Trevor Birdsall knew there was something different about his pal Peter. He seemed to have a thing about the girls on the game. He joked about them and sometimes with them, but something seemed to make him angry. And then there was the night in Bradford when he had left his friend in the car and returned a few minutes later saying he had had a go 'at one of the bags'. When he had tried to hit her with a brick in a sock, the sock had come apart and the brick had fallen out. He showed Trevor the sock. There must be an easier way.

The following year, 1970, sister Maureen became friendly with a soldier, Robin Holland, a private in the Royal Engineers. They were to marry three years later, and although they are now divorced, Mr Holland has distinctive memories of his brother-in-law.

'The four of us, Sonia, Maureen, Peter and me, used to go out regularly together for a drink. The Sutcliffe family often used to have parties for one thing or another and Peter always had plenty to say for himself. The favourite topic of conversation, more a sermon really, was men who two-timed their wives. He used to call them "beasts". In fact the rest of the family seemed to think Peter was a saint, sort of the perfect son. But I know he wasn't. I had regularly gone out with him drinking to pubs in the red light districts and his main topic of conversation had been sex and prostitutes. He regularly boasted about prostitutes he said he had been with, so when he used to be on his hind legs at family parties going on about unfaithful married men I used to sit there thinking "you hypocrite".

'I've been with him at a pub in the Lumb Lane district of

Bradford and known Peter get up and go out with a girl for five or ten minutes and then come back and sit down with a silly grin on his face. I stopped going out with him in the end; I couldn't stand the hypocrisy,' says Mr Holland.

By September 1970 Sonia was at last ready to take the positive step towards becoming a teacher. It had taken a while, for she was by then 20, but armed with seven 'O' levels and a Royal Academy of Music Grade 4 Certificate in piano. It was a time of contrasting emotions, for she was ready to leave the constraints of Tanton Crescent behind for the first time in two decades. Her father had insisted that when she was in London for the course at the Rachel McMillan college at Greenwich she should live with her older sister Marianne.

And then there was Peter, not too happy about her moving away from Bradford, although he didn't attempt to stop her. It wasn't far to London and he would try to get down every other weekend or so; and the holidays were long. There was talk of a possible engagement and the two of them always accepted that there would be a wedding one day. Depends if anybody asks us, Peter used to joke. But if Sonia could qualify as a teacher the money would be useful, with Peter always changing his job.

Peter's maverick ways continued and during Sonia's first two terms at college he had a number of casual labouring jobs, some of them in London, enabling him to spend more time with Sonia who wasn't having the easiest of times with her studies. She started her second year at Rachel McMillan in September 1971 and two months later Peter got a job with Trevor Birdsall on the packaging line at Bairds television factory in Bradford. He left when they asked him to go on the road as a salesman. He was personable and smart and could drive, but Peter wasn't interested; he didn't want to join the rat race and would rather stay on the production line with his pals. When it was time for Sonia to go back to college in September she wasn't happy; she hadn't been enjoying the course very much and would rather have stayed in Bradford with Peter. He told her not to worry, that he would travel down as regularly as possible; in fact he would go down and stay there a few weeks to keep her company.

As it was, Peter brought Sonia back to Bradford from London after she suddenly had a nervous breakdown in November and dropped out of the course. He was to nurse and care for her and show great concern. She was to remember that concern years later. At college, Sonia had started the course with painting as her speciality but had soon changed to pottery. As when she had been at school in Bradford she had seemed to have no close friends, content with sister Marianne's company when Peter was not about. The pottery teacher at the college, Miss Margaret Kerr, recalled, 'I don't think anybody got to know Sonia well. Although it was a small college where one tends to get to know most people, she was somebody who didn't make an enormous impact. Sonia was just a quiet girl; indeed she had a bit of a language problem. Her accent seemed to inhibit her somewhat.'

Susan Leigh and Elizabeth Johnson, who were students at Rachel McMillan College at the same time as Sonia Szurma, also remember her as quiet and withdrawn, with an apparent language problem, and a distinct foreign accent. 'Myself and my group tried to get her to mix a bit more, but it was a job,' Susan recalled. 'She didn't say anything at all in the dining-room at college,' Elizabeth added. Both girls knew of her boyfriend and it was generally known in the college that she had had mental trouble. 'We certainly knew there was this boyfriend, but she kept it very much to herself. We knew he came to

London to stay with her, but we never saw him because she would never come to parties,' one of the girls remembered.

Back at Tanton Crescent within the protective shell thrown around her by her mother and father, and with the solicitous attention of Peter, Sonia was told to rest. A few months later, she enjoyed a brief spell as a student teacher and subsequently enrolled to train as a State Registered Nurse, although she persevered only a few months. In April 1973 Peter took what was to be for him a steady job, working permanent nights for two years at the Britannia Works of Anderton International, again down by the river Aire in the heart of Bingley. He was in the heat-treatment section, strengthening metal clips by heating them and dipping them in a chemical bath.

Even Peter, whose record of bad time-keeping as a result of late rising was to plague him throughout his working life, managed to arrive on time for the night shift. He was regarded as a reliable worker but he seemed to go out of his way to keep most of the other men there at arm's length. When he left, some of the men on his shift pointed out that Peter Sutcliffe hadn't spoken to them once during the whole time he was there. There was one exception, however – Mr Peter Fitzgerald.

'I don't think he had a lot to do with many people because in a funny sort of way Peter was easily hurt. He readily took offence, although he would not make a fuss about it. He just withdrew into his shell. He didn't go in much for drinking like the rest of us and seemed to be careful with his money. In fact he ran a smart Capri GT but I could only afford an old banger. He can't have wasted his money like I did. Very occasionally he went out with a group of the lads to Bradford, and once one of them suggested after a night's drinking that we go off to find some girls who were on the game. Peter said he wasn't interested in prostitutes and so the two of us just came home. He always seemed a bit shy with girls but very devoted to Sonia. I know he was very upset after she had had what he described as a nervous breakdown and had had to leave college. He told me it had been due to pressure of work. The only other woman he used to speak about with affection was his mother. He seemed to dote on her.'

By 1974 people were beginning to ask questions. When were he and Sonia going to get married? Were they going to wait forever? He tried to explain that Sonia had always wanted to qualify as a teacher first to enable them to have two incomes and be in a position to buy a reasonable house, and that while there had been a set-back to her plans he was working regularly at Andertons and they were still trying to save money towards the distant objective of marriage.

But Peter did give it some thought and came to the conclusion that eight years after meeting at the Royal Standard disco, if they weren't sure now they never would be. But Sonia was still only 24, and had dreamed for a long time of being a teacher. That was still her ambition and would continue to be. But Peter had made up his mind, and her main worry was the uncertainty about her own future and, of course, the fact that they couldn't afford the deposit for a house. No doubt Kathleen Sutcliffe would have been happy for Sonia to squeeze into Peter's bedroom – make it a sort of flat, however temporary – but things were not as they should be at Cornwall Road between John and Kathleen; there were constant rows about his alleged womanizing, and talk of separations and the like.

In fact it wasn't to be long before John Sutcliffe did

leave home and move in with Wendy Broughton, the deaf mute who had taught him to understand sign language and who was by then herself divorced. Peter's sister Maureen recalls the period with sadness and thinks her father was with Mrs Broughton for approximately three months, although Mrs Broughton herself thinks it was nearer two months. 'There must have been 20 or 25 incidents involving other women over the years with my father. I just felt very sorry for my mother,' says Maureen now.

But for Peter and Sonia the decision was taken, and although Sonia and her father were not on the best of terms, Bodhan and Maria's offer of a solution to their housing problem was accepted. Sonia and Peter, after a honeymoon in Paris, would move into the house in Tanton Crescent with them. The date was set, Sonia's 24th birthday on 10 August, and the appointed place was to be Clayton Baptist Church, not far from the bride's home. Maybe not a Catholic wedding as Kathleen would have preferred, but, all the same, a happy day for her, the wedding of her first-born.

Peter went to see the Rev William Nelson alone, and explained that though they were not churchgoers, he and Sonia had once been to a Baptist wedding and had been impressed by the way in which it had been conducted. They asked for theirs to be carried out the same way. 'I remember Sonia was very shy and nervous but the wedding was very straightforward although there were not many guests. I never saw them again after the marriage,' recalls the Rev Nelson. As far as he was concerned the day varied in only one respect from such occasions in his church. He was not invited to the reception, which was held at a pub outside Bradford. But everyone at the wedding seemed agreed – they were a handsome couple. The best man was Ronald Wilson, an old schoolfriend from Cottingley

Manor, who wasn't insulted to be told that he was in actual fact third choice.

He recalls: 'I hadn't seen much of Peter for a long while, since we used to tinker with cars together. He certainly had closer friends than me and asked them to be best man, but they had given some excuse. He asked me to do it as a favour a few days before the wedding, saying he was stuck.' Sonia had worn white and Peter, a dark suit. The lime-green Ford Capri GT which had appeared in Tanton Crescent at irregular intervals, and at irregular times, became a permanent feature outside the Szurmas' house.

The young couple and the older couple had long and serious talks before the wedding, about the former's prospects and about their intentions of saving a deposit for their own home. They planned to save every penny they could for the deposit. Bodhan never made it clear what his innermost thoughts were about his youngest daughter's choice for a partner for life, but Peter was a hard worker and he seemed careful with his money.

It quickly became apparent to Peter that the job on permanent nights at Andertons was inconvenient for a newly married man, although it did have its advantages. He could spend the days tinkering with his car. Six months after they were married in 1974 Peter recognized the chance of a £400 redundancy pay-off as a way of ending the night-work but, more importantly, saw it as the key to a scheme he had been quietly nurturing for some time. He knew about engines and engineering and he could drive; in fact he was a damned good driver. So Peter took the £400 and within four months was the proud possessor of an HGV licence. He had spent £200 of the redundancy money to buy a total of 30 hours instruction with the Apex Driving School, Cullingworth, near Keighley.

He passed the HGV test Class 1 at Steeton driving school on June 4th, two days after his twenty-ninth birthday. Three days later he treated himself to a white Ford Corsair, with a black roof, although he still had the lime-green Ford Capri GT. There was plenty to celebrate: things were looking up.

One month later, in the early hours of Saturday 5 July, Peter William Sutcliffe drove to Keighley and hit Anna Patricia Rogulskyj three times over the head with a hammer, pulled up her clothing and left her with slash marks from a sharp instrument across the stomach.

Inspired by Peter's success in gaining his HGV licence Sonia decided to be positive about her unfulfilled wish to become a teacher, and enrolled at the Margaret McMillan college in Bradford for a teacher-training course. On Friday 15 August Peter Sutcliffe and Trevor Birdsall, the drinking friend he had never lost touch with, drove to Halifax and visited a number of pubs in and around the town. Late in the evening, after the pubs had shut, Peter left Trevor in the car for ten minutes.

Housewife and mother of three Mrs Olive Smelt was knocked to the pavement with two blows to the head with a hammer-type instrument. Her clothing had been pulled up and slash marks inflicted on her back. There were two lacerations above her eyes. It was to be more than five years before Trevor Birdsall told the police about that night. Ten weeks later Wilma McCann was dead.

On 29 September Peter started work as a driver, but not of heavy goods vehicles. He became a delivery man for a tyre firm and had to settle for a two-year-old rigid-bodied four-wheeler. He had discovered the harsh facts of HGV life. The jobs are there for experienced drivers, but where do you get the experience? Sutcliffe was to stay with the Common Road Tyre Company, of Oakenshaw, tucked into the angle formed by the junction of the trans-Pennine M62 motorway and the M606 spur into Bradford, for just five months. He left on 5 March 1976, after receiving an official warning for bad time-keeping on 2 February.

The firm's records for 29 October, the day before Wilma McCann was bludgeoned to death at 1.30 in the morning, show that driver Sutcliffe had completed deliveries to the Skipton and Barnoldswick areas and had arrived for work on time the following morning, 30 October, and proceeded to make deliveries and pick-ups to Halifax and Leeds. Three weeks later, 26-year-old Joan Harrison was to die at Preston in Lancashire, a murder which was later to be regarded as a possible Yorkshire Ripper killing. She was battered to death in a disused garage shortly after 10 p.m. That morning Sutcliffe had been six minutes late for work and records show that, on a full day, he had delivered tyres to Ilkeston in Derbyshire. The following morning, 21 November, he was eight minutes late and had then driven to Chester and back.

On the evening of 20 January 1976, Sutcliffe dealt housewife and part-time prostitute Emily Jackson two massive blows to the head in a disused cul-de-sac in Chapeltown, Leeds. He then proceeded to stab her 51 times in her stomach and back, some of the wounds being inflicted by a screwdriver. He stamped on her right thigh leaving a ribbed pattern with his boot.

That day he had been picking up tyres in Pudsey, between Leeds and Bradford, and on the following morning he was driving to the Pirelli depot at Burton-on-Trent as Det. Chief Supt. Dennis Hoban and forensic experts were viewing the desperately mutilated remains of Mrs Jackson and coming to terms with the implications of her death.

Seven months after leaving the tyre company, having received a number of rejections of his applications for jobs as a long-distance lorry driver because of his lack of experience, Sutcliffe was to give Sonia the great news. In October 1976, he got a job as a driver at last, with T. and W.H. Clark (Holdings) Limited on the Canal Road Industrial Estate, between Shipley and Bradford.

Tom Clark and his son William were soon to overcome any reservations they may have had about taking on an inexperienced new driver. The new man was quiet and polite and kept the most perfect records they had ever seen. As soon as anything was wrong with the lorry, no matter how small, he logged it. Very conscientious; a pity all the drivers weren't like him. Four months later, on 5 February 1977, Sutcliffe took Irene Richardson to Soldiers Field, Roundhay Park, Leeds, hit her three times over the head with a hammer, and slashed and stabbed her stomach so badly her intestines spilled out.

Dennis Hoban was perplexed. Was he seeking a man who simply enjoyed killing women in an overtly brutal way, who got some sort of sexual release from the very act of ending the lives of the McCanns and Jacksons and Richardsons of this world? Was it an orgasmic frenzy which manifested itself in ejaculation at the time, or soon afterwards, or did the memory of the act sustain the killer? Did it enable him to maintain sexual relations with his wife or womanfriend, over subsequent weeks and months, safe in the secret knowledge that his arousal was securely based on what had gone before? Or was he another sort of monster? Mr Hoban speculated publicly that the killer could have a pathological hatred of prostitutes.

Privately he expressed concern at the implications of such a prognosis. What if the killer was suffering from, for example, schizophrenia, and part of his being felt the need to cleanse the streets of undesirable to him women, women on the dirtiest game of all. Then every female would be at risk. Did he hear voices in his head urging him on? Would the street-cleaner see every woman walking along a pavement after dark as a whore, a life to be taken?

In May 1976, nine months before the Richardson killing, coloured prostitute Marcella Claxton had felt the weight of Sutcliffe's hammer at the same Soldiers Field, although the assault was not linked by the police with the McCann and Jackson deaths at the time. She was sure her attacker, the man with the dark, angry eyes, had stood and relieved himself sexually as she lay on the ground, the blood from her bursting head coursing into her eyes.

In September 1976 a barrister in Bradford decided he wanted to return to work in his home country, Pakistan; but first he had to sell his house, number six, Garden Lane, Heaton. It had been a happy home, a gathering-place for some of the élite of Bradford, friends and acquaintances of the popular and well-connected Nasim Rahman. A frequent visitor was the head of his chambers, Labour M.P. Edward Lyons, embryo Social Democrat. It shouldn't take long to sell the house which was probably the best in the road. A couple from Belgium seemed certain to buy.

CHAPTER 3

So Sweet, So Clear

In the pubs and clubs, in the shops and on the street-corners, indeed wherever the good-time girls gathered in Chapeltown, the Ripper legend had become fact. Have you heard what he does to them? Cuts them open, pulls their insides out; I've even heard he cuts their tits off. For a few short weeks after Irene Richardson's death the girls almost deserted the streets of Chapeltown, the brave or foolhardy ones trying to operate in pairs or threes, ostentatiously making it clear to any would-be clients that their friends were taking car numbers – so no funny business!

For a while the normally brittle relationship between police and prostitutes became even more strained, as detectives warned the girls off the streets and made repeated journeys to their flats and bedsitters, seeking elusive information about the killer. They felt sure that the man who had taken the lives of three women who had prostituted themselves must be known to others. But it was hard, and relationships were to be strained for a very long time. Many of the girls left Leeds, and even Yorkshire, altogether, going to stay in Manchester, Glasgow, Nottingham or London, hoping that things would become normal before they returned.

The Ripper was the subject of many animated conversations in Bradford's red-light area, the Manningham Lane–Lumb Lane–Oak Lane district. But Patricia Atkinson wasn't worried, with her own flat in

Bradford and not having to bother much with the car trade. She said she preferred to be called Tina rather than Patricia, and sometimes added the surname McGee; even when she married Asian immigrant worker Ray Mitra she regularly called herself Tina Atkinson. They were to have three daughters in quick succession – Judy, Jill and Lisa – but then the strain of being married to a Westerner, particularly one with Tina's waywardness, became too much for Mr Mitra and he sought a divorce.

Tina Atkinson was now free to drink and dance as often as she liked and have as many menfriends as she wanted. By the spring of 1976 she was operating quite openly as a prostitute from a small flat in Oak Avenue – Flat 3, at number 9, just round the corner from Oak Lane. She was slim and dark-haired and attractive, with a full sensual mouth.

The caretaker of the flats where she lived, Mr Jack Robinson, never actually spoke to Tina Atkinson but he had noted how smartly she dressed; strangely, in fact, she always seemed to be wearing the same outfit. On the night of Saturday 23 April, she had dressed in just the same way – short, black leather jacket, blue jeans, blue shirt – and was carrying a blue denim handbag when she left her flat and headed for the busy red-light pubs, where she was well known for her heavy drinking.

Tina had had a good Easter but that had been almost a fortnight earlier and her money was almost gone. She called in at the Perseverance, in Lumb Lane, a lively pub where the West Indians and Pakistanis were more interested in the games of dominoes than the girls looking for business in the saloon bar. As the evening wore on Tina Atkinson became more and more drunk and by 10 p.m. had made her way to a bar nearer home, the Carlisle in Carlisle Road, a short walk from her flat. The staff remember her announcing she was leaving at 10.15 p.m. and watching her stagger towards the door.

It was a warm evening and the ladies of the street were much in evidence. A number of them saw Tina walking around rather unsteadily until just after 11 p.m. But then she was gone, down Church Street, towards St Mary's Road, not far from Manningham Lane, the busy road out of Bradford which takes you up the Aire Valley through Shipley, with classy Heaton up to the left on the hill, and on towards Bingley and Keighley. Tina Atkinson made it a rule never to have to work on Sunday unless it was financially unavoidable. She said goodnight to the last Saturday night client and climbed into bed for a long luxurious sleep well into the Sabbath. Knowing her habits, long-time friend Mr Robert Henderson waited until early evening, 6.30 p.m., before walking round to Tina's flat hoping for a coffee and a natter.

He knocked twice on the door but there was no reply, and when he tried the door handle he found it open. He pushed the door gently and moved slowly into the flat, conscious of the possibility that Tina might have one of her friends with her. But that was unlikely. As he stepped through the door he noticed the pool of blood on the floor, just one stride inside the flat. There on the bed was a lumpy bundle covered in blankets, and Mr Henderson did not need to go any further to know that what he could see of the side of the still, white face, the arm and the blood on the pillow, meant Tina was dead. He rushed to Mr Robinson, in the caretaker's flat, and almost hysterically shouted at him in his distress that there had been 'a murder'.

Professor Gee made his way to Bradford from Leeds and when he slowly pulled back the blanket from the body on the bed the girl's face was almost unrecognizable. She

had initially been attacked as she stepped through her door
and had received four massive blows to her head. Her
killer had then removed her coat before lifting her on to
the nearby bed. Her faded denim jeans and pants had been
dragged down together but her jeans had later been
partially pulled back up. Her bra had been hoisted above
her breasts which were exposed. She had been stabbed six
times in her stomach and there were further signs of
stabbing attempts to her back, although the skin was not
broken, and some slash marks along the left side of her
body.

   Professor Gee thought the wounds had been caused by a
knife or chisel approximately $\frac{1}{2}''$ wide. A blood sample
showed Tina had consumed twenty measures of spirits and
had died probably at midnight. A vaginal swab revealed
the presence of semen but this was thought to be as a result
of sexual activity some time before her death. But the most
startling clue for the police was a size seven boot print
from a Dunlop Warwick wellington boot, the same as that
found on Emily Jackson's thigh, but this time on the
bottom bed sheet.

By any standards George Oldfield was entitled to
congratulate himself on the success he had attained in his
chosen career as a policeman by the summer of 1977.
When he left Archbishop Holgate Grammar School, York,
he had volunteered for the Navy and had served on
minesweepers in the Western Approaches, taken part in
the D-Day Landings and been demobbed as a petty officer
in 1946. He joined the old West Riding force and 31 years
later, most of the time spent in the C.I.D. in different parts
of the county, he found himself in his early fifties behind
the desk of the Assistant Chief Constable (Crime) at West
Yorkshire Police Headquarters in Wakefield.

He was overweight, smoked too many cigarettes a day, and liked a glass of Scotch. Thoughts of retirement and perhaps a lucrative security consultancy post in industry had crossed his mind, but being a policeman was a secure job and he and his wife Margaret were still educating their children. Their eldest daughter was at direct-grant Wakefield Girls High School, and one of George Oldfield's proudest moments was when she became Head Girl. She was to elect to study dentistry and, ironically, chose Newcastle University in a part of the north-east that was to occupy her father's thoughts considerably after she moved there. Their eldest son was at a private school, Silcoates, just outside Wakefield, and the other son was due to follow him later.

As for most people, life was not perfect for George Oldfield, but he was content that, despite the financial burden, he was giving his children a start in life full of potential for the future. But there were clouds. One which appeared annually, and which was in fact due the following month, was the anniversary of the death of Oldfield's first daughter, who had died from leukaemia when she was only six, fifteen years earlier. Mr Oldfield had a reputation for being a hard detective, among his own men as well as among the criminals he battled with, although friends say his bluff manner can be deceiving. He rarely talked about his daughter's death but readily concedes the tragedy could have affected his attitude to his job. 'It was a traumatic experience, but whether it affected my approach to the job, I wouldn't like to say; the whole thing certainly made me more mature. As a detective you often see and understand the agony of grief and misery the loss of life, particularly a young life, causes. It has never been difficult for me to feel for these people,' he says.

Of more recent concern to George Oldfield, in the

summer of 1976, in his role as overall head of the West Yorkshire C.I.D., were the deaths of three prostitutes in Leeds and another in Bradford over the previous 16 months. On the morning of Sunday 26 June, as he toyed with the prospect of a few hours' gardening at his home at Grange Moor, between Wakefield and Huddersfield, he received a telephone call which was to herald a change in his life so dramatic that its implications can only now be appreciated. The news was stark and terrible. The man who had taken the lives of Wilma McCann, Emily Jackson, Irene Richardson and Patricia Atkinson, had now claimed that of a sixteen-year-old girl, barely out of school. After a brief discussion with Chief Constable Ronald Gregory, it was agreed that the Assistant Chief Constable (Crime) should join the troops on the ground and personally spearhead the quickly escalating inquiry.

A bearded lorry driver's secret life brought fame to the Leeds area of Chapeltown and with it an almost universal misunderstanding of the area's characteristics. When journalists from all over the world descended on Chapeltown after a Ripper killing it suited them to describe it as seedy, miserable, decaying and dangerous. There was probably no conscious will to deceive the public, but the myth of the twentieth-century Ripper had been born, and it was more convenient to portray Chapeltown as a modern equivalent to the original Ripper's East End slums rather than what close examination shows it to be – a multi-racial suburb of considerable (albeit faded) elegance, leafier than most other parts of Leeds, with shops and cafés to cater to a range of ethnic cultures. And, very low down the list of characteristics, a fairly high proportion of prostitutes.

Before the Ripper killings, many respectable Leeds

people were probably only dimly aware that prostitutes existed in any number in Chapeltown. Chapeltown is in the north of the city and Leeds is, like many provincial cities, divided socially into two halves. South Leeds is considerably poorer and more industrial than the northern part. North Leeds has an inner band of motorway and light-industrial development with only a few small residential areas; then a band of once-smart Victorian suburbs, of which Chapeltown is one; and then, two miles from the city centre, essentially Victorian suburbs which have retained their elegance. After that, while still within three miles of Leeds Town Hall, come the suburbs of the 'thirties and later, which peter out into little-spoiled countryside.

Socially, Chapeltown may not be the choicest of places to live. You are unlikely to remain in Chapeltown if you can possibly afford to move. When Jewish immigrants, who settled in the now demolished Leylands slum, almost in the centre of Leeds, moved out to the Victorian mansions of Chapeltown, they had truly made it. Synagogues were built in Chapeltown, just as Sikh and Muslim places of worship are built today; but the Jews were not there to stay. Seeking fresher air, they moved on into outer suburbs like Moortown and Alwoodley between the 'thirties and 'fifties, and precisely as in London's East End, they left behind a large number of Jewish businesses and shops, some of which continue to thrive. Although a Jewish working-class community of mostly older people survives in Chapeltown (again, just as in the East End or the Lower East Side) most inhabitants today are poor Commonwealth immigrants and very poor whites, many of whom are eastern Europeans who settled in Leeds after the War. The area is lively and cosmopolitan during the day, but quiet and rather eerie at night, with people mostly passing through, perhaps stopping to buy bagels or Indian spices, on their way to more prosperous areas.

But Chapeltown does have a seedy side. Elegant houses crudely broken up into depressing little flats; pubs that are neither plastic-smart nor wood-and-glass-quaint, but simply shabby; hard-headed prostitutes who do it for a living – sad single women who drift into selling sex in order to support children. This is Peter Sutcliffe's Chapeltown.

On the evening of Saturday 26 June, teenager Jayne MacDonald bent down to kiss her father 'cheerio' as he sat in the fireside chair in their modest but happy home in Reginald Terrace, Chapeltown. Just behind him was the silver cup she and her brother and sister had bought him, inscribed 'World's Best Dad'. Jayne was happy. She was 16, had not long left school, had got a job in the shoe department of a local supermarket, and it was Saturday night, her favourite night of the week. Her freshly washed hair was shining, she had on her blue and white gingham skirt, and she was going dancing. As her father was later to say, 'She was almost bursting with optimism and the sheer joy of life.'

At 9.45 a.m. the following morning, Sunday, the sounds of an all-night West Indian party had not long faded away when two young children made their way into the adventure playground between Reginald Street and Reginald Terrace, an oasis for them in a sea of once-superb terraced houses just off the Chapeltown Road. Over near a wall the children found the body of Jayne MacDonald.

She was lying face down and the gingham skirt had been disarranged. Her blue and white halter-neck sun top had been pulled up to expose her middle. The police quickly established that Jayne had been struck on the back of the head as she walked along Reginald Street past the adventure playground. There were spots of blood on the pavement outside the entrance, and Jayne had been dragged 20 yards into the darkness of the play area. She had received three blows to the head and repeated stabbing to the chest through the same wound. She had been stabbed once in the back.

When it became apparent that warm Sunday that the killer of Yorkshire prostitutes had struck again (63 days after Tina Atkinson had died in Bradford), and that his latest victim was a 16-year-old, the nation sat up and took notice. Det. Chief Supt. Hobson, by now on familiar ground, identified Jayne from the contents of her handbag, and the mother and father, waiting unawares in their home just a short walk away, were told.

From that moment Wilfred MacDonald's own will to live began to ebb away, as surely as if someone had started to lace his food with poison. Just 28 grieving months later he was dead, killed by a broken heart, insisted his wife, Irene. Since Jayne's death he had developed nervous asthma, had been unable to work, and had simply lost the will to live, a victim of the Ripper as much as Jayne. As he was finally laid to rest, friends remembered his oft-repeated words as he stared endlessly out from his armchair: 'She smelled so sweet, so clean, when she bent down to kiss me goodbye. She was perfect, just like a flower.'

The police search in 1977 for the man who had cruelly crushed Jayne was quite relentless, and by September Jim Hobson was able to tell the Leeds Coroner, Mr James Walker, that by that time officers had interviewed residents in 679 homes in 21 streets in the immediate vicinity of the murder. Some 3,500 statements had been taken, many from prostitutes. In the previous 12 months

152 women had been arrested for prostitution. But the police were no nearer catching the Yorkshire Ripper, as he had by now been dubbed around the world, than when he gave Wilma McCann a lift to death 88 weeks earlier. He had chosen a non-prostitute as a victim, and made the mistake of attacking a woman on a public street. But he got away with it.

One thing about the Yorkshire Ripper particularly occupied much of George Oldfield's thinking. What was driving this man, why did he do it, what was wrong with his mind? He made a note to read up the possible explanations and to see some psychiatrists. Then two weeks after he had installed himself in the impressive new Millgarth police station to oversee the Jayne MacDonald inquiry, he was given a further insight into the killer's psyche.

As for Jayne MacDonald, Saturday night was always a big night for Maureen Long. On with her best dress, have a few drinks, and then some dancing. On Saturday 9 July, two weeks after the attack on Jayne, Maureen Long prepared herself at her home in Farsley, near Leeds. She chose a long black evening dress for her trip to Bradford. She called at a number of pubs, including one where she met her estranged husband, and made arrangements to stay at his home in Laisterdyke, Bradford later. She made her way to the Mecca ballroom, renamed Tiffanys, in Manningham, and settled down to some serious dancing and drinking in the Bali Hai discotheque. She was well known and a large number of people recall seeing her dance with a lot of men. They remember how she seemed to be very drunk by the time she left just after 2 a.m. the following morning.

Her plan was to wait in the taxi rank for transport to her husband's home. Instead, she remembers being offered a lift by a man in a white car.

A nightwatchman doing his rounds on premises alongside waste ground off Bowling Back Lane, Bradford was alerted by his barking Alsatian in the middle of that warm July night. He saw a Ford Cortina Mark II saloon, white with a dark roof, being driven away from the waste land at high speed. He looked at his watch and made a mental note of the time – 3.27 a.m. exactly.

At 8.30 a.m. two women walking near the waste land heard what sounded at first like the sound of a child whimpering. Maureen Long had been hit one blow to the back of the head and was then stabbed four times in the chest, stomach and back. Her girdle, pants and tights had been pulled down and a slashing stab wound stretched from her breasts to below her navel. The police fingertip search of the scene produced a bloodstained partial palmprint on a small piece of ceramic material believed to be from a broken sink. The police were convinced it belonged to Maureen Long's attacker.

The news was soon broken to George Oldfield that Maureen Long's injuries were the same as those inflicted on the other known victims, but now they had a survivor. Oldfield was anxious to get to the hospital bedside, but first the surgeons had to save Maureen Long's life. As well as hypothermia, they had to contend with the possibility that brain damage would result from the savage wound – a wound so deep that even now Maureen Long avoids going to the hairdresser's. She is too embarrassed when their hands discover the terrible indentations beneath her strong black hair.

Following the delicate three-hour operation in the neurosurgical unit of Leeds General Infirmary, a gentle question-and-answer session, three days after the attack, took the police very little further. The following Friday night Ripper-Hunt detectives arrived at Tiffanys night club and proceeded to interview everyone present about the previous week. The management made private offices available for the interviews and police spent a lot of time assuring those who were not there with their wives or husbands' knowledge of the absolute confidentiality of the information they might give.

Soon afterwards, as detectives were beginning to realize that the trail was going cold once again, the Home Secretary, Mr Merlyn Rees, who was also a Leeds M.P., visited Ripper Headquarters at Millgarth police station. He was told that the case now involved 304 officers working full-time. They had interviewed 175,000 people, taken 12,500 statements, and checked 10,000 vehicles. Mr Rees's words stated the obvious but were nonetheless welcome to the police, who were under ever-mounting pressure: 'Often piecing evidence together, considering it and analysing it, does take time, unless someone is there with a camera when the murder is committed.'

Over three years later Maureen Long says the attempt to kill her, while it failed, succeeded in ruining her life. She is afraid of the dark, and refuses to go out alone at night. She has a recurring nightmare of being attacked, but in her dream the man with the hammer held high above his head has no face. She swiftly pulls her jumper up to display the long, vertical scar travelling downwards from her breasts. When she walks in the streets she hears the young boys calling after her, 'Jack the Ripper-Lover.'

As the summer of 1977 turned into autumn George Oldfield began to seek the advice of psychiatrists. He felt they might be able to present a word-picture of the man he was hunting which could help with his identification. The art of being a successful detective is to avoid falling into the trap of tunnel vision, to maintain an open mind. Mr Oldfield had been doing his homework, and when he visited psychiatrist Stephen Shaw at Stanley Royd hospital, Wakefield, just a mile from West Yorkshire Police Headquarters, he quickly turned to the subject of the disease known as General Paralysis of the Insane, or G.P.I. Dr Shaw was impressed by Mr Oldfield's careful research into the possible motivations of a man who had felt the need to kill five women and attempt to murder a sixth in just two short years.

General Paralysis of the Insane is the third stage of syphilis, a condition in which grandiose delusions, false beliefs of a magnified nature, can occur. Mr Oldfield wondered whether it was possible for a young man to have contracted syphilis, maybe from a prostitute, not to have had it treated, and some 10 or 15 years later to be murdering women because of delusions. Dr Shaw's opinion was that such a state of affairs was unlikely, for syphilis in its later stages presents itself more commonly as dementia, that is, premature old age. Mr Oldfield pursued the argument. If this were so, could it be possible then that the man he was looking for suffered from schizophrenia – schizophrenic delusions causing him to kill? He was told again that that would seem unlikely. For if a man were suffering from schizophrenia to such a degree, it was argued, then he would surely be so grossly disordered as to have been brought to the attention of his family and his local doctor, and would be in a mental hospital.

Was there, asked Mr Oldfield, a personality type they should seek? The most likely type was a psychopath, but it is a fact that psychopathy is not uniformly nor universally defined. The Mental Health Act of 1959 stresses two aspects of psychopathic behaviour; that it will be either seriously irresponsible, or abnormally aggressive. Psychiatrists differ in their views, but in general will accept that psychopaths can be divided into three groups: the inadequate, who commonly become a 'down and out'; the creative, who can on occasions become highly successful in his chosen career; and the aggressive psychopath. The latter exhibits four main features: he or she cannot resist impulsive urges, cannot learn from mistakes, is cold and callous in many aspects of his relationships and, finally, tends to be a disruptive element in any social group. This type would be the most likely to commit a series of murders.

Mr Oldfield further wondered whether this aggressive psychopath would exhibit features which would explain the intervals between killings. As the series of attacks continued it became important to attempt to explain these hiatuses. Research work in America, where hundreds of male homicides have been studied, has revealed that these personality types could be further divided into two groups: the over-controlled aggressive psychopath and the under-controlled aggressive psychopath. The under-controlled man is an individual who does not have the necessary constraints from the higher centres of his brain, being involved frequently in acts of aggression and usually well known to the police, perhaps having a number of previous convictions for violence. Murder occurs quite simply as an extension of his aggressive behaviour. The over-controlled aggressive psychopath, however, is the opposite. He has many constraints from the higher parts of his brain which governs his behaviour. He tends to be a rather meticulous, rigid, often obsessional individual. At times of stress, however, he is unable to control the aggressive urges which rise from deep within his personality. At such times violent behaviour can occur, as though a safety valve has blown. Immediately after the pressure has been released, the man becomes his normal self once again. Factors which cause such outbursts vary from individual to individual. What will upset one will not upset the next man. As a result the intervals between murders can be as short as weeks, or as long as a year.

Having outlined this hypothesis, Dr Shaw had then to try and dampen any enthusiasm the police and the media had for the compilation of a psychological profile of the Ripper. In order to do this he cited the example of the 'Boston Strangler', a man who reduced the city of Boston, U.S.A., to a state of terror. As part of the murder investigation a panel of experts was convened, composed of psychiatrists, psychologists, social workers, criminologists and policemen. The panel decided that the man perpetrating the offences in Boston would, without doubt, be a schizoid, unmarried, latent homosexual with a disturbed psychosexual life and suppressed mother fantasies. When he was eventually apprehended, he was found to be a happily married man with two children. Dr Shaw said in 1977: 'No undue credence should be placed upon our psychiatric pontifications. We can only paint a broad picture, and as I have said repeatedly, the man responsible for the Ripper killings will be, to all intents and purposes, indistinguishable from the man next door.'

Meanwhile, in the Ripper murder-room, a white telephone stood alone on a desk at one end of the airy fourth-floor room overlooking Leeds market. George Oldfield and Jim Hobson were both strongly convinced that a friend or a relative knew or suspected the identity of the Ripper. The hope was that he or she would pick up a telephone and leave a recorded message on freephone

5050. In the first two weeks after Jayne MacDonald's murder the white recording-box was almost swamped with calls. Again there was a brief flurry of information when Maureen Long became a victim. But by the autumn it would stand idle for days at a time.

CHAPTER 4

Near, But Far

For Peter Sutcliffe, the good-natured jibing of friends and workmates, even relatives, did not end with his marriage to Sonia. It was not long before the echoes of 'When'll we be hearing wedding bells, then, Peter?' had been replaced by 'When'll we hear the patter of tiny feet?' But Peter had some sad news less than a year after the marriage. Sonia had suffered a miscarriage. As the months went by he was to tell his father, brothers and sisters, as well as drinking-partners, that there had been other prematurely ended pregnancies. He loved kids and he wanted some; so did Sonia. But worse was to follow. Sonia had been told there were to be none of her own, after all.

After the wedding and the move to Tanton Crescent, Sutcliffe surely but steadily was to move apart from most of his former friends and acquaintances. The one certain exception was Trevor Birdsall.

In 1972 Sutcliffe started insuring his cars through Mr Arthur Bisby, an agent, who lived at Cross Flatts, and continued to call occasionally at his house socially during the subsequent years. Says his wife, Mrs Anne Bisby, 'I always felt that Peter regarded Arthur as something of a father figure. He would ask his advice about many things, and used to bring Sonia, and they would sit and talk about things in general. Sonia was difficult to talk to; it was really hard work, because she seemed so shy and sensitive. Peter loved to play with the kids a lot. I can picture him now throwing his head back and laughing. He got quite excitable when he was laughing, but it was a very nervous laugh. Sometimes they would stay three or four hours but it would be a bit of a trial to try and keep the conversation going with Sonia.'

They talked about the women who had been killed in Leeds and Mrs Bisby mentioned that she had been to school with the husband of one of the victims, Mr Sydney Jackson. The spring of 1977 had been a time of despair for the police. The Ripper had claimed another victim, Bradford prostitute Tina Atkinson, but this time had changed his pattern by killing indoors, 11 weeks after Irene Richardson had died so gruesomely. Yet the same period was a time of hope for Sonia Sutcliffe. At long last she seemed in sight of one of her most cherished wishes; she felt confident of qualifying as a teacher at the end of her two-year course at Margaret McMillan that summer.

And then Sonia saw the house of her dreams – number six, Garden Lane. Peter wasn't so sure. £15,000 plus was a lot of money; they would be financially stretched, pushed to the limit. What if Sonia didn't get a job teaching after the summer holidays? But he agreed to go and look at the house. Mr Rahman, the Pakistani barrister who currently owned it, told them it had been for sale since the previous September, and that they were the third couple to show an interest. Mr Rahman remembers: 'Mr Sutcliffe was very calm, very collected and very polite. He didn't appear to be too enchanted with the house, certainly not as much as his wife and his mother-in-law. His wife was quite insistent. He came several times to the house, sometimes when my wife and twelve-year-old daughter were there alone. He told me he was a long-distance lorry driver and he was away for long periods so he wanted his wife to be in a quiet, pleasant area. His wife seemed a pleasant person. She said she was a concert pianist from Czechoslovakia, which seemed a little odd to me, a concert pianist and a lorry driver, but we agreed a price and there was no delay in the sale.'

In the end the agreed price was £15,350, and as the Rahmans were returning to Pakistan they agreed to include some bedroom furniture. It was however to be September before they moved in.

On the day of Peter Sutcliffe's very first visit to his new home, that Saturday in June, he went out for a drink – to Leeds, to Chapeltown. Wilfred MacDonald remembered the night well.

Two Saturday nights later Sutcliffe again left Sonia at home in Tanton Crescent with her parents and set off in the white Ford Corsair with the black roof to an area he knew better than Chapeltown. Manningham Lane and the red-light Lumb Lane district of Bradford would be even easier to get to once they had moved to Heaton, only about a mile away as the crow flies. At 2.15 a.m. on Sunday 10 July, Maureen Long got into a white car with a black roof, and an hour later Sutcliffe left her for dead on waste land off Birkenshaw Lane, Bradford. He had dealt her one massive blow to the head, and stabbed her in the chest, stomach and back.

It had taken ten years, and a nervous breakdown, but it was with a sweet feeling of satisfaction that Sonia Sutcliffe walked through the door of Holmfield First School, Bradford, at the beginning of September 1977. Could it be true? A teacher at last; a supply-teacher, maybe, but it was a start. Life was really looking up. They had exchanged contracts for the house in Garden Lane two weeks earlier, on 18 August, with Peter's restrained signature on the document alongside his wife's more flamboyant 'Sonia

Szurma-Sutcliffe'. His mother-in-law had signed as a witness. On Monday 26 September the Sutcliffes moved in and a few days later their new neighbours, Tom and Mary Garside, wrote to the Rahmans in Pakistan to say that the new young couple were very nice people and that all was well.

That Monday was a busy day for Peter because he had also bought another second-hand Ford Corsair, a red one, having sold the white Corsair with the black roof on the last day of August.

The following Saturday he worked on the car in his drive, just outside the kitchen door of the tall house, and in the evening set off to try it out. Sonia stayed in her new home.

By 9.30 p.m. Jean Jordan was climbing into the red Ford near her home in Moss Side and, yes, she did know somewhere quiet where the bearded stranger could take her for some 'business'. Dead quiet, as she and other Manchester prostitutes called the spot – land between allotments and the Southern Cemetery, two miles away.

It would be £5, in advance. She tucked the note into a secret pocket at the front of her handbag.

Jean Bernadette Jordan was known as 'Scottish Jean' by the prostitutes of Moss Side and Cheetham Hill because she came from Motherwell. She had no convictions for prostitution but she had received two cautions for soliciting. She was slightly built with long dark hair and a smile that lit up her face – a shy smile, giving her a look of vulnerability which many men had found appealing. She had arrived in Manchester from Scotland as a 16-year-old, with no money and nowhere to stay, five years earlier. She had been wandering aimlessly round the concourse of Manchester station when a young man offered a cigarette and asked her if he could buy her a cup of tea. Alan Royle was 21, a chef, and had met her on his way back from work. The waif-like creature in front of him in the station buffet said she had run away from home and had headed for the nearest big city outside Scotland. She didn't know anybody in Manchester, had nowhere to live, and was frightened the police would send her back to Motherwell.

Alan Royle had a small flat at Newall Green, in Wythenshawe, and Jean moved in. Two years later she gave birth to Alan, named after his father, and two years after that James. But their early happiness had begun to fade and by mutual agreement they kept part of their lives separate from each other. Alan would go off for what he described as two- or three-day 'benders' with his pals, while Jean had her own circle of girlfriends, whom Alan never met. Girls in the 'business'.

Jean would also think nothing of taking a bus to the motorway and then hitching a lift to Glasgow where she would stay with relatives, often for a week or ten days. But she always returned to Alan and the children. On Saturday evening, 1 October, they sat in the kitchen of the council house they had moved into at Moss Side a few weeks earlier, and Alan told Jean he would be going out for a drink with his friends later. She poured him a drink from a bottle of lemonade and then went to watch television. When Alan returned later, after the pubs had shut, he found the children were asleep but Jean had gone. He presumed she had gone to meet her friends. When she had not returned a few days later he took it for granted that she had thumbed a lift to Scotland to see her relatives – a break from him and the kids. It never occurred to him that she should be reported as missing. What he could not have known was that soon after he set off for his Saturday night out Jean decided that she would fit in a couple of hours' 'business'. There was nothing special on the television. She left their home in Lingbeck Crescent at 9.30 p.m. and soon afterwards was climbing into the red Corsair.

She directed Sutcliffe to the land between the allotments and the cemetery and soon after 10 p.m. Jean Jordan was dead. The slim woman with the long dark hair got out of the car at Sutcliffe's suggestion with a view to sexual intercourse taking place. As he eased out of the driver's seat he retrieved a hammer hidden beneath it and proceeded to hit Jean Jordan a total of 13 times over the head, before hiding her body in undergrowth near the fence between the cemetery and the allotments.

Sutcliffe drove back across the Pennines to Sonia and the new house and as the week passed busied himself with thoughts of the weekend, and the small house-warming party for the family they had planned for the following Sunday evening. But as the week wore on, and still no screaming newspaper headlines announced the discovery of another Ripper victim, other thoughts began to intrude into his troubled mind. The £5 note. What if the body was found and the police were to discover the brand-new note he had received in his pay packet and which had gone into the dead woman's handbag? Should he go back and retrieve the £5 note, or would that be too dangerous? Might he be seen?

If he was troubled he showed no signs of it as he distributed the drinks the following Sunday evening, 9 October, as the guests at the party were made welcome at Garden Lane. It was almost midnight, and Peter, thoughtful as ever, ran some of his relatives home in the red Corsair, while Sonia went to bed. It had been a tiring day.

But her husband didn't return straight away from Bingley, going on across the Pennines once again to the cemetery and the allotments at Chorlton-cum-Hardy, just off a link road to the M62 and M63. The dead prostitute was exactly where he had left her, her once-pretty face a contorted mask of dried blood, matted hair and pain. But where was her handbag?

He looked near the body and he looked under the body and then searching in increasing sweeps away from the corpse, but still no handbag. He searched further, more frantic with every passing moment, the dread implication of the possible discovery of the £5 note by the police gaining more and more urgency. And then there was no controlling his fury as he dragged the already rotting body away from its hiding place, tearing off Jean Jordan's clothes until she was naked.

What he did to her then was to make toughened police officers shake their heads in sadness and disgust when they first got to the scene. In a paroxysm of rage he stabbed her again and again, some 18 times, in her breasts and chest, her stomach and the area of her vagina – fierce slashing swipes, a terrible burst of rage which relented only when the vilified body was almost unrecognizable, its stomach obscenely ripped open as if slashed by the swiping claw of a beast-like creature from the pages of baroque legend. There were knife wounds from her left shoulder to her right knee, and there were six more wounds on her right side. Some of the gashes were 8″ deep. The storm eventually subsided, and ignoring his thumping heart Sutcliffe thought once again about the £5 note. In a few seconds, with the logic of the illogical, he conceived a plan to divert the Lancashire police from the Yorkshire Ripper's trail. If the dead woman's body did not have a head, they would not be able to identify her. He could dump the head somewhere where it wouldn't be found, at the side of the motorway. But the task was impossible with the tools at hand, and Sutcliffe set off back to Yorkshire and his newly warmed house in Garden Lane. 'Scottish' Jean Jordan's torment was over.

Twelve hours later, just after noon on Monday 10 October, the police at Chorlton-cum-Hardy received an emergency call from a highly distressed Princess Road allotment-holder. When they stared at the woman's naked body they could understand why. Her blackened head was unrecognizable, flattened with the severity of the many blows she had obviously received. Her belly was gaping open. Putrefaction was evident and there had been vermin in the field.

Det. Chief Supt. Jack Ridgeway, head of Manchester C.I.D., found no identifying documents in the woman's scattered clothing and by the end of the afternoon a brief description had appeared in the local evening newspaper. The dead woman had shoulder-length auburn hair and there were details of her clothing. Not much to go on. Mr Ridgeway felt sure she would soon be identified. He realized the awful implications of the day's discovery – had the infamous Yorkshire Ripper travelled to Lancashire?

In the early evening, after reading the brief newspaper account, Alan Royle telephoned the police to say he suspected the dead woman could be his common-law wife, Jean. He was taken to Manchester C.I.D. Headquarters and showed the police a photograph of his long-haired wife smiling shyly at the camera. He explained how he thought she had gone to Scotland to visit her relatives, as she had done in the past. Mr Ridgeway couldn't tell from the snapshot whether this was the same face he had stared at at lunchtime, with all its gruesome distortion. He was not anxious for Mr Royle to view the body and Det. Chief Inspector Thomas Fletcher, of the fingerprint branch, suggested to him that there might be something at their flat which Jean had touched shortly before she disappeared.

Royle remembered the glass of lemonade she had poured him eight days earlier, just before he had gone out for a drink, that Saturday night. The bottle was still in the same place in the kitchen. Within an hour Chief Inspector Fletcher had established that the fingerprints of the corpse matched the perfect set of latent prints on the bottle. Unbeknown to Mr Royle, one of Jean's girlfriends, Anna Holt, known by the police to be a prostitute, was also at the police station as a result of the information in the evening newspaper. They showed her the photograph and she told them, 'That's Scottish Jean. She's on the game; she worked the same patch as me.'

Despite a careful warning from the police she bravely offered to look at the corpse, sadly confirming it was Jean. She told the police that Jean had worked as a prostitute for approximately two years, and in the winter of two of them had taken clients to a city-centre flat owned by the friend. During the better weather they had occasionally used the Southern cemetery area, an area popular with many of the girls in their trade. But, said Anna Holt, Jean had not been really suitable for the rôle. She had felt guilty about the children and had recently told her that she planned to give it up, and settle down to a decent home life.

That would have pleased Alan Royle, for whom the nightmare was only just beginning. He was heartbroken by the tragedy and over the subsequent long months was to lose his job as a chef, being unable to concentrate for more than a few minutes at a time before his thoughts turned to Jean and what had happened. Son Alan, regarded as a bright child, was retarded by his mother's death and later, when he was in his fifth year, was still only able to speak a few monosyllabic words.

For Mr Ridgeway the girl's death seemed motiveless and unnecessarily savage. Was it a client who hadn't wanted to pay? Or had someone decided to take the money from her handbag, which had not been recovered? Or was it the work of a demented maniac with a grotesque appetite for death? She was a prostitute, so he had got in touch by telephone with Mr Oldfield and Mr Hobson in West Yorkshire at an early stage on the first day. An officer was despatched to Manchester. It was a time for open minds, particularly in public pronouncements. Some doubts were removed on the following Saturday, 15 October, when Jean Jordan's imitation-leather handbag was found almost 100 yards from where the body had been discovered. The £14 or £15 Mr Royle estimated should have been in the handbag was missing. But in a hidden pocket at the front of the bag police found a £5 Bank of England note. It was wet and had to be dried out, but it became apparent that the note, serial number AW51 121565, was almost brand-new. Before the weekend was over Bank of England officials had opened their files and established that the note was part of a consignment sent to the Shipley and Bingley branches of the Midland Bank, right in the heart of the Yorkshire Ripper area.

Mr Ridgeway's theory was reasonable and simple. Find the man who had probably received the note in his wage packet a day or two before Jean Jordan died, and you had found her killer. The note had been issued only four days before the Saturday she disappeared, so it was likely its bearer over the Pennines to Lancashire was the first member of the public to receive it from the bank via his employers.

And if Mr Ridgeway could find the killer of Jean Jordan then it was possible he would also have found the Yorkshire Ripper.

It was with real hope that Mr Ridgeway and 30 hand-picked Manchester officers travelled to Bradford within 48 hours of the handbag being found and set up a special incident room in a disused schoolroom at Baildon, having been given 30 West Yorkshire officers to help with his specialized line of inquiry. It was established that the £5 note in question had been part of a bundle of £500, had been one in a sequence of 69 notes, and was the note five from the end of the sequence. However, Mr Ridgeway's initial high hopes, and those of his West Yorkshire counterparts, were to turn to dismay when the enormity of the task they had set themselves became apparent.

The bank had distributed money from the batch of £17,500 to a number of firms in the Bradford and Shipley area, employing almost 8,000 men between them. They set about the task of seeing them all, always conscious of the depressing possibility that the £5 note in question could have left the wage packet within minutes of it being opened, could have been handed over in a shop, a pub, a betting office, or any number of outlets and then transferred to two or three pairs of hands before arriving in Manchester. It was unlikely, but a possibility that was to haunt the officers for over two years. They faced the additional handicap of a time-lapse of over two weeks since the note was issued and before it was discovered in the handbag. Long enough for memories to fade and alibis to take shape, accurate or otherwise. Three months after arriving in West Yorkshire the Manchester detectives left the schoolroom at Baildon and returned to Lancashire wiser but sadder men. They had interviewed 5,000 men but had come to accept that they did not have enough information about the suspected killer to isolate him, always presuming they had spoken to him at all.

One of the firms they had concentrated on was T. and W.H. Clark (Holdings) Limited in Canal Road, Shipley, and just before Christmas they had interviewed the men who worked there, including one of the firm's long-distance drivers, a Mr Peter William Sutcliffe, of Garden Lane, Heaton. There had been nothing about him or any of the other 5,000 men they talked to before they retreated to Manchester in January that had made them suspicious. They had been to the house, talked to his wife, and nothing she had said contradicted in any way his account of the night, or nights, they were interested in.

In the middle of that December, on the 14th, the police were positive the Yorkshire Ripper had struck again, and this time he appeared to have made two more errors which it was hoped would lead the police to him. It was just after 8 p.m. when convicted prostitute Marilyn Moore, plump, with long dark hair and an attractive smile, left a friend's home in Gathorne Terrace, near the Gaiety pub just off Roundhay Road, Leeds. She decided she would look for some business before returning to her own home in nearby Bayswater Mount. As she strolled along Gipton Avenue she saw a dark-coloured car being driven towards her in a slow, careful way she recognized as that of a potential client. She walked along Spencer Place and the car passed by. She thought it would turn into Louis Street and then turn back, and in anticipation she crossed Spencer Place and turned right into Leopold Street where she imagined the car would next appear. As she was about to cross a minor junction, known as Frankland Place, she saw the car parked close to the kerb and the driver, who was aged about 30, of stocky build, around 5′ 6″ tall with dark wavy hair and a beard, stood against the driver's door. He seemed to be waving to somebody in a nearby house.

The man was wearing a yellow shirt, a navy blue/black zip-up anorak, and blue jeans. As she walked past the car he turned to her and said, 'Are you doing business?' Marilyn replied, 'Yes' and the man said '£5?' The deal was struck and she got into the front passenger seat, noticing immediately that there were two rear-view mirrors on the windscreen. The man said he knew a 'right quiet place', some spare ground at Scott Hall Street, about a mile and a half away. As they drove there the man said he was called Dave, adding that he preferred it to David. Marilyn asked him what he had been doing in the street where they had met. He said he had been waving to his girlfriend who was ill.

The unease that Marilyn Moore, like every other prostitute in Leeds at that time, had felt when she got into the car, and indeed felt every time she struck a deal with a client following the killings, was eased slightly by the relaxed and friendly way the man was talking. He seemed to know the area well, and mentioned other prostitutes as if he was a regular client and widely known. Hardly the sort of information a killer would make available too readily, she thought. 'Dave' mentioned two prostitutes called Hilary and Gloria and said that Hilary was 'the one with the Jamaican boyfriend'. Marilyn also knew two prostitutes called Hilary and Gloria.

At the spare ground, well back from Scott Hall Street, 'Dave' suggested that they should have sexual intercourse in the back of the car. Marilyn agreed but when she stepped outside and tried to open the rear passenger door, found it was locked. The driver said he would come round and open it and as he passed behind her Marilyn Moore felt a searing, sickening blow on the top of her head. She screamed loudly, holding her head with her hands for protection, but as she began to fall to the ground, frantically grasping her attacker's trousers as she slipped down, she felt further blows before losing consciousness.

Her screams and the noise of a dog that had started barking persuaded 'Dave' to leave without completing his gruesome task. He returned to his car, which Marilyn Moore said was about the size of a Morris Oxford and maroon in colour, although it was difficult to tell at night, returned the ball-pein hammer to its hiding place under his seat, and drove away to Bradford. Marilyn recalls, 'I can remember hearing him walk back to the car and slam the door; the back wheels skidded as he drove off. After a few minutes, I think it was a few minutes, I came round a bit and managed to get to my feet. I started walking back to the road to get to a telephone. When I got to the pavement a lad and a girl saw me with blood running from my head and he ran to the phone to get an ambulance. A girl I know also came up and asked what had happened. I was taken to Leeds General Infirmary and had an operation. I still have a hole in the back of my head where he hit me, and scars all over my scalp. They shaved off all my hair and it has taken ages to get back to its old length. I left hospital just before New Year's Eve and went to stay with friends in High Wycombe. I couldn't stay in Leeds knowing that he might be in the same town.'

She eventually returned to live in Leeds but still suffers from depression and admits she is 'back in the business'. In hospital, as well as establishing that Marilyn Moore's injuries had included a depressed fracture behind her ear on the left side of her head, measuring $1\frac{1}{2}'' \times 1''$, and seven or eight lacerations up to $2''$ long, doctors told the police there had also been a $4''$ laceration on her left hand and bruises on both hands. Their view was that considerable force had been used by her attacker. If the police had any lingering doubts about linking the Jean Jordan death in Manchester with the work of the Yorkshire Ripper, there was no question of the link in the case of Marilyn Moore.

Scene-of-crime experts had established that the wheel-marks indicated the same track width as those recovered after Irene Richardson's death. The same half-worn India Autoway cross-ply tyres were on the front wheels. The photofit created from her description bore a remarkable resemblance to a long-distance lorry driver living at Heaton, Bradford.

In the third week of the following January (1978) a frustrated Jack Ridgeway decided to pull his men out of Baildon. He believed the £5-note clue was the best chance police had had to pinpoint the killer. He also realized that the most frustrating possibility of all was that they had probably looked into the face of Jean Jordan's killer, possibly the Yorkshire Ripper – and that they had not recognized him! When he had arrived in Bradford, Mr Ridgeway, a man who said no more to the press than he felt was absolutely necessary, commented, 'We are looking for a very strange man.' He felt Jean Jordan's attacker had been annoyed or disappointed when her body had not been found a week later and had returned and moved it to make sure of its discovery. He said he regarded the £5-note lead to be so vital that his men would 'interview every single person we need to, whether it takes a week or a month.' They would visit every factory in the area and interview every male employee. On 16 November 1977 he had been reported as saying, 'I am quite certain we have the name of the person to whom that £5 note was issued. We now have a list of people, organizations or firms to which the £5 notes were issued by the bank.'

When the operation was called off three months later the development was reported in the local press. 'Killer evades big dragnet' said the headline to one story on Tuesday 17

January, and the article quoted Mr Ridgeway as saying, 'There is always the chance that we have already seen that person. We have interviewed everybody who could have received that £5 note. It is more than likely that we have interviewed the person who received the fiver, but it does not follow that it is the same person that murdered Jean Jordan.' The following Saturday evening, 21 January, Peter Sutcliffe battered Bradford prostitute Yvonne Pearson to death with a lump hammer, a weapon so devastating police thought she had been killed with a boulder. But it was to be two months before her body was found.

The police were beginning to wonder if the attack that had gone wrong on Maureen Long had frightened the Ripper off – more a hope than a belief. And yet, he had seemed to panic. Was he losing his nerve? Would he go away? The Yorkshire Ripper may indeed have panicked that July night, but his drinking habits had not changed.

His next door neighbour in Tanton Crescent, Mr Ronald Barker, went out regularly with Peter Sutcliffe in the evenings. 'We used to drive to places like Manchester, York, Leeds and Bradford. I remember going round the Chapeltown area of Leeds with Peter. He was regularly changing his cars and always careful with his money. He was always talking to girls in the pubs we went in but I don't know what line he used to give them. I don't think Sonia had any suspicions about him playing around with other women. He seemed fascinated by the red-light districts and he used to tour them with his car window wound down, shouting things at the girls on the pavement. I never saw him actually pick a girl up, though he used to talk to lots of them. He would say to me that he liked girls in black underwear. I wasn't interested in the girls, mainly the drink myself. In fact I used to get in the back of the car and was often half asleep when we got back to Tanton Crescent. Sometimes he would drop me off and then go off again, I don't know where. I do remember once we went what he called "whoring" and were driving down Lumb Lane, in Bradford, and out of the blue Peter said, "This is Ripper country."'

Mr Barker says that during one visit to Chapeltown, Leeds, when he had been resting in the back seat of Sutcliffe's car, Sutcliffe had pulled up at the side of the road and left him for a few minutes. 'There was a girl walking up the road, and when he got out of the car he followed her.' Sutcliffe had driven back to Tanton Crescent and dropped Mr Barker off, saying he was going out again. Mr Barker is an inveterate diary-keeper and his diary for 1977 was of great interest to the police. The entry for 26 June that year, the night 16-year-old Jayne MacDonald died in Chapeltown, recorded that Mr Barker had been out for a drink with Peter. His brother, Mr David Barker, also a bachelor, and also present on some of the drinking excursions to red-light districts, now believes they were unwitting witnesses to Sutcliffe's reconnaissance trips.

'The weekend after the Wilma McCann murder Sutcliffe bragged to me that he once beat up a prostitute after having sex with her. He said the prostitute wanted £10 but he had just turned round and smacked her in the mouth, pushed her out of the car door, and driven off. Looking back he had just seemed to be getting to know the areas. All we did was drive round. We thought we were doing it for a laugh. Peter used to say he could get sex with girls without any trouble, and he seemed to like coloured girls. We went to Manningham and Chapeltown watching them. We did discuss the Ripper killings but his expression never changed. Peter was tight with money and would go out with only £3 in his pocket. He never bought a round for all of us, just his own drink. Yet he was always smartly dressed, done up like a dog's dinner.'

CHAPTER 5

Over-Controlled

Yvonne Ann Pearson, aged 22, was a serious professional – competent, attractive, experienced. She had worked the rich-businessman trade in most of Britain's major cities. Though a Leeds girl, her cream and gold diary contained names and addresses all over the country – men who were to be massively embarrassed by police inquiries. She was discovered, her head beaten unrecognizable, her body rotting, under an overturned sofa on waste land off Lumb Lane, Bradford on 26 March 1978, spotted by a passer-by who saw an arm sticking out from under the sofa. The putrid smell he encountered when he approached what he had thought was a tailor's dummy sent him rushing for the phone in a nearby garage.

Yvonne's death set the police a puzzle – so much so that they were inclined at first to discount the killing as being the Ripper's work. The first of the Ripper letters had arrived within the previous fortnight, and though the writer claimed to have killed Joan Harrison, he boasted of having killed eight women so far. Yet Yvonne had obviously been dead several weeks. The letter-writer was clearly not a man to be modest about his achievements, so why had he not mentioned this killing?

There was another question: Yvonne was killed by a large blunt instrument wound to the head; her assailant had then jumped on her chest repeatedly. Professor Gee's examination led the police to say that she had been hit with a boulder, not known as a Ripper trademark, and this view remained unaltered until Peter Sutcliffe explained three years later that he had used a heavy lump hammer on this occasion, instead of the usual lighter ball-pein hammer.

But there had been similarities too strong to discount. Yvonne's clothing – she wore black flared slacks, a black turtle-neck jumper and a woollen jacket on the night of her death – had been re-arranged in the tell-tale manner: bra and jumper above the breasts, other clothing pulled down. Secondly, it seemed that the killer had returned to the scene to make her body more visible, as he had done with Jean Jordan six months earlier. Sutcliffe later denied he returned to the scene of this killing, making a mystery of the fact that a copy of the *Daily Mirror,* dated exactly a month after Yvonne's death, was found apparently deliberately placed under one of her arms.

It was inconceivable that during the two months since the murder someone would not have spotted the arm beckoning grotesquely from under the sofa, unless a dog had moved it. Could Sutcliffe be assumed to be now covering up his return to the body for some reason? The corpse had certainly been well concealed. Soil, rubble and turf had been piled on top of it, and the abandoned sofa placed on top of the heap apparently some time after rigor mortis had set in because the arm was well entangled in the sofa springs. Horse-hair from the sofa had been stuffed callously into the mouth.

It was a humiliating end for a girl who saw herself as a cut above many of her fellow prostitutes. Yvonne was stylish and fashionable, wary and clever. A prostitute friend, another Yorkshire girl working in London, had been stabbed in a hotel room in Bayswater just two months earlier, and Yvonne was a drinking acquaintance of Tina Atkinson, whom the Ripper had killed less than a year previously. So Yvonne knew the dangers. Since both these girls had been killed indoors, she decided only to work outside, where at least there was a chance of escape. Even so, Yvonne had told a neighbour and friend of her fear of the Ripper. 'It would be just my luck to get knocked on the head,' said the girl whose taste for a touch of glamour had been reflected in her choice of name for her five-month-old baby – Colette.

Yvonne Pearson knew only too well about the other dangers of her business. Five days after her death, she had been due to appear in court on a soliciting charge. It would not have been her first conviction for the same offence, and she knew she stood a good chance of going to prison. Yvonne's personal life was not at a high point, either. Her Jamaican-born boyfriend, Roy Saunders, with whom she had shared a flat in Woodbury Road, Heaton (just a few hundred yards from Sutcliffe's house) since 1974, was visiting relatives in Jamaica, and their relationship had recently deteriorated almost beyond recall.

On the night of her death, a crisp January Saturday, she had been shopping in Bradford, and almost run out of money. She left a 16-year-old neighbour to look after Colette and Lorraine, aged two, and set off for the Flying Dutchman pub. She left the pub at 9.30 telling a friend she was 'going to earn some money'. Sutcliffe slowed his car to let the lissom, blonde girl with the big black handbag he saw in his headlights cross the road.

Yvonne Pearson responded to the stare from the bearded man and within minutes they were parked on a derelict area of waste land in Arthington Street. He killed her with the lump hammer, then dragged her by the collar to the abandoned sofa, and jumped on her until her ribs cracked.

At her flat the young babysitter, puzzled because Yvonne had said she would not be late, prepared to settle down for the night. It was Monday before Yvonne was reported to the police as missing. Naturally, there was fear for her life, but also a strong suspicion that she had jumped her bail because of her impending court appearance. Checks were made with police in London and derelict areas were searched. For Yvonne's parents, a warehouse foreman and his wife in Leeds, the anguish increased with the passing weeks. Two weeks after her disappearance another mutilated body was found in a woodyard in Huddersfield, but the apprehension which stirred in Yvonne's parents retreated when it became clear the dead girl wasn't her.

Helen Rytka, an attractive 18-year-old half-black girl, also had dreams about improving her lot in life. Her ambition was to be a soul singer. When she died, she was an unemployed sweet-factory assistant and was working as a prostitute. She shared an artistic bent with her twin, Rita, who had received a grant to go to Batley Art College. The two, whose Italian mother and Jamaican father had split up when they were young, had sent a well-constructed and touching poem to the editor of the *Yorkshire Post* in May 1975. It dwelt on the misery of being brought up in care – they were in a children's home out in the country, at Knaresborough, cared for but feeling unloved.

In fact, Helen Rytka was loved, possibly more so than some of the Yorkshire Ripper's more pathetic, lonely victims. Helen, or Elena as she preferred to be known, and Rita were the closest of twins. They shared a miserable room next to a motorway flyover in Huddersfield, spent their income on trendy clothes, and dreamed. There was still time to make their mark on the world.

The twins worked the streets of Huddersfield's prostitute district as a pair. The red-light district was concentrated at the time on the Great Northern Street area – a depressed, desolate section of the wool town, just a few hundred yards from the shopping and business centre. The railway arches under the Leeds to Manchester line formed *ad hoc* brothels, but Helen and Rita were one step above the railway-arch trade. They were strikingly attractive girls, who had no trouble attracting 'punters' with cars to take them somewhere quiet. They also had a system. They would be picked up separately outside a public lavatory, each give their client precisely 20 minutes, and meet outside the lavatory at the set time. They even took the car number of each other's client before they set off. They knew any man could have been the dreaded Yorkshire Ripper.

On the snowy night of Tuesday 31 January, however, something went wrong. Helen was back at the rendezvous five minutes early, at 9.25 p.m. The handsome man in the white Corsair offered the chance of another quick £5 perhaps before Rita returned. And if she was a few minutes late back at the toilets, Rita would understand. She did not go far away – just to Garrard's timber-yard, which straggles round the railway arches, and was a constant night-time haunt of down and outs as well as prostitutes, who found its nooks and corners quiet and convenient.

Helen Rytka and Peter Sutcliffe parked and got out of the car to move into the back. He spotted two men nearby, however, so his chance to hit her with his concealed hammer was lost, and he was forced to pretend that he would go through the motions of sex with her. As she left the front seat to get in the back, anxious to rendezvous with Rita, he raised his hammer and hurriedly swung it down in her direction. But the first attempted blow missed its target. The hammer struck the door of the car with a shock that jolted his entire body; he struck her head on the second attempt, and then hit it another five times. The attack was a few feet from the foreman's shed, the wall of which was spattered with blood, and Helen's body was left long enough for the blood to soak into the ground, before being stripped and dragged to the wood-pile where it was hidden.

Helen Rytka's clothes were scattered over a wide area – one shoe was found 20 yards away, up an embankment. Her bra and black polo-neck jumper were found in the characteristic position above her breasts, and her socks were left on. She was naked otherwise. Sutcliffe mutilated her horribly; there were three stab wounds to the chest, with indications of repeated stabbings through the same wounds. There were also scratch marks on her chest.

Back at the lavatory block, Rita Rytka was worried, yet her fear of the police prevented her from reporting Helen as missing immediately. A driver spotted Helen's black panties at the wood-yard in the daylight of the next morning, and the yard foreman saw the blood-soaked ground where Helen had died.

But 'all sorts of things went on at night in the wood-yard', they reasoned. It was to be Friday, with the full missing-persons procedure in operation, before a police Alsatian located Helen's body where Sutcliffe had left it. The dog had gone straight to the corpse after sniffing some of her clothing.

The dead girl had disappeared early in the evening in a relatively crowded area, and George Oldfield was convinced that someone must have seen the killer. More than a hundred passers-by were traced, and all but three cars and one stocky, fair-haired man were eliminated. The lavatories were a popular meeting-place for homosexuals, who were as unwilling to come forward as the prostitutes.

The fair-haired man, had he been found, may have been a witness.

After the Rytka killing, Oldfield spoke optimistically about being closer than ever before. He appealed to housewives on BBC Radio's Jimmy Young show a week later and pointed out that a wife, mother or girlfriend probably by then suspected the Ripper's identity.

Vera Millward, frail, ill and 41, died from three hammer blows. Peter Sutcliffe then slashed her so viciously across the stomach that her intestines spilled out of the wound. He killed her in a well-lit area in the grounds of Manchester Royal Infirmary, and a man taking his son for emergency treatment at the hospital was sure he heard her dying screams. Just 'Help', repeated three times, and then silence.

However, in this area, Det. Chief Supt. Ridgeway commented after the body was found, a scream at night was not uncommon. And yet the area of the killing was largely flood-lit, there were 800 patients and staff in nearby buildings, and the hospital car park was in regular use even late at night, both by staff and prostitutes.

Vera Millward, Spanish-born and a mother of seven, had come to England after the War as a domestic help. She lived with a 49-year-old Jamaican, Cy Burkett. Vera resorted to prostitution in Manchester's Moss Side and Hulme districts to support her children, but believed she was dying. She had only one lung and underwent three operations in 1976, 1977 and again in May 1978, just before she died. On the night of Tuesday 16 May Cy Burkett thought she was going out to buy cigarettes, and get pain-killing drugs from the hospital to ease her chronic stomach pains.

Vera left the couple's flat in Greenham Avenue, Hulme, bought two packets of Benson and Hedges, and waited in the street for her 'regular' Tuesday customer who used to flash the headlights of his old, white, Mercedes and then drive off with her, usually just to talk, and very occasionally to have sex. That particular Tuesday, however, the regular did not turn up.

When her fully-clothed body was found by a landscape gardener at 8.10 a.m. the following morning by a chain-link fence on a rubbish pile in a corner of the car park, he thought at first she was some sort of doll. Vera Millward was lying on her right side, face down, her arms folded beneath her and her legs straight. Her shoes were placed neatly on the body and rested against the fence.

She had been attacked twelve feet away, and Sutcliffe had dragged her across gravel to the fence after hitting her three times on the head. Apart from the obscene stab wound to the stomach, he had also raised her dress and underskirt and stabbed her repeatedly in one back wound, just below the lower left ribs. Her right eyelid was punctured and the eye bruised. She was still wearing her coat. The tyre tracks nearby were the same as those found at the site of the Richardson murder the previous February and the Marilyn Moore assault five months before this killing. The common denominators were two India Autoway cross-ply tyres and a track width of 4′ 2″. Typically for a Ripper killing, there was no sign of sexual molestation.

Greater Manchester Police again warned prostitutes of the risks they were running, that poor Vera Millward had ignored. No noticeable reduction in their activities was noted, however.

Detectives from Manchester travelled to Yorkshire, again this time believing the tyre tracks were an unshakeable link with the Yorkshire Ripper. They met Det. Chief Supt. John Domaille, recently appointed by Chief Constable Gregory as head of an élite twelve-man Ripper squad, to be based in Leeds. Mr Domaille, a Channel Islander, had followed Mr Gregory to West Yorkshire from the Devon and Cornwall force after Mr Gregory had been appointed West Yorkshire's Chief Constable. Some senior officers thought the appointment of Domaille as head of the new squad was a snub for Assistant Chief Constable George Oldfield, who had taken charge of the inquiry on a day-to-day basis following Jayne MacDonald's death almost a year earlier. There were also those who were grateful that Mr Gregory had not given them the thankless task.

There was another similarity between Vera Millward's case and that of Irene Richardson. They had both suffered grotesquely mutilated stomachs, their intestines spilling out from terrible wounds. The slashing and stabbing wounds to the abdomen had started with Anna Rogulskyj and had also been inflicted on Emily Jackson, Tina Atkinson, Maureen Long and Jean Jordan, while Jayne MacDonald and Helen Rytka had been repeatedly stabbed through the same wounds in their chests. While police thoughts were occupied mostly with who the killer was, they spent some time considering why he did it.

George Oldfield had looked at the possibility of General Paralysis of the Insane, associated with an earlier bout of venereal disease. But the continuing mutilation of the women's stomachs brought forward a further possibility.

However many previous killers and murderers had been studied the lessons learned would probably be only of fractional value in understanding the killer who had become the Yorkshire Ripper. The range of their characteristics was too great for a clear profile to emerge.

A psychiatrist cannot describe what a wanted man looks

like or his life-style. West Yorkshire detectives had been told they were looking for someone with a psychopathic personality, the characteristics of which were a failure to resist impulses, a failure to learn by mistakes, and a failure to provide love and affection. Such personalities were known to disrupt social groups, often their own marriages. They tended to be callous and unfeeling individuals who bore a grudge. Psychopathy is a failure to develop a normal moral sense, an inability to distinguish between right and wrong, rather than an actual mental illness. One psychiatrist told the police that they tended to be more prevalent in the lower social groups where problems of money and housing could be greater, and where it was easier to develop grudges.

At the trial of Ian Brady and Myra Hindley, the Moors Murderers, in 1966, both were shown to be characterized by strong psychopathic tendencies; the judge described the killings as 'calculated, cold-blooded murders'. Most psychopaths demonstrate a lesser degree of planning than Brady and Hindley in the murders they commit. They are like volcanoes, dormant most of the time, but sitting on domestic or personality problems which they cannot totally control and which occasionally erupt.

The possibility that intrigued a number of officers in the summer of 1978 was that the Yorkshire Ripper was married and that his wife could not have children. If this was a man who had set his heart on having children, was his anger transposed into the assault on his victims' stomach, or more precisely their womb? Was it his wife he was attacking? The possibilities were almost endless and speculation along these lines came to be regarded as something of an indulgence. Nevertheless, an explanation for the workings of the mind of the Yorkshire Ripper was, and is, of abiding interest to all policemen connected with the inquiry.

In the *Yorkshire Post* at the beginning of November, Dr Stephen Shaw offered the view that the Yorkshire Ripper had settled down and married and might not kill again. 'I realize I could end up with egg on my face, but I feel this is a real possibility. I have never felt this was a married man, but it may be that since the murder of Vera Millward [at Manchester, seven months earlier] he has found a woman and settled down. She would probably be the opposite of a tart, possibly very religious, or even a devout member of a religious sect. Someone he can pamper and at whose feet he can worship. Someone who is in his eyes a paragon of virtue.'

Dr Shaw believed the Ripper was an over-controlled aggressive psychopath, a usually rigid, quiet, vaguely paranoid man, who looked and acted normally until subjected to some form of pressure. 'We know for a fact that at the age of about 35 personality disorders can mature and sometimes settle down for ever. That could happen with this man, and we might never hear of him again. I don't want to tempt fate, but it is a possibility.'

In the same week tell-tale signs of the strain involved in the biggest murder hunt of the century became apparent. Two detective constables were suspended from duty following the discovery of irregularities in the way they had obtained a small number of statements during the inquiry. They tendered their resignations from the force and papers were forwarded to the Director of Public Prosecutions.

A week later, on 8 November 1978, a 59-year-old mother of six, Kathleen Frances Sutcliffe, died in Airedale General Hospital. She had suffered from angina for four years and on her death certificate, dated 9 November, the cause of death was described as myocardial infarction and ischaemic heart disease. Her eldest son, Peter William, the one who had clung to her skirts for so long as a boy, and the one at whom she had gazed so happily on his wedding day, was grief-stricken. And angry.

Brother Michael recalled, 'There was no doubt Pete was closer to her than any of us. He was heartbroken when she died. It really upset him. He was mad about dad and his womanizing, though. He claimed it had made mother ill in the first place. The rows and going off with Wendy Broughton to live for a few weeks, some years earlier, hadn't pleased him. Pete was really mad.'

And with Peter in his 33rd year, so she was gone, mercifully never to know her son's terrible secret. Peter and Sonia had been at Garden Lane for well over a year and had worked hard making a home of the house that they wanted. Sonia spent a lot of time in the garden. The neighbours, however, had been kept at a distance. An odd couple, thought some; he would speak to you if he had to, but he had been known to turn back up his drive rather than have to make conversation. He was always messing about with the car in the drive. By this time the red Corsair had been sold; busy as ever where cars were concerned, Peter had bought a metallic-grey Sunbeam Rapier a month earlier. The couple had number six pebble-dashed and coloured a very pale pink to match others in the street.

At Clarks Peter was sometimes confused. He was the most conscientious of their drivers, keeping immaculate logs and repair records. Police on the Ripper job had been back to see him – something about his car number being picked up in red-light areas. But he hadn't seemed bothered. Some of the lads were saying that Pete was a bit of a dark horse, claiming that he had got a girlfriend in Motherwell called Tessa, short for Theresa.

CHAPTER 6

'Nice Talking To You, George'

By the spring of 1979, the Yorkshire Ripper was believed to have been responsible for the deaths of ten women in Yorkshire and Lancashire and further attacks on four others who had survived. The police had compiled a daunting amount of information from the separate cases, but were concerned that they were not receiving the sort of quality feed-back they believed they needed to trap the killer.

In March, it had been ten months since the horror of Vera Millward's death in Manchester and more than a year since that of Helen Rytka, the last killing in West Yorkshire. Asst. Chief Constable George Oldfield was unhappy about the extent of public co-operation, feeling that apathy towards the prostitutes' way of life was causing a lack of concern. If people in general were reluctant to come forward with information, the men who had been with prostitutes in the relevant areas on the nights in question created other headaches for the police.

Detectives were loath to approach directly a man whose car number had been noted in a red-light area, but many had refused to respond to appeals from the police in the press. When approached, they would often flatly deny being anywhere near the towns involved, creating further complications. While some members of the general public may have quickly lost interest in the plight of prostitutes who had been eliminated while pursuing their profession, many were keen to nurture the legend of the Yorkshire Ripper, a legend based on the thinnest of authentic information.

Stories of women being slit open from stomach to throat, of various subsequent and terrible rituals, were repeated as fact and without hesitation over cups of tea and coffee in offices, homes and factories, and over pints of beer in pubs. Intestines were said to have been removed and wrapped round victims' necks; breasts, even the flesh of vaginas were being carved from the women and recovered 200 yards away.

In 1978, the students of Trinity All Saints College, near Leeds, carried out some unusual survey work on public attitudes to the Ripper, which suggested that people in West Yorkshire were becoming almost immune to the regular onslaught of information in the media about the killings. Entitled *The public need shocking, don't they*, the students' report noted that only 6 per cent of people questioned believed there had been too much coverage of the case. Over half thought there had been just enough, and a third thought more was needed. The students concluded that more sensationalism, more 'facts with an emotive slant', were needed in the media to keep the issue alive in the public mind.

At least one senior police officer believed the time had arrived to publish a photograph of one of the victim's injuries. He felt the stark reality of what the killer was doing, in the form of a photograph, might shock a mother, a lover or a wife into stepping forward and voicing her fears.

It was not uncommon for policemen of the lower ranks, unconnected with the inquiry other than in a general sense, to fuel the Ripper legend. It was almost as if no one wanted to admit that he didn't really know what the killer was doing to his victims. George Oldfield and other senior officers had insisted that no details of the victims' injuries other than the barest outline should be disclosed, on the grounds that a 'copycat' killer might try to emulate the Yorkshire Ripper.

The police were aware of the increasingly bizarre legend that had grown up around the series of deaths, and there were officers who believed a greater danger lay in the possibility of a seriously disturbed person trying to emulate the legend! The alleged hysteria surrounding the deaths, responsibility for which is now blamed on the media by some officers, was undoubtedly nurtured by the element of secrecy imposed by the police.

In March, exactly a year after George Oldfield had received a letter posted in Sunderland and signed 'Jack the Ripper', he received another. The first, along with a similar one posted to the editor of the *Daily Mirror* in Manchester, had given little firm evidence of a Ripper connection, other than referring to, and indeed claiming responsibility for, the Harrison killing. It had tried to strike up a rapport with Oldfield, dwelling on the fact that while the press had dubbed the Ripper a maniac, the police chief had called him 'clever'. Yet there had been nothing about the letters to distinguish them from hundreds of others received by the police and most newspapers, apparently from cranks. But then the third letter arrived on George Oldfield's desk, and a re-appraisal was obviously required.

Some detectives had expressed doubts about the authenticity of the first two letters. Although one claimed the Preston killing as the work of the Ripper, the detectives were puzzled by the absence of any reference to Yvonne Pearson, who had died two months earlier, but whose body had not been discovered until after the letters arrived. However, it was difficult to dismiss a significant reference in the third letter regarding a medical detail about victim Vera Millward. Saliva tests on the first two envelopes had produced no result. Often, bacteria from food particles are present and spoil such tests, but examination of the third envelope produced positive results. Saliva under the envelope flap indicated the rare blood group B, the same as that of the man presumed to be the killer of Joan Harrison, who had had sexual intercourse with her at the time she died.

The third letter warned that the Ripper's next victim would be 'an old slut' in Bradford or Liverpool (a point never subsequently released), but thirteen days later, on Wednesday 4 April, the prediction proved inaccurate, when building-society clerk Josephine Whitaker died almost in sight of her home in Halifax. Forensic evidence from her wounds indicated traces of a mineral oil used in engineering shops, and was similar to particles found on one of the envelopes from Sunderland. Handwriting analysis carried out at the Home Office Forensic Science Laboratory in Birmingham confirmed that all three letters originated from the same source.

So it was that the 'Geordie connection' was about to be well and truly implanted in the public's consciousness, although the writer had said in an unpublished section of the third letter, 'I suppose you think I live in Sunderland. I'm not daft, I just posted it there'.

The day Josephine Whitaker received her eagerly-awaited £65 silver watch from a mail-order catalogue, she was to be asked the time for the last time in her life. Seconds later, she was dead. It was Wednesday the 4th, and one of the girls she worked with at the magnificent Halifax Building Society headquarters handed her the box with the watch she had picked out of the catalogue so carefully two weeks earlier, and awaited impatiently. It was Josephine's treat to herself.

She walked up the hill that evening, a tall, striking dark-haired girl, to the family home in a stone terrace off Savile Park, high above the town. She lived there with her mother, stepfather and two younger brothers. Josephine was a creature of habit, and for many years had visited her grandparents' home a mile away, up the side of the busy Halifax-Huddersfield road, for Sunday tea. It was a ritual she enjoyed, an opportunity to give and receive the week's news and gossip. There was no question that Jo, as they called her, was the apple of Tom and Mary Priestley's eye; her infectious good humour and enthusiasm for life were a weekly tonic for the elderly couple. Tom Priestley was surprised, though nevertheless pleased, when Josephine walked into his house that Wednesday evening. He couldn't remember the last time she had visited them on a day other than Sunday. He told her that her grandmother was at a St Andrew's Church function and would not be back until late, probably 11 p.m. But Josephine didn't mind the wait, and she made them a pot of tea after showing her grandfather her new watch. Then she settled down to watch television with him for the evening; she was as comfortable in his company as in that of anyone she knew, and the time passed quickly and easily.

When Mary Priestley returned home from the church function she too was surprised to find Jo at the house, and wondered at first if there was something wrong. She then admired Jo's new watch. Jo began to make noises about leaving, and both her grandparents counselled caution, suggesting that she should stay for the night. There was even a bed there for her, one she had used frequently just before her schoolteacher mother, Avril, had remarried in 1972.

Jo told the elderly couple not to be silly, that she would be all right; she had walked the route many times, up the

Huddersfield Road a way, into Dry Clough Lane, on towards Savile Park, a short cut across the grass to the house where her parents and brothers would already be in bed. They knew she would be able to let herself into the house with her own key. The Priestleys tried again to persuade their grand-daughter to stay until morning, but she wouldn't hear of it. Apart from anything else, she told them, the box in which she kept her contact lenses while she was asleep was in her bedroom at home. Tom Priestley knew it wasn't much of an excuse, but also realized he wasn't going to be able to change the mind of his tall and self-confident grand-daughter. He offered to walk home with her, despite the wracking pain caused by his emphysema, but Jo told him not to be silly, that she would be home in ten minutes.

Mary Priestley stood at the front door and waved to Jo as she set off up the hill, calling after her 'Goodbye' and 'Take care'. The light rain that had been falling earlier in the evening had stopped as she reached Savile Park, an area of open grassland about half a mile square, almost totally surrounded by well-lit roads. Jo's friends were later to say that she would not have been frightened by any man trying to speak to her when she was on her own, even close to midnight, as it was that evening. Craig Midgeley, a former fiancé, said she was confident and fearless. She had loved life, loved her work, was clever and bright; a generous and kind girl, said Mr Midgeley.

Jo enjoyed meeting people. As she strode across the still, damp grass of Savile Park, she met a man with a black beard and dark wavy hair. Peter William Sutcliffe.

It was almost four years since Peter Sutcliffe had been drinking in Halifax with Trevor Birdsall and knocked

Olive Smelt to the ground with a hammer. He liked drinking in the old town, the Bull's Head being a particular favourite, and had returned there often on drinking expeditions with Birdsall, Keith Sugden, the Barker brothers, even Sonia and Birdsall's wife Melissa.

But tonight he was alone, Sonia in bed back at Garden Lane. The girl he saw was tall, just about the same height as him, and looked him steadily in the eye when he asked her where she had been. To her grandmother's, she told him. (Just like bloody Red Riding Hood, one detective said later, completely without humour.) He asked the girl what time it was, feigning admiration and surprise at her good eyesight as she looked towards a distant clock and told him. The dark-eyed stranger received no privileged glimpse of the new watch, but he had bought himself enough time to produce the hammer from its hiding-place in his jacket and crash it down on Josephine Whitaker's head, only a dozen strides from the roadway. Another blow as she lay on the grass, and then he dragged her some 30 feet, back towards the darkness, away from the road. Sutcliffe pulled her clothing back and proceeded to rain a total of 25 stabbing blows with a kitchen-type knife, its blade 4″ long, into her breasts, stomach and thighs, even into her vagina. She was left like a bundle of rags, her multi-coloured skirt with its white lacy trimming, pink jumper and heather-mixture hacking-hacket despoiled with mud and blood. One of her tan shoes still lay at the point of the initial attack.

Bus driver Ronald Marwood saw the bundle of rags at 5.30 a.m., when he drove the first bus of the day, a number 6, along Savile Park Road. When he reached the depot, he reported the mystery object at the office, but it was not thought necessary to inform the police.

Mrs Jean Markham was standing at the bus stop in

Savile Park Road at 6.30, when her early-morning, half-hearted stare at the bundle on the grass opposite began to come startlingly into focus when she took a few steps towards it and realized it was a young woman.

At the same time, Josephine's young brother, 13-year-old David, was, as usual, the first to rise at the Hiley household in nearby Ivy Street; on with his clothes and down to the paper shop for his daily paper round. As he made his way across the playing fields, he saw the policemen gathered round something on the ground, bent over, peering intently. Curiosity took him towards the group, his heartbeat quickening as he began to sense someone's misfortune. And then he saw his sister's shoe, the brown one with the stacked heel, and his young head was suddenly full of crowding, frightening images.

And then he turned and was off, racing across the grass, across the road, into the streets of terraces, bursting through the kitchen door at number 10 Ivy Street, gushing out his confusing story. Josephine's mother hurried upstairs to her daughter's bedroom and was mortified to see her bed had not been slept in. When she had risen herself she had presumed that Josephine was still asleep, as she had been so many times before. Distraught with fear and mounting grief, they rang Halifax police station.

The first policemen to arrive at the scene suspected the dead girl could have been the victim of a hit-and-run driver as she was crossing the nearby road. Had she then crawled onto the grass? Had she been dragged from under a car onto the grass? The police priority was to make sure that as little as possible was disturbed, to define clearly lines of approach to the scene, in an attempt to ensure that no more footmarks than necessary were imposed on the immediate area.

It was the following day, Friday, before the police officially confirmed that Josephine Ann Whitaker was believed to be the Yorkshire Ripper's eleventh victim. On the Thursday morning, soon after the body was discovered, George Oldfield's telephone rang, and he heard the words he was dreading; battered skull, clothes disturbed to reveal the front of her body and, yes, a frenzy of stab wounds. Like every senior detective, he had learned years earlier never to jump to conclusions, never to take anything at face value. Wait and hear what the pathologist has to say. But still, as he headed towards new territory, Halifax, he knew; in his heart, he felt sure the nightmare had been re-kindled.

Halifax clings to the side of a hill, with some of the steepest streets in Yorkshire – a dark, almost forbidding place to the new arrival from Leeds and Wakefield on a wet day. But why Halifax? Not even a hint of red-light district there, unlike nearby Bradford and Huddersfield.

The head of the West Yorkshire C.I.D. was joined on the grass of Savile Park by his right-hand man with the special Ripper squad since February, Det. Supt. Dick Holland, with his photographic memory for Ripper facts, and Det. Supt. Trevor Lapish. The three of them were big, burly and serious, grim-faced enough for the front row of the Halifax Rugby League team, its glory years long passed. A fourth man had more the look of a centre three-quarter. The Manchester C.I.D. chief, Jack Ridgeway, had wasted no time in travelling over the still snow-capped Pennines.

The four of them turned away, silent and sad, as the polythene sheet was placed carefully over Josephine's body, there to await the arrival of pathologist David Gee from Leeds. They had stared at similar desperate and terrible spectres over the previous long months and years. George Oldfield walked across the wooden duck-boards, a strange mixture of despair and optimism in his heart. He just hoped that this time, please God, the killer had made the mistake that was to take the police to him. But still there was the bitterness, another girl dead – Josephine Whitaker, not much older than his own daughter studying at Newcastle University, a long way from home, in the North East.

Within 24 hours, Oldfield's spirits had lifted. The realization that this girl was totally unconnected with prostitution or red-light areas had produced a previously unseen response from the public. Police switchboards worked overtime, as if the 90,000 good people of Halifax were being swept along on a tide of indignation and rage, as if a giant, slumbering conscience had at last been prodded awake. Oldfield and Holland considered reports of cars seen in the area at the relevant time, a man walking with a girl who answered Josephine's description, and information about a man in a dark Ford Escort saloon who had approached a woman in Halifax town centre earlier on the night of the attack. He had what was known as a Jason King-style moustache, as had Marilyn Moore's attacker two years earlier, but Oldfield warned that the photofit of the Ford Escort man should not be regarded as the face of the Ripper.

There were further reports of a white Escort being seen in Savile Park Road around the time of the attack. The following Sunday, 8 April, the Palm Sunday service at St Jude's Church, just along the road from Josephine's grandparents, was packed. Jo had attended Sunday School there, and her brother Michael had sung in the choir. Rev Michael Walker urged a truly Christian attitude, calling for prayers for everyone concerned in the tragedy,

George Oldfield with the famous tape-recording, now thought to have been a hoax.

Dear Officer,   March 23rd 79

Sorry I haven't written, about a year to be exult, but I haven't been up North for quite a while. I was'nt holding last time I wrote

That was last month, so I don't know when I will get back on the job but I know it wont be Chapeltown too bloody hot there maybe Bradford's Manningham. Might write again if up North.

                    Jack the Ripper

The letter received by Oldfield, believed originally to be from the Ripper.

George Oldfield showing the strain. For a time he left the enquiry because of ill health.

Jim Hobson in the incident room at Millgarth Police Station, Leeds.

Police officers interviewing a woman in the red-light district of Leeds.

Police play the Ripper tape in a working-man's club.

A police photographer prepares to take pictures of Wilma McCann's body (arrowed) as police officers erect canvas screens around the area.

The scene of Emily Jackson's killing in Leeds.

Garrard's timber-yard, Huddersfield, with the location of Helen Rytka's body arrowed.

Police mark the wasteland where Yvonne Pearson was killed.

The sofa under which Yvonne Pearson's body was found.

Detectives and forensic experts examine Vera Millward's body on waste ground near Manchester Royal Infirmary.

osephine Whitaker lies in Savile Park, Halifax.

pring crocuses provide an ironic foreground to the scene in Savile Park as
atrolling policemen guard the area.

The house in Bradford where the body of Barbara Leach was found, behind the low wall to the left.

Police at the scene of Barbara Leach's killing.

Jacqueline Hill's body lies in front of a police screen.

Flowers placed at the scene of Jacqueline Hill's killing.

The Ripper 'Super' Squad in November 1980: (*seated*) ACC Jim Hobson (West Yorks), (*standing, left to right*) ACC David Gerty (West Midlands), Commander Ronald Harvey, Deputy CC Leslie Emmant (Thames Valley), Stuart Kind (Home Office), ACC Andrew Sloan (National Co-ordinator).

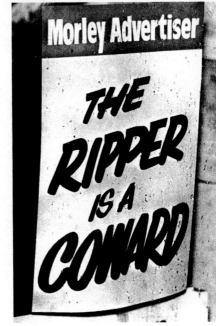

Ripper poster in Morley.

Sutcliffe at the wheel of his lorry, a publicity shot used on a T and W H Clark works calendar.

Melbourne Avenue, Sheffield, the secluded lane leading to where Sutcliffe was arrested.

PC Robert Hydes (*left*) and Sergeant Robert Ring, the officers who made the arrest.

George Oldfield and Ronald Gregory in jubilant mood at the post-arrest press conference.

lice guard the Sutcliffe house in Bradford.

igry demonstrators show their feelings as they wait for the Ripper to appear
tside Dewsbury Court.

Sutcliffe, covered by a blanket, arrives at Dewsbury Court.

cliffe's wife, Sonia, pictured at a party in 1979.

Mrs Sutcliffe is helped into Court.

including the Ripper. 'He needs help. He is someone's child, husband or father. Pray not only for Josephine and her family, but for the Ripper and his family. They may be unwittingly protecting him.'

Oldfield and Holland had spent many hours considering the implications of the three letters from Sunderland, particularly since forensic experts had established the possible mineral-oil link. Thirteen months earlier, in March 1978, George Oldfield had forwarded a copy of the letter sent to the *Daily Mirror* in Manchester and postmarked Sunderland to Northumbria police headquarters in Newcastle. They, like West Yorkshire, regarded the letter as a potential hoax, along with many others they had received. Still, they went through the standard procedure of checking their files for similar handwriting, looking at crank letters, threats and hoaxes as well as samples of known criminals' writing. But a year of intermittent inquiry produced no suspects. Almost two weeks after Josephine Whitaker was killed, however, on Easter Monday, 16 April, West Yorkshire Police announced that the following day's press conference was being moved from its usual time of 10.30 a.m. to 3.30 p.m. There were hints of a major announcement by George Oldfield, suggestions of a breakthrough in the inquiry. Despite complaints from evening newspaper representatives, used to having the day's fresh headline handed to them on a plate at the daily conference, Oldfield insisted on sticking to the new timing. He was anxious that this announcement should gain the maximum exposure over the widest area, which meant through the morning newspapers and the evening television news broadcasts.

The police in Northumberland knew all about it, because they had already been informed that the third letter, the one received 13 days before the latest attack, was being taken seriously by West Yorkshire police. An inquiry team of four detectives had been set up in Sunderland, the dates of the letters having been passed on to a largely sceptical North East force, and the team had been visiting firms in the area to gather details of Geordies who had been in Yorkshire on the attack dates, and Yorkshiremen who had visited the North East on the dates the three letters had been posted.

The Sunderland squad was enlarged and an incident room set up following a conference with Oldfield in West Yorkshire. The so-called Geordie connection was duly revealed at Oldfield's afternoon press conference, but Oldfield did not actually say that the Ripper had written the three letters. Some newspapers had picked up that information from their own sources, and the following morning the public knew of the strange North East connection. Mr Oldfield was faithfully reported as asking engineering firms to check their records in West Yorkshire to see if they had a man visiting the Sunderland area on 7, 8, 12 and 13 March 1978 and 22 and 23 March 1979. Similarly, he appealed to engineering concerns in the North East to contact the police if any of their workers regularly visited West Yorkshire.

A measure of the task facing the police was quickly established when it was realized that there were two million engineering workers in the British Isles, and in the North East alone there were thousands of small firms. But the police thought they were at last making progress, and the day after the press conference, Wednesday 18 April, Dick Holland, then 46, felt able to take two hours off in the afternoon.

Two months later, further correspondence was received by George Oldfield from Sunderland. This time the writing on the envelope was printed, and there was no letter inside, just a recorded tape cassette. One of the detectives present at the first playing of the tape said, 'It was bizarre. We were amazed at the sheer cheek of the little sod.' The tape was played through twice, copied, and then sent immediately for detailed examination by forensic scientists in London, who soon confirmed the handwriting and saliva-blood group tests matched a previous letter.

Two days later, in conditions of the utmost secrecy, a conference of top detectives from four northern police forces gathered at the Wakefield headquarters of the West Yorkshire police. Detectives from Manchester, Preston and Sunderland had been told at short notice to travel to Wakefield as quickly as possible. They listened to the tape five or six times, then listened just as carefully to the West Yorkshire view of its authenticity.

The rare B blood group (if it were to be accepted that on balance the killer of women in West Yorkshire had also taken the life of Joan Harrison in Preston) and the mineral-oil link had proved persuasive for the West Yorkshire police. A reference in the third letter to an aspect of Vera Millward's hospital treatment had also made a deep impression on George Oldfield, that he was to carry in the back of his mind for a long time. Officers from Lancashire at the conference repeated previous misgivings about the link with Preston, although their resistance had weakened considerably. There were also doubts expressed about the wisdom of going public with the tape. George Oldfield's view was that eventually the tape should be released to the media in an edited form, being mindful of the Ripper's explicit threat to kill again.

Some detectives said there was no choice other than to release the tape. 'If he kills again and the public finds out in a year's time that we have been sitting on this tape, then all hell will break loose,' was one view forcibly expressed.

An outline of the last killing, that of Josephine Whitaker, seemed to link it incontrovertibly with the others, via the evidence relating to the wounds and, crucially, boot-prints found near the body in Savile Park. They seemed to match those found at the Emily Jackson and Tina Atkinson deaths, and were from footwear with moulded rubber or composition soles, the type most often found in industrial protective or army-type boots. The sole impressions indicated size seven, with the right sole showing some wearing and twisting in the centre, possibly as a result of the wearer regularly pressing some sort of pedal, as when driving, with his right foot. Police established that although the impressions found were almost certainly size 7, persons with shoe size of up to $8\frac{1}{2}$ could wear the boots comfortably.

Yet after the 20 June meeting, George Oldfield remained uneasy about the taped message. If it was the man who had doubled the original Jack the Ripper's tally, this had to be the most sensational clue in criminal detection history. But was it really the actual voice of the killer being hunted by every policeman in the North of England? The heartrending 17-minute tape of Lesley Ann Downey, aged 10, begging the Moors murderer Ian Brady, 'Don't, please . . . God help me', was discovered after Brady and Hindley were in police hands. That too had ended in music – *The Little Drummer Boy*. That tape had been for Brady's personal gratification later. George Oldfield knew that the snatch of the obscure Andrew Gold's *Thank you for being a friend* at the end of his tape was there purely to mock him.

Whatever Oldfield's uncertainties about the tape, and the wisdom of whether it should be released in part, in whole, or not at all, he was overtaken by events, when, three days later, news of its arrival and details of its contents were leaked to the press. A hurried internal police inquiry conducted by the Deputy Chief Constable of West Yorkshire failed to trace the source of the leak, and the officers in charge of the hunt were furious because it forced their hand. They had to release the tape with no cuts other than the shortening of some gaps to facilitate the playing time on radio and television, as well as on the special telephone number that was set up to make it available 24 hours a day. Police from the North East had immediately identified the accent on the tape as that of a man from the Sunderland area. The leak to the press precipitated the sort of in-depth investigation by voice experts necessary to pinpoint the accent more accurately.

The decision was taken to go public and the following Tuesday, 26 June, saw the most memorable press conference those present had ever witnessed. Journalists from all over Britain assembled in the lecture theatre of the West Yorkshire Police Academy at Bishopgarth, Wakefield, to see George Oldfield lean forward and switch on the cassette player, place his spectacles on the desk beside him and stare straight ahead, his head resting on his left hand throughout the playing of the tape. The room, flooded with television lights, was suddenly full of an unmistakably Geordie voice, at one minute chiding Oldfield, the next almost conspiratorial.

'I'm Jack. I see you're still having no luck catching me. I have the greatest respect for you, George, but, Lord, you are no nearer catching me now than four years ago when I started. I reckon your boys are letting you down, George. You can't be much good, can ya? The only time they came near to catching me was a few months back in Chapeltown when I was disturbed. Even then it was a uniformed copper, not a detective. I warned you in March that I would strike again, sorry it wasn't Bradford. I did promise you that but I couldn't get there. I'm not sure when I will strike again, but it will definitely be sometime this year, maybe September or October, even sooner if I get the chance. I'm not sure where, maybe Manchester. I like it there. There's plenty of them knocking about. They never do learn, do they George? I bet you warned them but they never listen. At the rate I'm going I should be in the book of records. I think it's eleven up to now, isn't it? Well, I'll keep on going for quite a while yet, I can't see myself being nicked just yet. If you ever do get near I'll probably top myself first. Well, it's been nice chatting to you, George. Yours, Jack the Ripper. It's no good looking for fingerprints, you should know by now it's as clean as a whistle. See you soon. Bye. Hope you like the catchy tune at the end. Ha. Ha.'

The impact of the press conference, at which photographs of the envelopes showing the handwriting were also made available, was immediate. Fifty thousand calls were quickly received from the public, causing further strain on police manpower, already under stress as a result of having 250 officers working full time on the case in West Yorkshire alone. Whereas detectives in the North East surmised that greater exposure of the tape was necessary if the voice were to be identified, the assumption of their colleagues in West Yorkshire was that the Ripper's message had already received a considerable airing. While detectives in Sunderland took the tape round local firms, pubs and clubs, police in the Leeds-Bradford area tried to cope with the calls they had already received. It was some weeks later, when they too took copies of the tape onto the streets, that they discovered far fewer people than they had at first realized had actually listened to it.

In the summer of 1979, the message to the public was clear and simple. The Yorkshire Ripper was a Geordie, and, by implication of the frantic subsequent police inquiries on Wearside, lived in Geordieland. Oldfield was to say consistently over the subsequent months that he believed the killer lived in Leeds or Bradford, but there can have been few members of the public who would be able to conceive of the wanted man being born in Bingley and talking with a flat, almost slow, very Yorkshire accent.

The Northumbria police had been immediately happy that the speaker on the tape was a Sunderland man. The feed-back from West Yorkshire – that the speaker was the Ripper – produced mixed feelings. 'It seemed strange that a man operating in Yorkshire and Lancashire should appear to be a Wearsider,' says Northumbria's Assistant Chief Constable (Crime), Brian Johnson. Police guessed rightly that the effect of releasing the tape of the Ripper's voice on the public would be enormous. Before the watershed press conference, the Sunderland incident room had again been expanded. Eleven West Yorkshire detectives were installed in an hotel in Sunderland, bringing the total number of men and women standing by for the expected onslaught of tip-offs and enquiries to 100. After the release, six women officers in Sunderland were kept engaged on the telephones for 16 hours a day, and four were still needed to answer the calls that came in between 10 p.m. and 6 a.m. By the end of the second day, one thousand calls (not including mere requests to hear the tape) had been received in Sunderland. All leads were investigated, and detectives were still busy in August, when the Leeds University dialect expert, Mr Stanley Ellis, pronounced the mining village of Castletown, near Sunderland, as being almost certainly the Ripper's home town.

Mr Ellis is regarded as the principal authority on English dialect, and has more investigative experience in the field than anyone else in the country. In the 1950s he spent eight years travelling the length and breadth of Britain soaking up the subtleties and variations of the various forms of English speech. He listened to tapes of policemen from all over the North East of England, and then travelled to Sunderland before pronouncing his verdict. He and his colleague at the University, Mr Jack Windsor Lewis, an expert in the pitch features of speech, were both phoneticians, and they concentrated on the voice quality of the tape, the type of articulation and the pitch of the voice. They work by separating from any voice thousands of strands, almost in the way a fingerprint expert approaches a piece of evidence. They were unhappy that they had not been able to give the police their final verdict until well into August. Mr Windsor Lewis also turned his attention to the letters, in an attempt to build up an even more accurate picture of the writer and his background.

He was surprised at the fact that four out of the five or six figure 7s in the letters were crossed in the continental style, and astonished that Mr Oldfield had not chosen to make this clue available to the public. Mr Windsor Lewis said the general educational profile produced by the letters showed the writer to be of the superior working-class. But the two experts were hopeful that the tape would quickly lead the police to its author, once they had pinpointed Castletown in August. They felt the West Yorkshire police should not have seemed as adamant as they had in giving the impression that the Yorkshire Ripper was definitely a Geordie, and would have been happier for the public to have been left more options. They thought a 50-50 possibility was more likely; yet they were confident that the maker of the tape lived and worked in Castletown and would be apprehended within days.

The police in Castletown based themselves in a 16-foot

caravan, also used as a police post for Sunderland's home games at their Roker Park football ground. They first set out to visit every one of the village's 1,600 households. One of the 25 detectives would knock on a door, and if it was necessary, explain why he had come. He would then go through a detailed questionnaire, designated N/WYP, and play the tape. People who could not help were recorded on white cards, while suspicious names, or those needing checking for the most trivial of reasons, were recorded on pink cards. It took ten days to go through Castletown in this way, and officers on the case worked out that if they were to take in the entire north bank of the River Wear, the general suspect area, they would be knocking on doors for 18 months.

The residents of Castletown reacted with mild disbelief to the prospect of one of their fellows being unmasked as the Yorkshire Ripper, and with occasional anger to some of the publicity the village received. Some people, particularly those trying to sell property, were upset when a newspaper described Castletown as 'dirty and decaying', an unfair description, even though the area had begun to slide since the mine closed the previous year. The police, who were obviously relying heavily on the public's help, asked journalists writing about the hunt to refrain from such phrases. Some jokes were still made at Castletown's expense. A detective wag told his colleagues, 'All we've got to do is find the bugger here who can write and we've cracked it.' And a pub joker told a London reporter, 'If he's canny, he canna come from here.'

There was considerable public co-operation for the police. Indeed, people could be too willing to help. One woman told detectives that she knew the voice, and if they would now show her the man's picture, she would put a name to him. But back at Leeds University, Stanley Ellis and Jack Windsor Lewis began to feel their first flickerings of apprehension when the tape-maker had not been identified within a few days of the big police push in Castletown.

'We knew they would speak to the maker of the tape very quickly, and that if the police could not isolate him because he had firm alibis for the days of the killings, then there could only be one possible explanation,' says Mr Windsor Lewis. 'The maker of the tape was not the Yorkshire Ripper.'

The inquiry continued, the work painstaking, laborious and ultimately fruitless. It was still in progress over a year later, when a lorry driver from Bradford was arrested in Sheffield after being found with a prostitute in a car with false number plates. But Det. Chief Inspector David Zackrisson, the genial deputy head of the Northumbria Ripper squad, recalls the lengthy exercise as one that built a useful bridge into the sort of community detectives rarely probed, a community of decent working people, quite different from the low-lifes and inadequates that big city detectives were used to dealing with. The house-to-house inquiry covered 11,000 households in Castletown and its surrounding areas, and some aspects of the hunt were to beg certain questions. A letter appeared in a church magazine asking why detectives had bothered to interview a church warden who was crippled with angina. Police received an irate letter from an interviewee who had no legs.

What was becoming embarrassingly evident was a fundamental difference in approach between the Northumbria force and the men from West Yorkshire, or at least the senior men. While George Oldfield seemed sure that the speaker was the Ripper, Northumbria were keeping their options open. Brian Johnson stressed after the arrest of the killer that there was no question of his force having defied Mr Oldfield. 'Let's say we weren't as convinced as Mr Oldfield, and we took certain actions to establish our point of view,' he explained. The difference in approach could easily be detected. While West Yorkshire's posters made it clear that the letter-writer and the tape-maker were the Ripper, posters appearing in the North East were deliberately more cautious. Under the heading 'Important notice', the Northumbria poster showed a sample of one of the letters and the following message: 'The writer, who signs it Jack the Ripper, claims to be connected with the murders.' The bolder West Yorkshire posters read, 'The Ripper would like you to ignore this,' above a sample of the handwriting of the hoaxer.

On 2 September 1979, Stanley Ellis and Jack Windsor Lewis felt almost sure the police had interviewed the tape-maker and that he was not the killer. By 3 September, they were sure.

Near the end of July, the strain of the chase finally caught up with George Oldfield, then 55. His wife Margaret found him sitting on the edge of their bed early one morning, and he suggested she call the heart specialist he had seen a few days earlier. He had terrible pains in the hollows of his arms, and admits he was frightened. He urged his wife to give him a stiff whisky and believes the early-morning shock to his system probably kept his ailing heart beating. He was rushed into hospital at Wakefield, and it was to be the beginning of the following year before he was to recover sufficiently from the three heart attacks and return to his desk. His deputy, Det. Chief Supt. Jim Hobson, was also preoccupied with hospital thoughts on Monday 3

September; his wife had fallen down the stairs at their Wetherby home, fracturing her skull, and he was at her bedside in the intensive care unit at Chapel Allerton Hospital, Leeds, that Monday teatime when he was summoned to Bradford police headquarters.

The Mannville Arms pub is just 300 yards from Bradford's modern smoked-glass and concrete police headquarters, the other side of the green-domed Alhambra theatre, on the bend where Great Horton Road climbs towards the University. If there is such a thing, the Mannville Arms is a typical West Yorkshire pub – noisy, busy, friendly, with a fine pint of hand-pulled Tetley bitter. The sort of pub Peter William Sutcliffe liked; in fact one of the many he patronized during his years of pub-crawling in and around Bradford. The Mannville Arms was popular with students, as well as the locals, 'townies' as the more affected of the university types called them. On Saturday night, 1 September, the start of the winter term was still weeks away, but there were enough students who had remained in the city throughout the summer to make it a typical Mannville Saturday night, the punks and the students competing good-naturedly for time on the juke box.

Barbara Janine Leach was one of the students, a vivacious, sunny girl with a stunning smile. Two years earlier, she had left her parents, Beryl and David Leach, in Kettering, where her father was a bank clerk. With her A levels in English and Religious Knowledge, she had a choice of several universities available to her, but decided to study social sciences at Bradford. She told her family she wanted to mix with real people, to be part of a world she had never known, to be among, she hoped, the working-class friendliness of ordinary people – the other half, as she put it. Her brother Graham, two years older than her, said Barbara had 'a totally cosmopolitan type of feminism'.

Two years at Bradford had largely satisfied her expectations and aspirations, so much so that she had stayed throughout the summer at the flat in the terrace of stone houses not far from the Mannville Arms to press on with her studies for her third year, and hopefully a Bachelor of Science degree. She loved it at the house in Grove Terrace, just across Great Horton Road from the University campus, where she lived with other young male and female students. She happily did much of the cooking and occasionally caught the bus to the ancient village of Tong, just off the Bradford-to-Wakefield road, for an afternoon's horse-riding at the weekends.

Saturday 1 September was Barbara's father's 53rd birthday, and she was horrified when she realized she had forgotten to send him a card. She went to the telephone box at the end of Grove Terrace, spoke to her mother, and asked her to apologize to her father for her forgetfulness. She said she would stay in Bradford over the weekend, but travel to Kettering on the Monday, and could her mother fix up a hairdressing appointment for her at the salon she used there.

The day was bright and warm, and the streets running parallel with Grove Terrace, up the hill and off Great Horton Road, were becoming busy with students. Most of the houses were owned by the University and divided into flats. Many of the sash windows were up, and at least one 'welcome back to Bradford' party was planned for that evening, including one in a ground-floor flat in Ash Grove, at the top of the hill. But for Barbara Leach, that evening would be spent in the Mannville Arms, where the music was good. She was there with five of her closest friends from the flat; some of the boys often helped behind the bar when it was busy. At closing time, 11 p.m., they helped the landlord, Roy Evans, collect the empties and generally tidy up. He rewarded them with a drink, after time, but they were his personal guests, and it was time to relax after a busy, noisy evening. When they finally left the pub at 12.45, they stepped out into Great Horton Road, turned left and walked slowly up the hill to the junction with Grove Terrace.

Barbara hesitated and despite the rain told one of her flatmates, Paul Smith, that she wanted to go for a walk. He declined her invitation to join her, but when she asked him to wait up for her, because she had no key, he promised he would. An hour later, when she had still not returned, he presumed she had called at the flat of one of her friends, or been invited into a party, and went to bed. When she had not returned late on Sunday, her friends reported her missing. One of them, Gabrielle Rhodes, told the police she had arranged to meet Barbara at the Bradford interchange at 12.30 p.m. on Monday. They asked her to keep the appointment in case Barbara turned up, but she didn't. The police decided to mount a search in the streets off Great Horton Road, starting with the ones nearest to Grove Terrace and her flat. It is one of seven similar streets, running parallel to each other in an area between Great Horton Road and Morley Street, which come together in an apex near the bottom of the hill, just before the police station. In one of the streets, Claremont, stands the home the composer Delius lived in a hundred years ago. Further up the hill is a similar thoroughfare, Ash Grove, but before you reach that, there is Back Ash Grove, a narrow alley-like lane serving as a rear approach to the houses in Ash Grove.

At 3.55 p.m., P.C. Simon Greaves walked down Back

Ash Grove and entered one of the open yards, just a few feet from the main road. He approached a low wall at the back of the house, a place where dustbins were usually kept. He pulled aside an old carpet on which some stones had been placed and found a girl, dead, in a distorted jack-knife posture. Barbara Leach's cheesecloth shirt and bra had been pushed up to expose her breasts, and her jeans had been undone and partly pulled down. She had been stabbed in the stomach and shoulder blade a total of eight times, and Professor Gee told Mr Hobson that the knife, with its four-inch-long blade, $\frac{5}{16}''$ wide, was identical to the one that had inflicted similar terrible injuries on Josephine Whitaker.

After asking Paul Smith to stay up for her just before 1 a.m. the day before, Barbara Leach had walked only 200 yards in the rain before Peter Sutcliffe dealt her one blow with a hammer to the back of her head at the end of Ash Grove, then dragged her along the cobbled alley, into the back yard and the ignominy that awaited. If the Ripper had taken two steps sideways and looked up the side of the house, he would have seen straight through the open window of number 16, where a bottle party was by then well under way. Instead he got in his car and drove the two short miles back to 6 Garden Lane.

Yet another police name came to the fore: Det. Chief Supt. Peter Gilrain, given the job by Mr Gregory of heading the Leach case, Mr Hobson continuing to have overall responsibility for the wider investigation as temporary A.C.C. Crime. If some had likened Mr Hobson's looks to the missing Lord Lucan, Peter Gilrain was to be dubbed another Sir Alf Ramsey, not so much for the physical resemblance, but because of his calm and carefully modulated way of answering questions. The statistics facing the West Yorkshire police by now did not have to be pointed out to them in heavy black newspaper print. There were 12 dead women and four survivors, all alleged victims of the Ripper. Those so-familiar faces, some smiling, some grim, were again leaping out from the printed page and the television screens. It was like a re-run of an unfinished nightmare, yet this time it was different.

It was not just that Barbara Leach was another non-prostitute. What after all is the alternative to an innocent victim? If Jayne MacDonald, Josephine Whitaker and now Barbara Leach were innocent, of what were the others guilty? Being women? Were women who were prepared to try to satisfy men's sexual needs any more deserving of a sudden, brutal end? Of course, the police were using a form of verbal shorthand, and the media were guilty of the same lack of precision with words, but it was not difficult to comprehend the sense of the police message. After Barbara Leach, things were never to be quite the same again for the police, either with the public or the press. However little real detail a man or woman in the street knew about the killer, until now, from September 1979 they were faced with an unremitting reality; whoever or whatever the Yorkshire Ripper was, in the space of a summer, 150 days, he had struck down two young women whose lives and life-styles were in the starkest contrast to the Wilma McCanns, the Tina Atkinsons and the Helen Rytkas. Consciously or unconsciously, that did make the whole affair different, a subject for increased concern in many minds.

Dick Holland had been obliged to return from Scotland, where he had hoped to take his first holiday break in many months. He had only been in Glenrothis for a few hours when he heard the news on the television that another woman's body had been found. He jumped into his motor caravan and drove back to Bradford through the night without even having unpacked his fishing rods.

There had been murmurings about the West Yorkshire police's inability to catch the Ripper after Josephine Whitaker's death, even suggestions that someone else should be given a chance – Scotland Yard, for example. The fact that Scotland Yard, unlike 20 years earlier, no longer had any more expertise to offer than other large forces was either ignored or was not understood. However, it still came as a surprise to the police a few days after the latest death when the first overt thrust from the Scotland Yard lobby came from an unexpected direction, the *Daily Express*, which had long been known as the Copper's Friend for its years of seemingly blind support for anything and everything concerning the police service, whether in West Yorkshire, Lancashire or London.

When the *Express* carried a front-page story saying that the Home Secretary was to set up a squad of senior officers, including some from Scotland Yard, to take charge of the four-year-old investigation, Ronald Gregory was furious. He dismissed the claim as false, adding, 'I deplore this irresponsible imputation against the professional abilities of my officers.'

It seemed that the paper had been confused by a meeting called at Wakefield by Mr Gregory three days after the Leach death, to which he had invited a wide variety of senior officers, including some from other forces. Among them was Mr John Locke, a Scotland Yard Deputy Assistant Commissioner, who was at the meeting in his entirely separate role as the national co-ordinator of the Regional Crime Squads. Those at the meeting, like the press and the public, believed the threat to kill again in September or October, contained in the most recent Ripper letter, had been carried out, and that the killer was a Geordie, not a bearded lorry driver with a Yorkshire accent who lived a five-minute drive away from the Bradford police headquarters.

On Thursday 13 September, the West Yorkshire police issued a confidential 18-page report to other forces outlining the 16 known attacks on women believed to be the work of one man. It was intended as a means of eliminating suspects. The 'special notice' entitled *Murders and Assaults Upon Women in the North of England* was planned as a guide to any officer who might be confronted by a man he suspected of being the killer. It outlined the relevant facts of each attack, but in just over 100 words at the beginning disposed of the exaggerated myths and legends flourishing elsewhere. It read; 'It is significant that although most of the early victims are prostitutes or women of loose moral character, in the majority of cases no obvious sexual interference has taken place, and the motive for each time is a pathological hatred of women. In the most recent cases, innocent women have been attacked. In the majority of these offences, vicious hammer blows to the back of the head have occurred, and it is generally thought this precedes the stabbing of the victim. In some cases the clothing of the victim is moved to expose the breasts and lower abdomen, prior to stab wounds being inflicted. No stabbing has occurred through clothing.'

In just a few lines, the murder hunt of the century, as it was by then being called, was reduced to the barest, baldest scenario. Explanations of tyre positions at the scene of the Richardson, Moore and Millward killings included a daunting list of potential cars of the same track width. There was an example of handwriting from one of the

letters sent to George Oldfield, the contents of the cassette
tape, and a five-point list for purposes of elimination. This
indicated that a person could be eliminated if 1) the man
was not born between 1924 and 1959, making him over 20
and under 55; 2) if he was an obvious coloured person; 3) if
his shoe size was nine or above; 4) if his blood group was
other than B; and most crucially, 5) if his accent was
dissimilar to a North Eastern (Geordie) accent.

There were stated to be three common factors (a) the use
of two weapons, a 'sharp instrument' and an alleged $1\frac{1}{4}$-
pound ball-pein hammer; (b) the absence of sexual
interference and (c) clothing moved to expose breasts and
pubic region. The greatest irony, with the benefit of
hindsight, is contained in the very last paragraph: 'It may
be that the man responsible has come to police attention in
the past for assaults on prostitutes and women which did
not result in serious injury, and suggestions regarding the
identity of the person responsible, or any other
information about similar assaults, not necessarily fatal,
would be appreciated.'

Stanley Ellis and Jack Windsor Lewis were so concerned
by the time that special notice was circulated that the writer
of the letters and the Geordie on the tape were not the
Yorkshire Ripper that they drafted a letter outlining their
fears and on 23 September sent it to the West Yorkshire
police. They laid great stress on their belief that the police
would have already interviewed the tape-maker in
Castletown within days of going to the village, but that he
had been eliminated simply because he could provide
satisfactory alibis for the nights of the attacks.

If he were not the killer, he would have no problem
accounting for his whereabouts, they argued. The two men

became doubly dismayed when the Ripper, Geordie or otherwise, killed again at the beginning of September, and their mood turned to despair later in the month when Chief Constable Gregory revealed details of what became known as the £1 million publicity campaign to catch the Ripper. They did not so much disagree with the concept of bill-boards, advertising hoardings and even a special Ripper newspaper to be delivered to every home in West Yorkshire, Lancashire and the North East in an attempt to force millions of people to concentrate on the matter at hand; nor did they object to the sample of handwriting and the reminder of a £30,000 reward; nor even the emotive language of one handbill ('He's a vicious, deranged maniac who returns time and again to perform a method of murder so sick that it has turned the stomachs of even the most hardened police officers'.)

It was the emphasis on the North East, the conviction that the killer spoke with a Geordie accent, which made them unhappy. A few days earlier, after their unsolicited report had reached the police, they were invited to go to Bradford police headquarters where Mr Hobson and Mr Gilrain were holding a conference with C.I.D. heads from all over the North of England. Mr Windsor Lewis recalls: 'We sat in a room all day and spoke to many of the individual senior officers involved in the inquiry. They listened carefully to everything we had to say, but at the end of the day I'm afraid we had to agree to disagree.

'They went through the evidence of the saliva and the blood group and some other things and told us that on balance they felt they had to stick to their original option. We told them that we were convinced they were after the wrong man.' Some of the officers had, however, admitted they agreed with one perplexing aspect of the case which Ellis and Windsor had also raised. If the sender of the tape was the Yorkshire Ripper, why had not any of his surviving victims, particularly Marilyn Moore and Maureen Long, with whom he had had lengthy conversations, spotted his Geordie accent?

When the author went to see Mr Windsor Lewis for the *Yorkshire Post* shortly afterwards, he gloomily predicted that the effect of the £1 million publicity campaign would be to guarantee that the Ripper was *not* caught. He felt this so strongly that he was prepared to be quoted discussing in detail his theories. He contacted Det. Chief Supt. Gilrain to tell him of his intentions, but he was urged to withdraw his co-operation from the *Yorkshire Post* for an indefinite period. It was to be 13 months, two more deaths and two further attacks before the *Post* was to run its sensational front-page 'splash' revelations about the rebel police expert. By then, Mr Windsor Lewis felt under no obligation to clear the interview with the police.

A further front-page exclusive the *Post* was able to print in 1979 was that at the end of November, eleven weeks after Barbara Leach's death, a top Scotland Yard man was to join the inquiry after all. Commander Jim Neville, the distinguished former head of the Yard's Terrorist Squad, was the man appointed to the task of travelling to Yorkshire to review the situation. He had undergone major heart surgery a few months earlier, and a suspicion that the move was little more than a cosmetic exercise seemed confirmed when the much-vaunted, and in some areas demanded, Scotland Yard presence returned to London after just one month.

A few weeks earlier, at the time of the inaccurate press reports of a super-squad being sent to the North by the new Home Secretary, William Whitelaw, a senior civil servant at the Home Office personally assured Gregory that there was never any question that a 'solution' would be imposed on his men. At the end of November, Mr Whitelaw had visited Millgarth police station in Leeds, the headquarters of the Ripper hunt, and had been given a secret briefing on the latest highly sensitive methods being adopted in a bid to catch the most notorious killer in British criminal history. The apparently strong links with Wearside were emphasized to the Home Secretary.

He was briefed about a Home Office-approved special programme on the Police National Computer to back up an extensive covert surveillance operation of vehicles in West Yorkshire; the use of birth and school registers to list all males born or living on Wearside since the 1920s; and police access to highly sensitive computer records held by government departments such as the D.H.S.S. to trace all males who had lived or worked on Wearside in the previous fifty years. Such details had remained a closely guarded secret. Aware of the sensitivity of the operation, senior police officers feared an over-reaction by civil-liberties pressure groups, which could have seriously frustrated their task. Special authorisation was sought for access to computer records on the basis that it would be a 'one-off' exercise.

The previous Home Secretary, Mr Merlyn Rees, M.P. for a Leeds constituency where the Ripper had killed four times at that point, believed that as little red tape as possible should be placed in the way of the hunt for the killer. 'It was vitally important that, given certain safeguards, no constraints should have been imposed. The police had a very difficult task, and we had to get our priorities right,' he says. With access to births, deaths and medical records stored on the computer, the police believed there was a high probability of their catching the Ripper through an elaborate system of elimination, by which they could trace the whereabouts of every male living or born on Wearside, and could record whether he had moved from the area. The theory was that the relentless system of elimination would focus on men who had moved away from Sunderland, particularly to West Yorkshire.

Meanwhile, Ronald Gregory set in motion the £1 million publicity campaign, which in reality only cost £20,000, a bill that nevertheless was to bring forth some flak for the Chief Constable from some members of the West Yorkshire Police Authority. When the *Yorkshire Post* broke the news of Jim Neville's impending arrival on Tuesday 20 November, very few senior West Yorkshire officers were aware of the development. Gregory's consistent view had been that he was happy to accept advice from any direction, though he remained adamant that with the standardized systems of detective training, and with the individual experience gained by a number of senior officers during other complex and protracted murder inquiries, his detectives were as capable as any of solving the Ripper inquiry.

A recent change of strategy had involved a reorganization of the surveillance operation undertaken by plain-clothes police in the red-light districts of Leeds and Bradford. People in both towns had become increasingly aware of the exercise, and some criticism was voiced when the subject was discussed on a phone-in programme on Pennine Radio, the Bradford commercial station. A caller said the police were being made to look foolish because too many people knew the location of the surveillance points. This seemed to suggest that the Ripper could also know of the trap awaiting him. The next killing, of Barbara Leach, took place just outside the red-light district in Bradford. However, the precise nature of the surveillance operation was much more sophisticated than many realized.

Its most important component was a special programme
fed into the Police National Computer under the direction
of two police branches of the Home Office, the Research
Services Unit and the Scientific Development Branch. For
some time, the police had wanted to demonstrate the use of
the computer in an operational setting, and in June 1978
the way had been cleared for West Yorkshire to break new
ground. The programme worked on a retrieval system of
vehicle makes and registrations based on index numbers,
which were fed into the PNC from the surveillance
exercise.

The computer was able to chart precise flow-patterns of
individual vehicles, in addition to providing descriptive
search information, a facility already available to all police
forces. It was hoped that the special programme would
make that descriptive search facility more manageable. It
was felt, for example, that if at a particular killing a
witness informed police about a blue Ford Cortina Estate
which passed close to the scene of the crime at a particular
time, the computer's scope would be far-reaching enough,
hopefully, not only to spill out details of all blue Ford
Cortina Estate cars, but also to isolate those which had
been spotted in the surveillance area.

In addition the memory bank would also be able to
recall all the other times, dates and locations on which that
particular car was spotted. Ultimately, the police hoped
that the computer would throw up the vehicle the killer
used. After Barbara Leach's death, they were hopeful that
the index number of the Ripper's car would have been
logged in Bradford that night. But it had not. It had,
however, already produced the number of a car belonging
to a lorry driver at Heaton, who had pointed out that many
of the sightings in Bradford could be accounted for by his
having to travel through the red-light district to his place of

employment. His explanation for the other nights in question was accepted.

The computer had aided in the speedy elimination of almost 200,000 vehicles, an otherwise thankless task which could have tied up many detectives for months. Yet what had become quickly and depressingly apparent to the police was that while the computer would give on the one hand, it would take away with the other. It was as if the inquiry was presented with too many facts and figures, an endless stream of information from the machine. The more sophisticated the questions asked of the computer, the greater would be the police work-load in checking the information provided. One example was the Home Office computer search, which listed all prisoners who had served sentences in the years separating the killing of the Ripper's 10th and 11th victims. It produced 17,500 names. The police themselves say they were acutely aware of the sensitivity of these techniques and their implications – an interference with the liberty of the individual to go about his business unhindered. Senior officers seemed at pains to make it clear that their only objective at the time was to track the Yorkshire Ripper. They stressed that when armed with the delicate details of an individual's visits to red-light districts, they were concerned only with eliminating the man as a suspect. The information was treated confidentially, and to this end, discretion, tact and diplomacy had to run hand in hand with the detective's more usual characteristics of suspicion and vigilance.

At the end of his secret briefing, Mr Whitelaw had felt able to give his backing to what was a most unusual line of inquiry, after satisfying himself that the public's right to maximum privacy was being safeguarded. Ronald Gregory had no doubts about the wisdom of using the new methods of detection, claiming that the public had to ask itself what price it was prepared to pay in catching the man who terrorized women. Having paid the price, the public would clearly have insisted on seeing the fastest possible result. G.K. Chesterton might even have been tempted to change his aphorism, that society was at the mercy of a motiveless murderer, to accommodate the computer age. Mr Gregory's and Mr Whitelaw's satisfaction with the use of computers in this controversial way can now be seen to have been justified, in as much as the cross-checks led the police to Peter William Sutcliffe. But sadly, as with the £5 note clue, they looked into the face of the Yorkshire Ripper without realizing it.

By the time the 1980s were taking root, the police were faced with millions of facts (five million in the case of car numbers) and had realized that they were being swamped. A decision was taken to discourage media coverage on the grounds that every story, however small and innocuous, produced a flurry of telephone calls with additional information. The police were aware of the danger of never actually catching up with the checking of information already in their possession. Unfortunately, none of the senior officers felt willing or able to explain the situation frankly to the media.

Some officers, as the year wore on, expressed the view that 'pressure' was being exerted on the Yorkshire Ripper which might produce a mistake. But what sort of a mistake? It was to be January 1981 before the lorry driver from Heaton made the most consequential mistake of clumsily affixing false number-plates to his brown Rover for an assignation with a Sheffield prostitute. During the 12 months leading up to that night, he was to attack four more women, killing two of them.

In January 1980 Sutcliffe was to have first-hand experience of how accurate police theories about the £5 note had been. The Manchester team, led by Det. Chief Supt. Jack Ridgeway, had spent three months in the Bradford area before returning to Lancashire. They had been faced with 7,764 'suspects', and a number of firms, including Clarks, where Sutcliffe worked. He was one of the many men interviewed. Soon after they returned to Lancashire, West Yorkshire officers returned to Clarks and other engineering firms, particularly Parkinsons and Butterfields, both in Shipley, a number of times.

Bosses Tom and William Clark recall visits from officers in June 1978 and again in the autumn. On both occasions, they checked drivers' log-books, including Sutcliffe's. They returned in June 1979, after the Geordie tape had been received and the engineering link established from one of the letters, and again in the autumn, following the Leach killing. On each occasion, they carefully studied log-sheets and took drivers away to be interviewed, including Sutcliffe, recalled the Clarks.

William Clark says: 'They became a bit of a nuisance really, and on one occasion, I remember Peter shaking like a leaf after he had been interviewed. In fact some of us used to jokingly call him The Ripper because of the interest the police seemed to take in him. Once when I had to give him a bit of a telling off, he seemed as if he was about to burst into tears. He was feeling really sorry for himself and said something about "even the police think I'm the Yorkshire Ripper".' West Yorkshire officers saw Sutcliffe at least twice between 1978 and 1979 in connection with his vehicle having been recorded in the red-light districts of Leeds and Bradford, although not on the nights of any of the attacks. At the beginning of 1980, the £5 note clue was resurrected with the re-appearance in Bradford of the Manchester officers. They remained for almost two months, interviewing Sutcliffe and others at Clarks. They took away samples of his clothing, but blood tests were not introduced because, police have said since, they felt the laboratories would not have been able to cope. In total Sutcliffe was seen nine times by the police during the course of the inquiry.

They insist that Sutcliffe was never in their leading group of suspects, largely because he was able to produce convincing alibis and, of course, because he was patently not a Geordie. Yet he was of the right B blood group, even if, as a non-secretor, he could not have deposited the semen recovered from the body of Joan Harrison (still regarded as a Ripper victim, particularly in West Yorkshire, at this stage). The police *were* looking for a man of that blood group.

The post mortem on Joan Harrison had demonstrated that she had had intercourse with two men on the day she died, and that her attacker had a gap in his upper front teeth. Traces of semen showed that one of the men had blood group A, and that the other was of the much rarer B group. The first A-group man was quickly seen by detectives and eliminated. Tests revealed that the act of intercourse involving the B-group man took place very close to the time of death, although saliva tests on 6,000 men in the Preston area failed to trace the killer. Since the 1920s, scientists have been able to detect blood groups from tests on saliva and semen, provided blood cells are secreted into these bodily fluids, as is the case with 80% of people. From the Harrison post mortem, the police presumed that her killer was a B secretor, one of only 6% of the male population. Saliva tests on the first two envelopes from Sunderland failed to show a reaction to blood group tests, which indicated that they had either been sealed by a non-secretor or that there was an excess of moisture or bacteria which occasionally produces negative results. The bacteria are transmitted from minute food particles on the tongue when brought into contact with the gum on the envelope. Forensic scientists run a controlled test, matching the gum on the side of the envelope which is not licked with the saliva on the flap. The ideal conditions for producing a positive test occur when the saliva is dry.

Peter Sutcliffe also had a gap in his front upper teeth.

When the Manchester officers returned to Bradford in January 1980, they were armed with a much more comprehensive framework of known facts about the Yorkshire Ripper than they had had two years earlier. They were, for example, able to be certain about the killer's boot size, having had confirmation from ground near the Whitaker killing site of earlier findings at the Jackson and Atkinson sites. But of greater interest to Jack Ridgeway was the prospect of narrowing down the numbers of potential payees who could have received the particular £5 note found in Jean Jordan's handbag.

In some six weeks, Ridgeway's team reduced the original list of nearly 8,000 payees to 300. They had returned to the bank and had even gone to the lengths of recreating the circumstances which had occurred on the day the money was handed out. They used the same counter-staff and arranged for them to count out the same amounts of money again. It became clear that some cashiers count money from the front of a pile and some from the back. With the assistance of the experienced bank staff they were able to establish more accurately, via the ledgers, where the money had gone. At the end of the six weeks, the 60 officers had narrowed the firms down to Clarks and two others, Butterfields and Parkinsons. Management at both these firms claim the attention they received from the police at the time seemed minimal. But the police went repeatedly to Clarks, talked to the Yorkshire Ripper and failed to recognize him.

How did this happen? There is little doubt that when Jack Ridgeway and his team first arrived in Bradford, no one expected the list of suspects to be almost 8,000 names long. The police admit that two years later, when it was reduced to around 300, among them Peter Sutcliffe, they know how they went wrong, but not precisely why. At the time they returned to Manchester defeated because of a fear of the unknown. They concluded that because any one of those 300 people could have handed on the £5 note within minutes of opening their wage packet, the trail, now more than 27 months old, was too indistinct for them to be able to follow it. Should they have taken blood samples, taken into account boot sizes and gaps in teeth, disregarded the lack of Geordie accents for once, and carried out 24-hour surveillance on the few, or even the many, who fulfilled the right criteria? Could they have? Did the Geordie connection prove too big a red herring? Would they have been able to mobilize the large number of men required for such surveillance, always assuming that the payees in question had not disposed of the note elsewhere? And then, could such an operation have been kept going indefinitely? Or even for six months, until August 1980, when Peter Sutcliffe set off from Garden Lane to drive to the red-light area of Chapeltown, Leeds, on the evening of the 20th? Would they have seen him suddenly turn off the old Bradford-to-Leeds Road at Farsley and park his brown Rover up a side street? Would they have seen a dark-haired, middle-aged woman walking down New Street, towards his waiting car?

None of the Douglas family – father, mother, nor the 24 bairns – had ever come across anybody as gentle or sophisticated as the dark stranger from down south in Yorkshire. Pete Logan had appeared in the village of Holytown, near Glasgow, in April 1979, charmed the family, swept the fifth daughter of mammy and pappy Douglas, 32-year-old divorcee Theresa, off her feet, delighted brother Gerry's tiny children with his affection and generosity, and eventually gave all of them the shock of their lives. For Pete Logan, they discovered when they looked at the *Scottish Daily Record* on 6 January 1981, was actually Peter Sutcliffe.

Gerry Douglas, young and unemployed, looking like a down-at-heel George Best with a wife and three children, was later to recall an amazing incident involving Pete Logan. 'One night Pete was at my mammy's house,' Gerry remembers, 'and my brother William said to him, "Pete, you know your eyes look evil tonight. I don't know what it is." Pete just looked at him and said, "Well, I am the Ripper." We all had a laugh.'

Peter Sutcliffe's connection with Holytown, which is about 12 miles from Glasgow on the Edinburgh side, seems to have given him particular comfort. He was a regular visitor to the village and its nearby General Motors plant, now a German tractor company's factory, to which he would be delivering engineering parts. It was in Holytown that Sutcliffe revealed more about himself than anywhere else. During his hours of conversation with Theresa in the cab of his lorry he claimed he had a potency problem; in Holytown, he was able to enjoy the company of Gerry Douglas's children, with whom he would play all evening, eventually carrying them upstairs at bedtime. And it was there that he felt able to make his extraordinary statement about being the Ripper, knowing that his audience had neither the evidence nor the inclination to take him seriously.

Peter Sutcliffe met Theresa in the Crown Bar, a pub standing on its own in Holytown's unassuming Main Street. Jean Kerr, Theresa's friend from around the corner, known as 'Big Jean' in the village because she is nearly six feet tall, was also in the Crown Bar that evening. Though it was Theresa who was to become Sutcliffe's special friend, when he invited her down to Yorkshire to stay in his big house (he claimed he was divorced) the invitation was also extended to Jean.

The Crown is like many other bars in Scotland, a no-nonsense drinking-house, with none of the carpet and horse-brass commonly found in even modest English pubs. The lino is white, the walls painted yellow. The notices up on the walls emphasize that the landlord is very much in charge: 'No club colours to be worn!', 'This TV is controlled by the bar staff!' There is a darts trophy in a cabinet on the wall in the public bar, but it is in the lounge, a narrow room at the back with brown, plastic-padded seats, brown laminate-top tables, a few low plastic stools, a bowl of plastic flowers and an old gas heater high up on the wall, that charming Pete Logan took a liking to dark-haired Theresa. Big Jean remembers that night: 'He was just quiet and ordinary. He sat blathering with Theresa for all the evening over about half a pint. I think he said he was divorced, but he might have said his wife was dead. When he came later on they'd sometimes go to the social club. He'd play records on the juke box. I remember how he liked Buddy Holly.'

Yet Theresa herself, known as Tessa to the family, had little insight into the real Peter Sutcliffe. Two short letters Sutcliffe sent her reveal more than her own observations, for he tells in them how much he enjoyed coming to Scotland, and in one tells Big Jean that she was not looking well when he was last in Holytown, and to look after herself (Jean was pregnant at the time). In one letter, he writes romantically, 'If I could be with you in five seconds, it would not be soon enough.' Theresa's replies, penned by a young cousin, Karen, were sent to Sutcliffe via his father's flat in Bingley.

Gerry Douglas recalls: 'He was a real gentleman. I wouldn't say a word against him. My sister Mary once swore when she was making some chips, and Pete turned round and told her off for it. He said she shouldn't swear. I told Pete any time he was up here and couldn't find digs or didn't want to sleep in his lorry to come and stay with me and my wife. He stayed with us two or three times. One night he sat with my two kids – they were five and three then – on his knees, and he gave them thirty bob each when they went to bed. The kids really took to Pete, but I don't know if it was just the thirty bob. The funniest thing was the little one, Amanda, sitting there on his knee. I've never known her to do that before with a stranger. He laughed and joked with the kids. He was like that, always good for a laugh and a joke.

'Peter didn't drink a lot. We might get through ten or twelve cans in a night. He liked a drink after he'd been driving, but never if he was on the road. He told me he loved that job more than any one he'd had before. He used to talk about the big house he'd got and how well he was doing. One time he showed me two wage packets he hadn't even opened. He was very generous as well, not just giving the kids money; but one night he took Tessa to Edinburgh in his lorry just for a drink and a meal in a restaurant. I don't know if he was in love with Tessa. I remember he sat with her on his knee once for an evening. That was at her house, and I don't know what they did after I went home, but he used to sleep on the sofa in my living-room when he was with me. I can tell you, he'll always be welcome in my house again. I still wouldn't say a word against him.'

Mary Douglas, middle-aged and plump, looks after her aged parents in a council maisonette in O'Wood Avenue, a better-class estate, although still sprayed with the occasional pro-IRA graffiti. Theresa lives in the same household, but she is now engaged to the brother of a policeman from nearby Motherwell, according to Gerry. Mary runs the O'Wood Avenue household, a motherly lady who had more reservations about Sutcliffe than her brothers and sisters.

'Pete was the best man we'd ever met,' Mary recalls sadly. 'The best type of man you could ever want to meet. I was making chips that time and I swore at one of the kids. He said to me, "That's not nice talk, Mary." I can tell you that we made a friend of him, but now we're ashamed. I wish we'd never met him now. I've always said you should never make friends. Just to think that he was in my house, in my kitchenette, for four hours when my mammy and pappy were out. But you wouldn't have known what he'd done. Soft spoken, kind. A real gentleman.'

Contradictory in many ways, Peter Sutcliffe had proved something of an enigma to everyone who had known him. Generally regarded as a handsome man, with his continental, dark good looks, he was apparently uninterested in women apart from prostitutes until he met Sonia. Sisters and girlfriends of friends almost without exception found him somehow strangely unattractive. Yet Sonia had been different. When they met, she was only just emerging from 16 years of almost claustrophobic attention at Tanton Crescent under the watchful eye of her parents, particularly her father. She was quiet and shy, yet interested in Peter, although theirs was to be a low-key relationship for many months. And she was also immature, unworldly, inexperienced in the ways of many of her peers, who had rushed headlong into puberty and young womanhood. She was sexually naive and made no demands on Peter, which seemed to suit him. He was happy to display the educated, dark-haired Sonia to his family, friends and acquaintances, almost relieved to be demonstrably like everyone else, with a girlfriend, although some of his contemporaries were already married with children. Yet none of these male acquaintances can ever remember Peter talking about, or even suggesting, any sexual impropriety with Sonia, in contrast to his often lurid accounts of adventures, real or imaginary, with girls in 'the business'.

One of the very few females, other than Sonia or prostitutes, that Sutcliffe ever had any sort of relationship with was factory-worker Carol Jones. She was two years younger than Sutcliffe, and they had first met in a pub when she was 16. Like Sonia, she was impressed by his restrained, almost old-fashioned approach to courtship. During the four years they knew each other, before Miss Jones moved from Yorkshire to the Midlands, they went out on an irregular basis. She says their relationship was almost platonic, sexual intercourse never taking place, and Sutcliffe rarely making any attempt to establish physical contact. They met in a pub called the Eastwood Tavern, in Keighley, where she had been with a lot of girlfriends and where he had come with some of his own friends. They went out with each other sometimes two or three times a week, and at other times hardly at all, with weeks and months separating their meetings. Miss Jones says they were almost like brother and sister.

She recalls: 'On the first night we met at Keighley, we just sat around having a drink and talking, or more accurately, I did most of the talking. I am a bit of a chatterbox, so Peter couldn't really get a word in. He didn't have much to say for himself, anyway, which is possibly why he liked me.' She says it was months before Sutcliffe showed any signs of sexual interest, and then it was restricted to a passionate kiss at the bus-stop after a night out. His embrace had been swift, even urgent, taking her a little by surprise, although his kisses were cold, as if he had no experience.

Sutcliffe's courtship, if courtship is the word, was routine and predictable. An evening at the pictures, a drink, sometimes on to a downstairs coffee bar in Keighley where there were just soft drinks and dancing. Carol Jones loved to dance, but Sutcliffe never would. All the same, she was happy to be out with him, a smart, clean, always tidy beau, who didn't swear and never showed any sign of violence, to the extent where she was sometimes annoyed at his habit of agreeing with people rather than falling out with them when he didn't really share their views.

'When we were out, I did most of the talking, but when Peter did say anything, it was usually to do with his family or cars. He took me out once and I met some of his family. I remember his mother was a really nice person, a good Catholic. But we were never very serious, and during that period, Peter knew I had other boyfriends. He knew I didn't want to be pinned down to anyone, but he was not the jealous type. He was generous and would always buy the drinks when we were out, although I never saw him get drunk. He was considerate and always remembered my birthday and Christmas. He'd send me cards, but never presents. I never really thought about it at the time, but it would be true to say that Peter never tried to touch my body. He was just content to be with me making no emotional demands.'

Years later, having worked in Stoke-on-Trent and then

in a holiday camp, Miss Jones returned to live in Cross Flatts, Bingley and work at a paint factory near her home. She bumped into Sutcliffe at the Boy and Barrel pub in Bradford in 1975 when she went there for a drink with a few girlfriends. It was the first time she had seen Sutcliffe, who was alone, in six years, and by then he had been married six months. They fell into conversation and Sutcliffe offered to give her a lift home to Keighley, first dropping a friend of hers off at Clayton, where Sonia was already in bed at Tanton Crescent. Polite and courteous as before, Sutcliffe dropped Miss Jones outside her home before driving off. 'He didn't even try to kiss me goodnight,' she said later. 'If he'd asked to come in I wouldn't have minded.'

Five months later, he drove down the Aire Valley again, to Keighley, to leave Anna Rogulskyj with a fractured skull. Yet the manifestations of overt violence had been so rare throughout Sutcliffe's life that the rare occasions when he displayed such tendencies tended to be remembered vividly. Gravedigging friend Laurie Ashton was to recall years later, still hardly able to believe it, the occasion in their favourite Royal Standard pub in Manningham Lane, when Peter had sat with a pint of beer in front of him. 'I began to realize that Peter was staring straight ahead, totally motionless, like in a trance, for quite a few minutes; then he suddenly took hold of the handle of his glass, stuck it up in the air and crashed it down on the table. There was beer and bits of glass everywhere and some of it splashed a bloke's trousers. Peter never moved a muscle, just kept staring into space. The bloke said something to Peter but he didn't answer so he went and poured his drink over Peter's head. He still didn't do anything, just sat there lost in his thoughts. It was weird and he never mentioned it again.'

Sutcliffe's relationship with Bodhan Szurma had turned full circle by 1980. Few fathers, of course, could ever put their hand on their heart and say they were totally satisfied with the man a precious daughter gives her heart to, but for Bodhan Szurma, 16-year-old Sonia's choice for the first and only man she was to bring to Tanton Crescent had not filled him with joy. The 20-year-old with the flashy good looks in his black leather outfit was everything Bodhan wasn't. The Czech immigrant was cultured, educated and intelligent, and had succeeded in imposing rigid standards on the Szurma household in Clayton. His displeasure with Sonia was at one point to lead him to converse with her indirectly only, through her mother. He was a man of principles and discipline.

Yet fourteen years after the first meeting with his son-in-law they had settled for a more cosy compatibility. They even played chess together occasionally, Sonia having taught Peter. Bodhan had been impressed over the years by Peter's willingness to work, and the purchase of a fine detached house in Garden Lane had confirmed in his eyes Peter's desire to provide the best for Sonia. But the turning point had come earlier with Sonia's nervous breakdown, and the way in which Peter had immediately gone to stay with her, nursing her devotedly for many weeks, until she was well again – the action of an honourable man, a man fit to marry his daughter, even.

At Clarks, Sutcliffe had taken his workmates by surprise with his talk about Tessa, the girl in Glasgow, and the letters that were being sent to him via his father's flat in Bingley so Sonia wouldn't find out. He had always been so circumspect about sexual matters, never showing any indication of a wandering spirit. In fact he had been unlike the other lorry drivers, a maverick breed in the main, in a number of ways – quiet, thoughtful, always neatly turned out and fastidious about his log-sheets and reporting faults with his lorry, which he had christened Wee Willie, fixing the name to his cab, a source of much ribald comment. If colleague John Hill had not been shocked, he had at least been surprised when Sutcliffe said one day at the depot that he was 'knocking off a girl in Glasgow and enjoying it'.

They had driven in convoy to London on a few occasions, parking up at the LEP transport depot at Charlton and going for drinking sessions in local pubs later. They had talked to women in the pubs, but Sutcliffe had never gone out of his way to do so. 'He was a good-looking guy, and women would often make it clear they wanted to talk to him, but he was always very low-key about it,' Mr Hill says.

At Clarks' depot, the drivers often used to talk about the Yorkshire Ripper case, but Peter never joined in. 'On one occasion some of the drivers said they bet Peter was the Ripper, but he just laughed and said nothing.' Sutcliffe did, however, talk about the Ripper killings with another driver, John Johnstone, perhaps the closest he came to making a friend at Clarks. He regularly gave Mr Johnstone a lift to his home in New Hey Road, Bradford after work. Sutcliffe had never lost his habit of going out drinking most nights of the week, and he and Mr Johnstone would regularly meet up again after work, sometimes three nights a week, for an evening's drinking.

Mr Johnstone found Sutcliffe less reserved when talking about the Ripper case, though he had noticed his companion always insisted on referring to the killer as a 'headbanger'. On one occasion in a pub, Mr Johnstone says Sutcliffe became quite emotional about the killing of 16-year-old Jayne MacDonald, saying she had been an innocent victim and that whoever had been responsible had virtually killed two people, because her father had never got over the death, and had died himself of a broken heart. 'He said something about it being "terrible", and "Whoever is doing all these murders has a lot to answer for",' says Mr Johnstone. On another occasion, they had been driving past the former home in Bradford of Donald Neilson, the Black Panther. 'I pointed to the house and said, "We lost a lot of money there, Peter", meaning we could have claimed the reward if we had realized who lived there at the time. He just said "Perhaps." We got on about the Ripper, and I mentioned the reward that they were offering, and Peter just laughed. He said "Yes" but showed no signs of emotion at all. After Barbara Leach was killed we talked about the Yorkshire Ripper again, and I wondered out loud if the police were any nearer catching him. Peter said, "They are no nearer getting him now than they were at the beginning".'

But there were occasions when Sutcliffe's mind seemed to be elsewhere. 'Sometimes when we were playing pool he would stare off into the distance as if he was somewhere else. He would pot the black ball instead of the white one without realizing what he had done.' Mr Johnstone says that Sutcliffe had talked frankly to him about his friendship with Tessa, saying she had slept in the cab of his lorry with him, but had not gone into any more detail than that. Sutcliffe was not a man to talk crudely about sex or anything else. He had once shown Mr Johnstone a letter from Tessa, and said he used the name Pete Logan so that the girl could write to him at his father's address. He would pretend that the letters were for a friend, and that he was acting as a middle-man, a kind of postman. 'He once told me over a couple of beers that Sonia had found out about the girl in Scotland, but that he had managed to smooth it over. He never gave me any impression other than that his marriage to Sonia was a happy one. In fact after he was breathalyzed he used to say again and again that they had a dream of going to live in the country and opening a pottery, where Sonia would be able to make things and sell them. He said they had wanted children but Sonia had had two miscarriages and had been told she would not be able to have any.'

Sutcliffe had often spoken about the dream of the pottery, telling workmates that the scheme would be financed from the money he and Sonia would make from selling the house in Garden Lane. They hoped they might raise £40,000, a good profit on the £15,350 they had laid down for it in 1977. They had worked hard on the house. It was fully furnished and Sonia kept everything immaculately in place. Some neighbours wondered why the couple always seemed to be in the kitchen, rarely disturbing the other rooms. They slept in a double bed in the back bedroom, with a view across the adjoining Bradford Salem rugby field, keeping the main bedroom at the front reserved for guests, they said. The third bedroom was decorated with children's wallpaper in readiness for the day a child arrived. Peter had told friends and relatives that they could not have one themselves and were thinking of adopting two Vietnamese orphans.

The Sutcliffes managed to avoid too much personal contact with the other residents of Garden Lane. To one side of their house was an electricity sub-station (they had once tried to get the rates reduced on that account) and then the rugby field, and because of the house's high, almost aloof position, small-talk with people passing the gate on foot was easily avoidable.

On the other side of the house were Tom and Mary Garside, whose kitchen door faced the Sutcliffes', so that they almost unavoidably saw more of the young couple than others. The new neighbours, who arrived in 1977, had certainly been different from the Rahmans, and Mr Garside even thought the man looked like a bit of a 'spiv' the first time he saw him, with the sharp suit, white shoes and the thin cigars he smoked. They were to grow more used to seeing Peter Sutcliffe in a cardigan, jeans and white clogs, but their most regular view of him was tinkering with his selection of cars in the drive and garage of number six. Again, because the bathroom was to the side of the house, it was noticeable that when Sutcliffe did get out of his old clothes to go out it took him a long time to prepare himself; he would pay particular attention to his hair.

If the Garsides ever did bump into the Sutcliffes in the drive, where just a low fence separated them, Sutcliffe would speak, not unpleasantly, if it was absolutely unavoidable, but on occasions it had been noticeable how he had gone out of his way to make sure their eyes didn't meet and he didn't even have to say hello. As a result, Mr Garside had been surprised on one occasion when Sutcliffe accepted an invitation to pop in and have a glass of whisky. Indeed, at least nine hefty whiskies later Mr Garside says, he had to drop hints to get Sutcliffe to leave. The incident did not set a trend, however, and despite working so hard to get the house into pristine condition the Sutcliffes rarely seemed to have any visitors. 'They didn't seem to go very far, other than to see her sister in London. Her photographs were kept in the living-room. I can't recall them having a holiday, and in fact in the spring of 1980 Peter had three weeks off work and spent most of it under the car in the drive. He used to go out very regularly of an evening, usually on his own, and I did think it was queer that he often seemed to go out very, very late at night. When other people went to bed, Peter always seemed to be just setting off to go out. I have to confess that it did cross my mind that he could be a burglar. It never occured to me that he could be the Yorkshire Ripper. One point of course was that he did not have a Geordie accent; in fact his was a thick, Yorkshire accent, quite high-pitched really.'

It had puzzled and amused Mr and Mrs Garside that Sutcliffe regularly washed his own clothes in the kitchen sink, holding woollens up to the light to see if they were properly clean. Sonia told Mrs Garside that Peter did not like his woollens to be hung outside on the line, and anyway he wanted to get them 'nice and fluffy'. Like her husband, Sonia had not been a regular visitor to the Garsides' home, but she once turned up in their kitchen for a cup of tea and a chat wearing a nightdress and thick woollen socks. Mrs Garside thought it was a little odd, but then she thought her neighbours were an odd couple.

'I didn't think there was anything particularly wrong with them, or anything to dislike about them, they were just different,' she says. 'When they first came, Sonia used to dress like a bit of a hippy, but then she was very arty. He told us she had some miscarriages, but she never discussed it. The only time I saw Sonia upset was when Peter's mother died and she came to our house in tears.' The Garsides once asked the Sutcliffes to look after their pet rabbit when they were going away for a few days, but Sonia had said it was not possible, it would have been too much trouble. The Sutcliffes had once briefly got themselves a dog, but had kept it in the garage and only had it for two days. Apart from the seemingly endless work on the cars, there was little sign of any other activity. Loud rock music could occasionally be heard coming from number six, and Peter always got the local *Telegraph and Argus* newspaper on a Saturday evening. Sonia had once surprised Mrs Garside when she turned up at the back door with a swede in her hand that her father had given her, asking for advice. She didn't know how to cook it, she said. Sonia had talked quite openly to Mrs Garside about the police having taken Peter away to interview him after the £5 note was recovered from Jean Jordan's handbag, and on other occasions, but they were speaking to everyone else at Clarks and she obviously thought it was not very significant.

Peter had seemed resigned to his fate when he told Mr Garside about the breathalyzer charge, and the neighbour remembered the night earlier in the year when he had heard a heated discussion at the end of Peter's drive, in which a man said to Peter, 'Come on, I've had enough of this, you're coming with us.'

Apart from the Garsides, none of the other neighbours in Garden Lane were invited into number six, although occasionally Sonia accepted an invitation for a cup of coffee at Mrs Barbara Bowman's house across the road at number fifteen. 'Sonia always spoke highly of Peter and seemed to love him a lot,' Mrs Bowman said. 'She told me he was fed up with his job and they were thinking of buying a cottage with some land in the country to start a small pottery business. At the end of last year [1980] I remember Sonia telling me they had been in Leeds soon after the last Ripper attack. They were shopping and Sonia said she had said to Peter that she was frightened and that he said he was frightened, too.'

At Clarks at the beginning of 1980, Sutcliffe must have felt he had got a really secure job, even a job for life. The firm had been forced to sack all their drivers for alleged theft from the loads, but not Peter. He had been the one exception, the one driver chairman Tom Clark felt he could trust. 'He could have made quite a bit of money for himself, but he never got involved with the fiddles,' Mr

Clark said. Yet there were those at Clarks who had noticed Sutcliffe's habit of occasionally turning up at work with false number-plates on his car, a fact considered insignificant by his workmates, at least until the first weekend of 1981.

The management had been so impressed with Sutcliffe, regarding him as possessing all the virtues required by the best lorry drivers, that he was chosen to appear in a promotional brochure for the firm. He is shown, hair in place, beard neatly trimmed as usual, behind the wheel of 'Wee Willie', and a giant enlargement of the photograph was given pride of place in the entrance to the firm's offices.

The only female working at Clarks during Sutcliffe's time there was 19-year-old Susan Kelly, who divided her time between being a clerk-typist and operating the switchboard. She was used to lorry drivers' banter, but never heard it from Peter Sutcliffe. Surprisingly, she never knew he was married. On a few occasions, he had given her a lift in the Rover from Clarks, on the Canal Road Industrial Estate, to the city centre interchange in Bradford. She was always struck by his pleasantness, his politeness, and particularly by the fact that she had never heard him swear, something of a record among lorry drivers. He was the sort who did not speak unless he was spoken to.

'I saw him at the office perhaps every other day,' she says, 'but we didn't have much to say to each other. One time he asked me if I had been out anywhere good the previous evening, and on another occasion I offered him a mint, which he took.

'He always looked clean and tidy and normally wore brown corduroy trousers, a plain-coloured tee-shirt and a bomber jacket and working boots. He had a fresh complexion with sideburns which grew into his beard. He also had a Mexican-type moustache. He used to stand with his hands in his pockets, always relaxed and casual, with perhaps a rolled-up newspaper in his pocket. He was in the office on occasions when we discussed the Yorkshire Ripper, but he never showed any reactions, and it was the same after he had been interviewed by the police. He didn't seem at all worried.'

Melissa Birdsall knew Peter Sutcliffe better than Miss Kelly, being the former wife of Sutcliffe's best friend, Trevor Birdsall. A year before the lorry driver was arrested, dark-haired Melissa was shaken rigid by something Trevor had said to her – that he thought Peter was the Yorkshire Ripper. 'I didn't believe it, but I said that if he felt that way, he should go to the police,' she says. 'Trevor said he couldn't split on a mate. He told me to say nothing about it. He has told me since he thinks he was with Peter on the nights he attacked two women.'

She had met Sutcliffe and her husband-to-be at the same time, when they worked together on the same packing-line at the Baird television factory in Bradford in 1971. The feature she had noticed most about Sutcliffe was his dark, staring eyes. Soon after she and Birdsall were married in the mid 1970s, she claims her husband confessed to her that he and Peter regularly toured the red-light districts when they were out drinking. 'We used to go out as a foursome with Sonia and Peter, and after he told me that, for five years I wondered whether I should tell Sonia what was going off. But I didn't. Sonia is such a nice girl, and Peter seemed to like her a lot, but yet he was regularly unfaithful to her. When she was studying in London and staying with her sister, Peter and Trevor used to be out drinking nearly every night. I asked myself hundreds of times if I should say anything to Sonia, but I just didn't know what to do. I didn't want her to be hurt in any way.

'I don't know why Peter felt the need to go with prostitutes. I didn't really believe what he said they got up to, so one night he said he would prove it to me, and we followed Peter in our car down to Manningham Lane. I saw him pick up what was obviously a prostitute in Lumb Lane.'

She says the two men were like brothers, and that after she and her husband separated she still continued to see Peter. 'After we were divorced, Peter came to see me and sat on the settee next to me. He put his arm round me and kissed me gently on the cheek. Peter said I was his sort of girl, and that if Trevor had not married me he would have. He said I was "decent". In many ways Peter and Trevor are similar. They even looked alike when Tevor grew the same sort of beard. They are both very quiet and keep their thoughts to themselves. When Peter would drive Trevor back to where we were living in his car, they would sit outside for ages, an hour or two sometimes, just talking. God knows what they found to talk about. We only went to Peter and Sonia's house at Heaton once for tea. It was full of dark furniture, which looked like antiques. They seemed perfectly happy, with a big house and a good job, and just the fact that they didn't have any kids to trouble them. Sonia told me she had had three miscarriages but she did not seem bothered about having children like Peter was.'

Mrs Birdsall was not the only person to whom Trevor Birdsall revealed his fears about Peter Sutcliffe in 1980. In the summer he had been drinking with his brother-in-law, Mr David Boldy, a Gas Board worker who is married to Birdsall's sister, Carol. With Sutcliffe, they had formed a drinking threesome in recent years, although they had not been out together for some time. Mr Boldy recalls a conversation with Trevor in a pub in Bradford: 'Trevor suddenly turned to me and said, "I wouldn't be surprised if Peter was the Ripper". We just laughed it off and said nothing more, but it seemed a strange thing to come out with at the time.'

By now, Peter William Sutcliffe's toll was 12 women dead and at least five injured.

CHAPTER 7

Different Voices

Despite the massive investment in police manpower and funds that the hunt for the Yorkshire Ripper obviously entailed, one man decided to take on the task of catching the killer on his own, and later believed he came nearer than the police to finding him. Jim Lyness, an Ulster-born private detective based in Oldham, Lancashire, launched his search after Barbara Leach's father telephoned and asked him to find the man who had killed his daughter. Lyness was to be dismissed as a crank, particularly by some policemen, who saw him as a Don Quixote figure, using an eccentric approach to try and help a man desperate with grief.

The Ulsterman's office is a threadbare room above a shop in Oldham's Union Street. The faded lettering 'Lyness Detective Agency' appears on a grimy first-floor window. Lyness also runs a security company, is almost 50, and is prosperous. He has never been a policeman and was once on Bradford City Football Club's books. He works, he explains, by instinct and 'feel' as much as by routine detective methods. His business has done very well and he was able to take the best part of a year out, without payment by Mr Leach, to pursue his ideas.

Barbara Leach's father had telephoned him on the recommendation of a journalist shortly after his daughter had died. Lyness says his life changed from the moment the tremulous voice on the other end of the telephone said, 'I haven't got much money, but I want you to find whoever killed my daughter.' He went to the Leach home in Kettering and found the family very ordinary people, who lived for their children. He observed that Mr Leach kept a bottle of whisky locked up, clearly for special occasions, but took it out and poured him a drink before locking it away again.

From such touching actions he decided to do his best to find the Yorkshire Ripper for the heartbroken couple, and even for all the other ordinary people whose lives had been blighted. Lyness was to conduct his inquiry, not unexpectedly, without the benefit of the police reports on the murders. He claims that Det. Chief Supt. Gilrain telephoned him when the news of his personal Ripper Hunt was published to say that he would not be able to see police files but should contact them if he came up with anything interesting. That conversation, as he relates it, angered Lyness and made him more determined to beat the police at their own job.

His starting point was Anna Rogulskyj, believed to be the first Ripper attack victim. She was regarded as a not totally reliable witness by the police, but Lyness coaxed from her a description of a Michael Gill, who had taken her to dinner at a steak bar in Bradford some time before the attack. She remembered him being a local man, from his accent and knowledge, who had surprised her twice during their date – first, when they drove back to her home in Keighley, he had asked her to point out all the places in the town she liked to visit; and second, he had not even kissed her goodnight when he dropped her off at her home. However, as she was attacked from behind some months later, she could not say whether 'Michael Gill' was the person who knocked her to the ground.

Lyness was to say later that Anna Rogulskyj subsequently identified Peter Sutcliffe from a picture in a foreign magazine as the man who had taken her out for a meal.

What Lyness regarded as his second substantial clue came from Olive Smelt, whom the Yorkshire Ripper had attacked 40 days after Mrs Rogulskyj. She described her attacker, or at least the man who had approached her in the street with a pleasantry about the weather, and whom she presumed had hit her almost as soon as she had passed, as a man with a Yorkshire accent, 'black, crispy hair', and long sideburns. 'From the day I walked out of her home,' Lyness said, 'I deleted any thought of the Yorkshire Ripper being a Geordie. I went on the radio and on the record in the papers as saying the tape was a hoax.'

Later in the year (1980) Lyness says Olive Smelt telephoned him to say she had received a 'phone call from a man saying, 'I missed you once, but I'll get you the next time.' She said she was almost certain the voice was that of her attacker, but the police had said that if he did not have a Geordie accent he must have been a hoaxer.

So Lyness formed his own picture of the Ripper, a picture quite different from that of the police who were, he says, obsessed with the taped message from Sunderland. 'I was looking for a good-looking guy, five feet eight inches tall, with jet-black, crinkly hair. He should have long sideburns and a Yorkshire accent because Olive Smelt was the only person who could honestly say who attacked her. I was also looking for the kind of guy who could help a girl to choose a record on a juke box, or accidentally knock over her drink and get chatting to her that way. We equate ugliness with evil, and the police seemed to be describing someone who was ugly. A good-looking fellow wouldn't have any difficulty picking up girls, or certainly falling into casual conversation with them,' speculated Lyness.

One mystery he came across was the story told by a Swedish girl, Raili Niemeta, who claimed she had met a man in a hotel in Benidorm in 1980 who said his wife was asleep upstairs, and at one stage during their evening together said he had been breathalyzed in June and was going to lose his job as a driver. He later became emotional and said he was the Yorkshire Ripper and lived in Bradford, or Barnsley, the girl could not remember which. After Sutcliffe's arrest the girl refused to talk about the incident, but later said that the story was a hoax. Lyness looked into the possibility of checking the records of people who were breathalyzed in June 1980, but says he was told it would be too difficult.

More than a year after taking on the assignment, in November, he received an abrupt telephone call at his office. He had received hundreds during the course of his investigation, many of them from cranks, some with the message 'Leave the Ripper alone, he is doing a good job'. But he was to recall this one – made with real urgency, it was only eleven words long: 'The Ripper is a driver and has got a brown Rover.' Another, soon afterwards, said: 'He lives within a mile of the prostitutes' area of Bradford.' But Jim Lyness had not been alone in trying to impose his will on the mystery.

Not for the first time in the history of crime detection, hundreds of clairvoyants, mystics, astrologers and mediums tried to lend the police a hand. And as the police had come to expect, they shared an irritating inability to conjure up anything other than the vaguest of clues from the beyond. A Yorkshire-based writer on the paranormal, Mr Joe Cooper, accepts that 'these peoples' track records in this kind of thing is appalling'. Mr Cooper, who recently retired as a sociology lecturer at Bradford College, spoke to an audience of psychics during the hunt and remembers annoying them by saying, 'The police don't ask for much – just his name and address.' He adds: 'They're all terribly jealous of one another, and a lot of them are frankly hopeless.' Mr Cooper eventually offered to help the police set up a screening service to weed out the cranks and the frauds who were threatening to submerge them with useless information. Four days later, however, the Yorkshire Ripper was arrested. Mr Cooper believes that an analytical study of true psychics' feelings about the murders could have produced results, but the bulk of the help that was given now appears entirely wrong.

In August 1979, a Dutch engineer, Wim Virbeek, said the Ripper was a 27-year-old washing-machine mechanic living in Aberdeen. A few months later, the Swindon medium, Dennis Kirkham, travelled to Bradford, went into a trance, and decided the Ripper was an electrician from Durham. At Christmas 1980, Mrs Doris Stokes said on Tyne Tees Television that the Ripper was 32, dark, five feet eight inches tall, and called Ronnie or Johnnie. In January the same year a Scottish astrologer announced that the Ripper was 39, a former sailor, now an electrician, with big feet, and who loved music and dancing. At the same time the Dutch clairvoyant Dono Meijling cancelled a skiing holiday in the Swiss Alps after seeing what he believed to be the Ripper's face in the corner of a photograph of the envelope containing one of the Ripper letters when it was published in his country.

Meijling spent Christmas and the New Year walking round Chapeltown in search of clues, emerging with a series of eight fairly specific leads, almost all of which turned out to be wrong. The most contentious was that the Yorkshire Ripper was somehow related to Det. Chief Supt. Jim Hobson. Meanwhile, a 'meeting of minds' in Southport supplied the police with what was believed to be the Ripper's name, age and address. He was, they said, a father of two from Morley, near Leeds. The 'psychic investigator' Bob Cracknell added to the confusion by describing the Ripper as a man who worked in a pumping station and had a dog. He lived in Bradford and had a link with Raynor Terrace in Pudsey.

Even after Sutcliffe's arrest psychics clung to the Ripper trail. The Dutchman Meijling returned to Leeds, again visited some of the scenes of death, as well as Garden Lane, and returned home to pose the question in a Dutch magazine, 'Is this the real Ripper?' However, despite the weight of spurious material heaped on the police by clairvoyants, one disturbing question remains.

A south London woman, Mrs Nella Jones, whose psychic powers have been exploited by Scotland Yard to good effect, predicted in an unpublished (for fear of inspiring a copycat killer) interview with Shirley Davenport of the *Yorkshire Post* London office in October 1979, that the Yorkshire Ripper was a lorry driver called Peter who drove a cab with a name beginning with 'c' on the side. In January 1980, according to Ms Davenport's notes, Mrs Jones said the killer would live in a big grey house in Bradford (Sutcliffe's house appears grey in yellow street-light, though it is a pale pink colour by day). The house, she said, would be elevated above the street, behind wrought-iron gates, and with steps leading up to the front door. It would be number six in its street.

Mrs Jones said the Yorkshire Ripper would prove to have been a tearaway in his youth, and to have committed other crimes. She also said that the Containerbase at Stourton, south of Leeds, was connected with the Ripper (Sutcliffe had indeed driven there as part of his job). Perhaps the most startling of Mrs Jones's predictions came at the beginning of November 1980 when she predicted the date of the next Yorkshire Ripper attack – 17 November. The day Jacqueline Hill was to die in Leeds.

Back on the earthly plane, Commander Neville had returned to London after spending just one month in the North reviewing the biggest murder-hunt the country had ever known. While Commander Neville had impressed everyone with his charm, courtesy and unflagging interest, it was realized that one month was hardly long enough to produce any radical recommendations. He only saw voice expert Jack Windsor Lewis once, and then briefly. As he left for Scotland Yard he demonstrated his diplomatic touch, saying, 'It would not be proper for me to go into details at this stage, but I will say I have been very impressed by the way all the police forces involved have been carrying out their most difficult task. I would like to say that their spirit and determination are still sky-high.'

Significantly, however, at the time of Commander Neville's departure, Chief Constable Gregory announced a major change at the head of the West Yorkshire team hunting the Ripper. Det. Chief Supt. Peter Gilrain, a former head of the old Wakefield City Police C.I.D. before amalgamation ten years earlier, was given overall charge of the inquiry. It was made clear that even when the still-absent George Oldfield returned from his illness, as he was to do soon afterwards, he would not be expected to involve himself in the day-to-day running of the inquiry. There were those who were to condemn Oldfield later, but the course he adopted would have been difficult to avoid if the taped message from Sunderland was to be taken seriously.

On balance, in the summer of 1979, the police were entitled to think that the person who had killed Joan Harrison had written the letters and sent the tape, and was the Yorkshire Ripper. But was George Oldfield, with the Chief Constable's encouragement, right to emphasize that probability so strongly? The press conference where the tape was unveiled was a moment of high drama, and the subsequent £1 million publicity campaign, about which Mr Oldfield was less happy, left the public with no room for manoeuvre.

If the man you suspected – whether it was your friend, lover or workmate – did not speak with a Geordie accent, then you could ignore him, couldn't you? The police said so. So some friends and acquaintances of Peter William Sutcliffe mentioned almost guiltily to each other (or even just to themselves?), in passing, that they would not be surprised if Peter was the Yorkshire Ripper. His best friend even told two of the women in his life his worst fears but did not act, unitl it was too late. Now they all say the same thing – he did not have a Geordie accent, so it couldn't have been him. How many policemen down among the door-knockers and foot-sloggers may have reached the same conclusion? When Peter Sutcliffe was seen travelling too quickly for the satisfaction of two motor-patrol officers in Manningham Lane, Bradford in the spring of 1980, they pursued him to his house.

As a lorry driver, whose living depended on his having a licence, Sutcliffe had not been keen on the prospect of being breathalyzed. He had a row with the officers in the drive of number six; neighbours recall the raised voices. But the outcome was a positive test and Sutcliffe knew he would be banned from driving any sort of vehicle for at least a year. He was due in court a few days after his arrest in January to answer the charge.

An officer connected with the case on the night of the breathalyzer affair was sufficiently aware of the Yorkshire Ripper case to forward a memorandum suggesting Peter Sutcliffe as a man worthy of further examination in the context of the Ripper inquiry. A short time later he was told that the lorry driver from Heaton was already in the index file but had, in effect, been eliminated. Two months later Sutcliffe drove along the old Bradford–Leeds Road and saw a dark-haired, middle-aged woman turn into New Street, Farsley, from the main road. The Yorkshire Ripper saw her and decided he wouldn't bother going to Chapeltown but would confuse the police even more.

Almost a year had passed since the death of Barbara Leach when 47-year-old civil servant Marguerite Walls was found strangled and severely bludgeoned in the densely wooded grounds of the imposing stone house of a local magistrate in Farsley, Leeds. There had been talk of the Yorkshire Ripper having matured as a psychopath. He might not murder again, it was suggested. He might even have committed suicide quietly somewhere without anyone suspecting what he had done. In fact Peter Sutcliffe was preparing to enter the most prolific and devastating phase of his five-year reign of terror.

What effect Det. Chief Supt. Jim Hobson's announcement after the Walls killing that 'We do not believe this is the work of the Yorkshire Ripper' had on his subsequent behaviour is still unclear. Hobson and the forensic experts who advised him in this announcement had thought long and hard before making it. There were obviously Ripper-like signs, such as the bludgeoning with a 'blunt instrument', yet the strangulation with a ligature was something new.

Miss Walls, known as Margot to friends and colleagues at the Department of Education and Science office in Richardshaw Lane, Pudsey, had worked late on the evening of Wednesday 18 August 1980, leaving her office between 9.30 and 10.30 p.m. She was starting a ten-day holiday on the Thursday, and typically did not want to leave any loose ends at work. Her plan was to go to a colleague's funeral in Newcastle on the Friday, and then go walking in the Lake District. She was a member of the Leeds and Bradford Fell Walking Club, and her daily mile walk to work and back from her detached stone house in New Park Croft, Farsley was her way of keeping fit.

Margot was a friendly woman, yet little was known about her by colleagues. Her brother Robert Walls travelled from his home in Lye, Stourbridge to identify Margot's body. He told police how close he had been to his sister. Their mother, Mrs Kathleen Walls, who lives in Worcester, said, 'Margot was very special to us all.' She had not liked the idea of Margot moving north from Leicester where she previously worked, but accepted that she was improving her career. Margot's broken-hearted father, Thomas Walls, died four months after she was killed. A second victim, perhaps, of the vicious assault in a quiet Northern street.

Margot had worked at the VAT office in Leicester between 1973 and 1978. Her only close friend at work had been Mr Tony Nash, who is now with the Customs and Excise in Northampton. He recalls how Margot kept colleagues at arm's length in Leicester as she later did in Farsley. She had been Mr and Mrs Nash's baby-sitter, and after moving north used to stay with them for weekends.

In her black, hooded trench-coat and carrying her black canvas shopping-bag through a respectable Leeds suburb, Margot was nearly home when she passed the high stone pillars at the end of the sweeping drive of Claremont House, home of Mr Peter Hainsworth, whose son Richard was one of the *Yorkshire Evening Post* reporters soon to be covering the killing. Sutcliffe looped a ligature round Margot's neck and dragged her just inside what local children called 'The Secret Garden'. Two gardeners

found her the following morning, her clothing partly
ripped off and torn, her body roughly hidden under a pile
of grass cuttings. He had dragged her 20 yards from the
point of attack and dumped her at the foot of a garden
wall, just yards from the garden of the local police house.

Headingley was not the sort of place where the Yorkshire
Ripper was expected to strike. Noisy and crowded with
traffic in parts, Headingley still has a gracious, bourgeois
air about it. A jumble of large houses in Yorkshire stone,
red-brick villas, little terraced houses and charming stone
cottages, the suburb also finds room for a large, ugly but
useful shopping centre – the Arndale – one of the world's
top cricket grounds, a major Rugby League ground, and
such Leeds institutions as Brett's Old Headingley Fish
Shop, where Charlie Brett serves some of the finest fish
and chips in the world every year to visiting Test cricket
teams. Brett's dining-room is where elderly Headingley
residents of the old school are served on rickety wooden
tables covered in bright check cloths, alongside the
students, teachers and media people who now dominate
the area. Leeds University and Becketts Park Teacher
Training College, now part of the burgeoning Leeds
Polytechnic, are within a stone's throw of Headingley,
giving the impression that it is only a student area. Yet
students who have long since graduated tend to remain in
Headingley because of its cosmopolitan atmosphere, and
mature students spending a time at the University are
similarly attracted to the area.

Dr Upadhya Bandara, aged 34, was one of these
students, spending time in Leeds from her native
Singapore as part of a World Health Organization
Nuffield Foundation scholarship. She had been visiting

friends in the north of Headingley, in trendy Cottage Road, and was on her way home. She had walked a long way; down busy Otley Road, past Salvo's Pizzeria, along the front of the Arndale Centre, and past the brightly lit Kentucky Fried Chicken shop, a relative newcomer to Headingley. As she strode by she noticed a man staring at her from inside. The doctor carried on past North Lane, where Brett's is, and turned right into St Michael's Lane opposite the Original Oak pub. As she turned into the dimly lit cobbled street called Chapel Lane, an alley that was a useful short cut through to Cardigan Road where it emerged by the cricket ground, she was hurled to the ground. Her attacker knocked her unconscious with his hammer, and held her round the neck with the ligature to prevent her getting away. As she lay on the ground, her head and the cobbles began to soak with blood. Peter Sutcliffe retrieved her shoes and handbag and took them several yards away. Within minutes, at 10.30 p.m., Mrs Valerie Nicholas, whose house in St Michael's Crescent backed on to the spot where Dr Bandara was lying, heard a noise and came out of her back door to see what it was. She called the police, who said they did not feel the attacker was the Ripper, adding that they were looking for a man aged about 25, 5′ 4″ tall with black hair, a full beard and moustache. Dr Bandara returned to Singapore to recuperate.

Peter Sutcliffe's Bonfire Night assault on 16-year-old Theresa Sykes at Huddersfield was to help lead to his downfall when he was arrested in Sheffield eight weeks later. He attempted to kill her on a path alongside grassland on the council estate at Oaks, Huddersfield, where she lived with her 25-year-old boyfriend, Jimmy Furey, and their three-month-old son, Anthony.

Theresa was happy just before the attack, because Jimmy, Anthony and herself had managed to get a council house in nearby Willwood Avenue. Though she was barely out of Deighton Secondary School, she was coping well with life. On 5 November she was cutting across the grassland from a late-opening estate grocery shop when she was struck on the head from behind. Her life altered for the worse from that instant. As she fell she turned, and distinctly remembers seeing a man with a beard and a moustache hit her again. She still has a half-moon-shaped scar of that blow high on her forehead.

The attacker ran off as Theresa screamed desperately. A neighbour, Mrs Rita Wilkinson, ran out to see what was happening, heard the girl's voice whimpering, 'Won't somebody help me?', and followed the sound. The attack was at first not considered to be the Ripper's work, though the police later changed their minds. Theresa spent several weeks in the neurosurgical unit at Pinderfields Hospital, Wakefield, and early in 1981 returned to live with her parents. Her father, Mr Raymond Sykes, landlord of The Minstrel pub in Huddersfield town centre, always insisted that it was the Ripper who had attacked Theresa, and says that she has changed drastically since the attack. 'Her whole personality has changed; she was always quick with a smile, but now she seems to flare up at the slightest thing. She only seems happy in the company of the baby, Anthony. She argues about every little thing. In fact I am sad to say that she has become a bit of a tyrant. It will never be the same for any of us again. Even now we tell each other when we go out and where we are going. We are all very nervous, particularly with Theresa.' Theresa had returned to her parents when she found it was impossible to live in the same house as her boyfriend after she left hospital. 'I have a great mistrust of men at the moment. Jimmy and I had planned to get married in the near future, and when I came out of hospital we got back together for a while, but it just didn't work out. I am on edge all the time and frightened at being alone with him. All that mattered was that he was a fellow, and I didn't feel safe. I preferred being with my mother and sisters. I am obsessed with having my back to the wall all the time, even when I am surrounded by friends. I have tried to stop myself, but I simply can't stand anyone to my back.'

It was a wet, unpleasant Monday evening in November when Peter Sutcliffe 'phoned his wife to say that he was still in Gloucester, where he had been making a delivery, and would not be home in Bradford until late. It meant another evening alone in front of the television for Sonia. Peter had been working late a lot recently, but life was soon going to be changed, ironically because of the drunk-driving charge which was bound to be coming up in court soon. The couple's money problems might get worse, of course, but if they got a good price for the house, which she had to concede was a bit large for just the two of them, there was always the hope of the pottery business in the country becoming a reality. In the meantime, Peter could always get a temporary labouring job to keep a bit of money coming in, and she might see some more of him.

Unfortunately, her husband was lying. He had clocked-off from work at 7.03 p.m. and was on his way to the Headingley area of Leeds in his brown Rover. He thought he might go back to the Kentucky Fried Chicken place in the Arndale Centre and have a bite there. As he drove into drizzly Leeds, a young languages student from the village of Ormesby, near Middlesbrough, was listening in her earnest, serious way to a seminar on the probation service in Cookridge Street, Leeds. Jacqueline Hill was a quiet, sensible girl, the eldest of three children, and had been hoping to join the probation service when she graduated the following summer.

She was doing well at her studies, and had a boyfriend serving in the RAF in Lincolnshire. Unlike many young people, she had opted to attend one of the nearest universities to her family home. She had heeded her art teacher-mother's advice to make some concession to the fact that Leeds was the heart of Ripper territory, and moved from a flat on the city's outskirts to the safety and security of an all-girl flat in Lupton Court, part of a large modern complex of university residences behind the Arndale shopping centre in Headingley.

Peter Sutcliffe saw her from near the Kentucky Fried Chicken shop as she got off the number 1 bus at the stop opposite the Arndale at 9.23 p.m. She had picked up the bus in Cookridge Street 20 minutes earlier. She crossed the road, turned left, walked along the front of the shops, and then right up the gentle incline of Alma Road for the 100-yard walk to the Lupton Flats. Alma Road, though dimly lit, is a pleasant street, with a mixture of stone mansions in the course of renovation, the university flats, whose high old wall is often used by student rock-climbers for practice, and, under a local council preservation order, one of the best rows of 'thirties Bauhaus-style semis in Britain.

Just yards from busy Otley Road, Sutcliffe struck the back of Jacqueline's head and dragged her 14 yards onto some spare land behind the Arndale, up to within two yards of the concrete wall of the shoppers' car park. Here, shielded from the street by trees and bushes, and protected by the hum of traffic from the main road, he stabbed her repeatedly. Though she must already have been dead, one eye remained open, so in fury he stabbed through the eyeball. Within minutes of killing her he left, forgetting that her cream raffia shoulder-bag was still on the pavement of Alma Road, and her glasses intact nearby.

At 10 p.m. an Iranian student, Amir Hussain, spotted the bag as he walked back to his flat in the Lupton complex. He took it with him and showed it to his five flatmates when they returned later. One of the friends, a mature student of 49 called Tony Gosden, a former chief inspector in the Hong Kong police, was alarmed to see that nothing had been stolen and that there were fresh blood-spots on the bag. The Barclaycard carried the name Jacqueline Hill, and he suggested that they 'phone the police. Another student, Paul Sampson, made the 999 emergency call at, he says, about 11.30 p.m., though the police insist it was logged at three minutes past midnight. Two uniformed officers eventually arrived in a Panda car. Mr Sampson pointed to the blood on the bag, but says the policemen seemed more interested in filling out a lost-property form than anything else. 'I kept saying, "What about the blood?", and I kept thinking that somewhere there might be a young girl bleeding but breathing,' he said.

He suggested a number of times that the officers search the area where the bag was found, but only after a cup of coffee did they go out to search with Mr Hussain. They looked for about three minutes with their torches before leaving, and it was not until 10.10 on the Tuesday morning that a worker at the rear of one of the shops in the Arndale saw what looked like a woman lying on her back under a coat on the waste ground. She was less than 30 yards from where the bag had been found the previous night.

Speculation grew all day on Tuesday that the Ripper, who was not thought to have struck in 14 months, had killed again. Det. Chief Supt. Peter Gilrain visited the scene and left. Det. Supt. Alf Finley, handling the new investigation, told a bad-tempered press conference late on Tuesday afternoon that there seemed to be nothing to link Jacqueline's death with the Ripper series. Within two hours, as Prof. David Gee continued his post mortem examination, Assistant Chief Constable (Crime) George Oldfield, who by now had been back on duty for almost a year, left a senior officers' conference in Derbyshire and rushed back to Leeds.

On the Wednesday morning he announced the dreadful news – Jacqueline was a Ripper victim after all. Oldfield said, 'This man is obviously very mentally ill and has got this sadistic killer-streak in him. He can flip at any time. We hope fervently we can catch him before any more lives are lost.'

The ensuing massive press coverage of the killing was largely the result of the lengthy interval since the last attributed Ripper outrage, and partly due to the type of girl Jacqueline was and the kind of area Headingley is. Within a few hundred yards of the site of her death live a large portion of the intelligentsia of Leeds. More than ever before, the reality of the Ripper was pressed home to people perhaps more outraged by it than when he struck in less favoured areas. It also took the Jacqueline Hill murder to stir Britain's militant feminists into a violent, raging demonstration in Leeds on the Saturday night after the killing. Cinemas were attacked and red paint thrown at the screen; cars were fist-pounded. There had been previous demonstrations by the 'Reclaim the night' movement in Leeds, but they had been quiet, torchlit processions against male violence. There was a sad irony in the fact that, while the feminists justifiably deprecated the police attitude to the Ripper's prostitute victims, it seemed to take the killing of a middle-class non-prostitute, with whom the feminists could really identify, to provoke them into a violent demonstration of women's by then strictly curtailed right to walk around safely at night.

Meanwhile, the handbag clue had produced large headlines, and the police were interested in contacting the driver of a 'dark, square-shaped car' seen reversing hurriedly down one-way Alma Road before the killing. When the driver did not come forward, the police assured him publicly that he need not fear prosecution for the driving offence. Someone moaned through the columns of the local papers that this was morally wrong.

At Jacqueline Hill's memorial service, at the tiny church in her home village, they played her favourite record, Simon and Garfunkel's 'Bridge Over Troubled Water'. The vicar stood on the same spot where he had presented Jacqueline with a book-token in appreciation of the work she had done for the church. He read from St John's Gospel, where Jesus spoke to his disciples words of comfort before he was crucified. And in Leeds the police received over 8,000 letters, 7,000 of them anonymous, most of them naming suspects. The writer of one unsigned letter, posted in Bradford, named a lorry driver. Two weeks after the letter was posted, Trevor Birdsall, the long-time drinking friend of that driver, made the effort to call at Bradford Police headquarters to repeat his allegation to the constable on the reception desk. The report was fed into the system. Mr Birdsall was to say later that he had become suspicious about his friend Peter Sutcliffe after the attack on Olive Smelt when he had left him for a few minutes that night in Halifax five years earlier.

'But he was a mate, a real close friend, and you don't

think that the bloke you are going round with is a killer. When the police made a big show of the tape and the letters in 1979 I did not think it could possibly be Pete. I knew his handwriting was nothing like that, and to cap it all they said the Ripper had a Geordie accent and was born in the North East. I knew Peter was not born there and was certainly no mimic.' Mr Birdsall says he wrote anonymously to the police after the Jacqueline Hill murder at the insistence of his girlfriend, Ms Gloria Conroy, who two weeks later also persuaded him to go to see the police personally. The anonymous letter had simply suggested the police hunting the Yorkshire Ripper should have a look at lorry driver Peter Sutcliffe of Heaton, Bradford. 'When I heard no more, Gloria persuaded me to go personally a couple of weeks later and the officer took the details down in his notebook. By Christmas I presumed they had checked him out and he was OK.'

So much so that he accepted Sutcliffe's invitation for a lunchtime drink in a Bradford pub the Sunday after Christmas. Sonia had not been able to join them as she was preparing for the dinner party that evening for her husband's father, brothers and sisters at Garden Lane – the last time his father was to see him before the arrest.

While Mr Birdsall's information was hidden in the mountain of information almost overwhelming the police, the so-called Super Squad of outside advisers was settling in in Leeds. It included Thames Valley Deputy Chief Constable Leslie Emment; David Gerty, Assistant Chief Constable of the West Midlands; Commander Ronald Harvey, adviser to the Chief Insector of Constabulary on Crime; and forensic expert Mr Stuart Kind, Director of the Home Office Central Research Department at

Aldermaston. There was also ACC Mr Andrew Sloane, national co-ordinator of the regional crime squads, a former West Yorkshire officer who had once worked under George Oldfield. But Mr Oldfield was no longer in charge of the inquiry, having been replaced by Jim Hobson a week after Jacqueline Hill died.

In the December issue of the West Yorkshire Police newspaper – the *West Yorkshireman* – there was a full-page message for the force under the headline 'Let's Nail Him'. Hobson said he was anxious to involve every officer in the force in the hunt, creating luck for themselves by doing something constructive every day towards the Ripper investigation. 'Hopefully, some officer will be in the right place at the right time and give us the break we need.'

He ended his message to the 5,000 force members: 'So much about the Ripper is ifs and buts – one cannot be 100 per cent certain, for instance, that all the murders are linked. What we are saying is that they are all similar and are the ones we are most interested in. For reasons obvious to all officers there is a certain amount of information that has to be kept back for the vital confrontation with the man responsible for the killings.

'On the balance of probability the man who sent the tape and wrote the letters is the Ripper but there can always be a question mark and it would be wrong for officers to eliminate suspects because they had not got a Geordie accent. We give certain guidelines but in the end, I feel, it will be some officer's intuition that leads us to the killer.'

In the middle of that December Sutcliffe made a trip in his lorry that for him, as a long distance driver, was unusual. As far as workers at the remote depot high up on the moor north of Sheffield were concerned, it was a bearded driver's first delivery there. He made a considerable impression on them. 'Because of the Christmas log-jam he had a long wait to get unloaded, but he was unusually calm about it,' recalls the depot manager. 'Instead of effing and blinding and kicking the walls like some of the drivers do, he just sat patiently.'

Sutcliffe spent some of the time in the depot office and then went over to a nearby loading-bay where he spent much of the afternoon chatting with the warehousemen, mainly about himself. He told one of the packers, Lol Housley, that both he and his wife were handing in their notice at the end of that December and were going off to start a new life in the country. He impressed Mr Housley as being a bit of a cut above the normal lorry driver, friendly and quietly spoken. 'The only odd thing about him, though, was that he never seemed to quite look you straight in the eye,' said Mr Housley. Another packer at the loading-bay remembered talking to the driver and recalled him as handsome and bearded and wearing an immaculate blue boiler-suit.

On a notice board in the bay was pinned a cutting from a Sunday newspaper. On it was an indistinct drawing of a bearded man; the poster read: 'WANTED. THIS MAN HAS KILLED THIRTEEN WOMEN. REWARD £50,000.'

'He stared at it for quite a long time,' the young packer recalled. 'I said to him, "See they haven't caught that twat yet." The bearded fellow just said "Yeah". He went on about his big house – he even said it cost £16,000 – and about his wife being a teacher.' Another packer said the driver had been like a 15-year-old boy who had just got his first girlfriend when talking about his wife. 'What she did and what she didn't do, what she liked and didn't like. He seemed very taken with her. He was right polite, not cussing and blinding like the others. Put a halo on him and he could have been Jesus Christ by the look of him. He kept asking about some deserted land you can see below the depot. He kept saying "It's quiet here." '

Two weeks later, on Friday 2 January, Peter William Sutcliffe returned to Sheffield. Just after 4 p.m. he said goodbye to Sonia in the kitchen of number six, Garden Lane. He reversed the brown Rover down the drive and was gone. Sonia Sutcliffe did not see him again for more than 48 hours, when he was to sit in a small C.I.D. office at Dewsbury police station and speak the most awful words imaginable.

CHAPTER 8

Lost Weekend

The British Iron and Steel Producers Association (BISPA) Headquarters in Sheffield is a fine, large and imposing stone building with a magnificent view across the city from its position on the hillside just below the Glossop Road. Light Trades House, built originally as a home for a wealthy industrialist, is approached along Melbourne Avenue, a public road with the look of a private drive. Only 300 yards long, it has twin stone pillars at each entrance and it might never occur to a stranger to pass through. Olivia Reivers had never been along Melbourne Avenue in the daylight, but she knew half-way along its tree-lined and leafy length was the perfect place for 'business'.

Light Trades House was deserted at night, the sloping drive dark and sheltered. Olivia Reivers was 24, a mother of two, brown-skinned and slim, with a mass of hair, and had moved to Sheffield from Birmingham seven years earlier. She was experienced with men of all types, and lots of her customers were married men, shy men, nervous men, and occasionally men who proved difficult to arouse. This man was like that, the man with the dark beard and hair, and almost black eyes. Just three hours earlier she had kissed her two children, Louise, 5, and Deroy, 3, goodnight at their home in Wade Street and made her way to the nearby Havelock Square district, Sheffield's so-called red-light area, a patchwork of tight terraced streets, full of compact houses. After dark you could be in Fulham, if it weren't for the steeply sloping ground, and the incongruously modern Little Mesters pub, all bright lights and formica and out of place. More the sort of area you would expect to find a Rovers Return, *à la* Coronation Street.

It had been almost 9 p.m. when Olivia met her friend, Denise Hall, 19, another coloured girl, and they set about patrolling Wharncliffe Road a few yards apart. Within minutes Denise had a potential customer, a brown Rover 3500 with a black vinyl roof pulling up alongside the kerb. She bent to talk to the driver and there was something about his eyes, dark, almost black, which seemed to pierce through her own. He wasn't bad-looking, with his neatly trimmed black beard and dark wavy hair, but his eyes frightened her. So she just said, 'Sorry' and walked away. Even the ladies of the street reserve the right to say no.

The car left, but it was back an hour later and this time a bargain was struck. Olivia looked into his eyes but did not see what her friend had seen and, after all, £10 was £10 to a working girl. She knew it wasn't the ones who looked odd that you had to worry about; it was the ones who did seem all right that could sometimes surprise you. She had had a few bruises in the past to prove it.

Three minutes later they were in the drive of Light Trades House. The man proved little different from many of the other married types she had known – more concerned about his wife than anything else. 'I asked him if he was married and he said "Yes". He spoke about his wife quite a lot. He seemed worried about her. He told me there had been a couple of miscarriages and that seemed to make him sad. It certainly seemed to me that he loved her a lot but that there were possibly some personal problems between them. After a while, you know, I tried to warm him up, but there was no response, he was cold as ice,' says Olivia. She leant across between the two front seats and whispered encouraging endearments as she fondled the man's penis, but to no avail. Was it the sudden intimacy of total strangers that quite often defeated the men who sought her favours, their ambition totally outstripping their reduced ability? This one wasn't drunk, so it couldn't be that. Was it guilt? Or was his circulation bad? It was a cold night. Never mind, they would try again later. So the man fastened up his trousers and settled back in his seat to talk. Had he felt the knife in the lining of his car coat, easily reached if he put his hand in his pocket and felt through the special hole, pressing into the small of his back? Or the piece of rope? Or the hammer under his seat – the 1¼-lb ball-pein, with one flat side and one rounded? The view through the trees at the bottom of the drive was almost romantic, with the lights of Sheffield sprawled below.

Sgt. Robert Ring and P.C. Robert Hydes had started the dreaded 10–6 'night' shift almost an hour earlier at Sheffield's nearby Hammerton Road police station. After the ritual of the 'parade' they had sorted out a Vauxhall Chevette 'Panda' car and set off on general patrol, expecting that Friday for a change to be quiet, what with New Year's Eve just gone and a Saturday night coming up. When he and his partner cruised along Melbourne Avenue at 10.50 p.m. that Friday evening, 2 January, there was little doubt in Sgt. Ring's mind what the dark, square-shaped car was doing parked half-way up the drive of the BISPA headquarters.

The man said his name was Peter Williams and the dusky woman was his girlfriend. But Bob Ring never forgot a face – wasn't she a convicted prostitute, under a suspended sentence for soliciting? As they transferred Olivia Reivers into the police car Sutcliffe climbed out of the Rover and said he was bursting for a 'pee'. Without waiting to be given permission he walked the dozen paces to the extra darkness alongside the towering house. A large stone entrance porch formed a right angle, and in it was an oil storage tank for the central heating system. He walked round three sides of it and was out of sight of the two policemen. He took the knife and the ball-pein hammer and bent down, both weapons in one hand, and placed them on the ground against the wall, hoping they hadn't heard the clinking sound. And then he returned to the car. Like every policeman in Britain today, Sgt. Ring and P.C. Hydes were only a radio call away from £50m of highly sophisticated computer technology, the Police National Computer at Hendon, which serves as a massive memory bank. It stores 25½ million registered vehicle numbers, 2½ million sets of fingerprints, 60,000 missing persons, 3½ million criminals and their records, 180,000 disqualified drivers and 300,000 stolen vehicle numbers. The original police computer system had been totally inadequate because of unexpected demand. Now they can deal with 15,000 inquiries an hour and each year 50 million inquiries are made. There are more than 500 terminals in police stations throughout Britain, directly linked by Post Office line to Hendon. Each of them is equipped with a visual display unit and a keyboard similar to a typewriter. It is simply a matter of the operator tapping out the details and the response from the computer will appear within fractions of a second on the small display screen. It is estimated that from the time a man on the beat in a patrol car calls for information the average answer, including peak periods, is received in less than two minutes. Previously such a check would have taken several hours.

The message Sgt. Ring and P.C. Hydes received back on

the night of 2 January was that the registration number
they had given from the Rover in fact belonged to a Skoda.
They re-checked it but received the same answer. A closer
inspection of the number-plates produced a surprise for
the two officers; they were held on with black tape. The
vehicle excise licence disc on the windscreen supplied some
of the answers they were looking for. And the driver
confirmed the details. His name was Peter William
Sutcliffe, and he lived at 6 Garden Lane, Heaton,
Bradford.

The man didn't want his wife to know he went with
prostitutes so they said, 'You had both better accompany
us to the police station', and the Rover, real registration
number FHY 400K, was left in the drive – a tow bar,
scruffy and untidy; a boot full of tools, bits of rope, a
spare speedo, windscreen wipers, a block of wood and a
piece of old carpet; some correspondence in the front, a
letter from a finance company in Nottingham; and an
incongruous red and purple paper flower on the dashboard
in front of the passenger seat.

At Hammerton Road it was separate interview rooms
for the man and woman. They were to soon let her go, but
he, they reckoned, would be there for a while. Sutcliffe
told them he had stolen the number-plates of a car in a
scrapyard at a place called Cooper Bridge, near Mirfield,
West Yorkshire. Where was Cooper Bridge? Police at
Sheffield knew that if a charge of theft was to be pressed
against Sutcliffe he would have to be handed over to a
neighbouring force. They were also conscious of the
repeated requests they had received from West Yorkshire
to draw their attention to any man from the area
spotlighted because of his connection with a prostitute or
prostitutes, or even red-light districts. Telephone calls to
Wakefield, Bradford, Leeds and eventually the police in

Dewsbury, at 5.12 a.m., satisfied them who would be dealing with an alleged theft charge from a scrapyard at Mirfield.

Arrangements were made for officers to travel to Sheffield from Dewsbury after the fresh shift came on at 6 a.m. A call was made to the man's wife at Garden Lane, Heaton, Bradford, from Hammerton Road police station, informing her of the whereabouts of her husband. By 2.30 a.m. on Saturday 3 January 1981, the Yorkshire Ripper was asleep in a Sheffield police cell. He had taken off his yellow and black car coat and his shoes, but was sleeping in his blue jumper and trousers. He had earlier asked to go to the toilet and while there had stood on the seat and placed a second knife in the cistern.

Three West Yorkshire officers travelled to Sheffield, one to drive the brown Rover back, and while they were away the station sergeant at Dewsbury rang the Ripper Room at Millgarth at 8 a.m. to tell them of the night's developments. While it was strictly a routine call, the officer was conscious of a recent directive from Ronald Gregory. The Chief Constable and Jim Hobson had spoken to almost every officer in the force, in groups of 500. It had been a severe pep-talk and had left no one in any doubt that alertness of the highest order was expected, that no detail was too small to be ignored. And that men found with prostitutes in suspicious circumstances had to be drawn to the attention of the Ripper Squad.

At 8.55 a.m. the West Yorkshire police car pulled around the back of Dewsbury's flat-roofed and low-slung police station, at the side of the road out of the town to Mirfield. Coming from the M1 motorway from Sheffield, the car had passed the soot-stained town-hall which housed the Magistrate's Court, 200 yards away. Sutcliffe and the two officers had hardly spoken on the 35-minute journey and he was quickly transferred through the double security doors into the station's 'Safe' cell and interview-room area.

At 8.59 a.m. the police had logged the new arrival. A strip-search of the prisoner found some money not noticed at Sheffield. Just after 9 a.m. a Mrs Sonia Sutcliffe rang from Bradford inquiring about the whereabouts of her husband. She was told he was being questioned about the alleged theft of car number-plates and she didn't ring back. Her husband had been offered breakfast from the police canteen but was soon talking to Dewsbury C.I.D. officers who, like everyone else in the force, were aware of the standing instructions to look carefully at any man with connections with prostitutes. They were told that he was a lorry driver from Bradford and about his interest in cars. They noted his dark, almost frizzy hair, the gap between his teeth, and his calmness.

Inter-force memoranda had noted a number of areas of reference, including the crucial Geordie accent, regarded as one of five points for elimination. Yet that did not deter the Dewsbury officers. Circulated police documents also insisted that the killer was believed to live or work in West Yorkshire or close by, and have a connection with the North East of England. Lorry driver Sutcliffe told them he had made regular deliveries to Sunderland in his 32-ton 'artic'. From all their collated knowledge the police had also drawn up a short-list of vehicles from which they believed the Yorkshire Ripper's came. They suspected it could be of B.M.C. manufacture with a Farina body style, probably a Morris Oxford type. That could include an Austin Cambridge, a Wolseley 15/60, an MG Magnette MK3, or a Riley 4/68. Three other possibilities were a Ford Corsair 2000E, Hillman Minx MKVI, or Singer Gazelle Mk VI. The lorry driver from Bradford, by now chattily telling the officers about all his cars, recalled the white Corsair (which they were to discover had since been scrapped), the one with the black roof. Hadn't Maureen Long talked about a white Ford with a black roof? And why was this man so calm, despite the disproportionate amount of interest detectives were showing in him for the theft of number plates worth only 50p?

Sutcliffe was questioned by a detective and it was discovered he had been seen by the police at Clarks about the £5 note and the red-light checks. He was a size 8 shoe, maybe even a 7. And there was a gap in his teeth. At 10 a.m., another call was made to the Ripper Squad in Leeds.

The so-called Ripper room at Millgarth police station, Leeds (officially the murder incident room) had by January 1981 become a cell for many officers, familiar with every item, from the charts on the walls to the last coffee mug. There had been weeks and months of repetitive, tedious work, processing the seemingly endless flow of data – indexing, filing, cross-indexing – the largest amount of such material on one case ever compiled in the U.K. The mountain of details almost mocked them, challenging them to fit the pieces together. There can have been few officers who had not put their jackets on at the end of the 12-hour day and surveyed the serried ranks of filing cabinets and asked themselves the same question. Is he in there somewhere?

Soon after lunch Det. Sgt. Des O'Boyle, a Task Force officer attached to the Ripper Squad, and once a detective at Manningham, Bradford, was on his way to Dewsbury. The files had shown that Sutcliffe's name was already known to the Ripper Squad. He had been seen a number of times during the course of the investigation, at first

regarding the £5 note checks following Jean Jordan's
death in Manchester, later because of the red-light checks
when his car number had recurred in Bradford, Leeds and
Manchester, and also because he worked for an
engineering firm. As Sgt. O'Boyle drove the ten miles to
Dewsbury, he mentally indexed Sutcliffe under 'Not happy
about'.

Sgt. O'Boyle approached Sutcliffe in the time-honoured
way – softly, almost gently, probing all the time but
conscious of the need to establish the firmest of
foundations for what might lay ahead. If anything lay
ahead, that was. There were many things to be looked into,
but early that Saturday afternoon Peter Sutcliffe was no
more likely to be the Yorkshire Ripper than many others
who had been thoroughly checked out over the five long
years of inquiry. And, after all, he wasn't a Geordie.

But slowly and carefully, with Sgt. O'Boyle in constant
touch with fellow Ripper Squad officers back at Millgarth,
the police were piecing together the life and recent times of
Peter William Sutcliffe. Although he did not think he was
necessarily talking to the Yorkshire Ripper, Sgt. O'Boyle
was sufficiently confident at 6 p.m. to stay with the inquiry
when he should have gone off duty for a well-earned
Saturday night out. He told his immediate senior officer,
Det. Insp. John Boyle, who himself had taken over at
the murder room at Millgarth at 6 p.m., that he was
staying with the case. A blood test late in the afternoon
had shown Sutcliffe to be the rare B group.

The Inspector, who had not been on the inquiry long,
and who had formerly been a Det. Sgt. at Halifax, agreed
that Sutcliffe was in the 'frame', but much more had to be
found out about him. Yet there was no rush, certainly no
need to emphasize to Sutcliffe that they were interested in
the Yorkshire Ripper case. After all, he wasn't going

anywhere. In fact by 10 p.m. Sutcliffe had gone to bed, locked in his cell for the night.

At the same time, Sgt. Bob Ring was back at Hammerton Road police station ready to start another 10 p.m.–6 a.m. shift. That afternoon he had had some friends to his home for a New Year's drink, the unusual timing an occupational hazard for a policeman. One of his friends said 'Wouldn't it be a turn up if the man Ring had arrested the night before with the prostitute, was the Yorkshire Ripper?'

After the 10 p.m. parade at Hammerton Road Sgt. Ring was told that the man he had arrested with the prostitute in the brown Rover the night before was still in custody at Dewsbury police station and was being questioned by Ripper Squad officers. He then made the most crucial decision of several lives – his own, perhaps, but certainly that of Peter William Sutcliffe. Within the next few hours it was to have an enormous bearing on the lives of others also: Ronald Gregory, George Oldfield, and Jim Hobson; countless other policemen involved in the hunt; and a large number of people in Bingley and Bradford. Even journalists. And most certainly that of a dark-haired woman at Garden Lane, Heaton, Bradford, who was at that time thinking of going to bed early. There had been no further news of her husband and the business with the motor car.

Bob Ring decided he would return to Light Trades House. He remembered the man with the beard had gone for a 'pee' behind the stone porch. Had that been a metallic clink? What if he was the Yorkshire Ripper? Would he, 26 years a policeman, look foolish if he had been tricked so easily? He had better check. Bob Ring didn't tell anyone where he was going but very soon afterwards his superior officers knew. When he got to

Light Trades House he walked to the side of the porch, around the oil-storage tank. He shone his torch on the ground by the wall and there he found a ball-pein hammer, one side of the head flat, the other rounded. And a knife.

Det. Supt. Dick Holland's telephone rang at ten minutes past midnight at his home in Elland, near Huddersfield, and he heard the words he had dreamt about for too long: 'I think we've got him.' Dick Holland was in overall charge of the Ripper squad that weekend and it was significant that D.I. Boyle did not inform him that Peter Sutcliffe was being questioned as a possible Yorkshire Ripper suspect until after the weapons had been recovered in Sheffield. Until he himself had received a call from a Det. Supt. at Sheffield, Sutcliffe had been one of the many who, while obviously a man with a mounting number of question marks against his name, had to be eliminated. Too often detectives working on the case had become prematurely excited about a suspect for whom more pieces of the jigsaw had appeared to fit than with Sutcliffe – until the hammer and the knife were found at Sheffield.

As a result, Dick Holland was cautious, quick to control the initial flicker of excitement, eager that if this was the man, they get things absolutely right. A short list of priority instructions was issued to John Boyle and his men, including an instruction that they talk as quickly as possible with Olivia Reivers and the other prostitute, Denise Hall, who had spoken to Sutcliffe the night before. And an officer was to be stationed in the prisoner's cell.

D.I. Boyle was to be joined in Sheffield by Sgt. O'Boyle, who by now had abandoned any thoughts of sleep that night. Mr Holland arranged to be briefed on the night's events at Bradford police headquarters at 9 a.m. the following morning, and by 9.30 a.m. he, Sgt. O'Boyle, Det. Chief Inspector George Smith, and Det. Constable Jenny Crawford-Brown were outside number six, Garden Lane. Mrs Sutcliffe had no objection to them looking round the house and when she left with them at 10 a.m. they moved a number of tools (including ball-pein hammers) from a workshop at the back of the garage.

For the next 13 hours Sonia Sutcliffe was to be questioned extensively, with a brief break in the middle of the afternoon for refreshment. Her husband had breakfasted on coffee and toast at the Dewsbury police station before being taken from his cell to the nearby interview room again. Dick Holland had specifically asked that Det. Sgt. Peter Smith of the Regional Crime Squad, who had been attached to the Ripper Squad longer than almost anyone else, be involved in the questioning. His deep and detailed knowledge of all the attacks, and the thousands of facts surrounding them, was regarded as a crucial element in the cat and mouse game to be played out with Sutcliffe.

Throughout the morning, without overtly mentioning the Yorkshire Ripper attacks, the officers tried systematically to close possible avenues of escape for Sutcliffe. He was friendly and he was articulate, and very calm. He was never once to ask for bail or a solicitor.

But behind the scenes special tasks designated by Mr Holland were being tackled. While some officers attempted to contact the firms Sutcliffe had worked for during the period of the attacks, others were setting up special incident rooms in key areas. One was at Odsal police station, Bradford which took in the area of Tanton Crescent. If they had got the right man the Yorkshire Ripper had operated from a semi-detached council house in the suburb of Clayton for two of the five years.

By Sunday afternoon at Dewsbury police station, Boyle, O'Boyle and Smith suspected they were approaching the climax of what had been an extraordinary 24 hours. Sutcliffe's resolve and astonishing calmness were showing signs of faltering.

By now increasingly sure that they had the right man, the officers had been concentrating their questioning on the evening of 5 November – Bonfire Night – 1980, the night that Theresa Sykes was attacked. Sutcliffe had clocked-off at Clarks at 5.03 p.m. and was adamant he arrived home at Garden Lane at 8 p.m. He had called for a drink but it had been no later than 8 p.m. when he had got home.

Unknown to Sutcliffe the telephone lines between Dewsbury police station and Bradford police headquarters were kept almost permanently open. He was also unaware that his wife's recollection of that evening was very different from his own. She was quite clear – it had been 10 p.m. when Peter had walked through the kitchen door. Theresa Sykes had been attacked at 8 p.m., and for the first time in the period they had been talking to him the officers felt Sutcliffe was struggling to remain plausible.

So much so that a telephone call was made to George Oldfield's home seven miles away at the village of Grange Moor. He had not started lunch and was left with a strange, almost empty feeling when he was told of the momentous developments. And again soon afterwards, when the moment had arrived and Sutcliffe had conceded defeat to Messrs Boyle, O'Boyle and Smith.

In theory George Oldfield was no longer in charge of the inquiry, Jim Hobson having been made acting Asst. Chief

Constable soon after the Hill killing, amid all the renewed clamour about the seemingly never-ending reign of the Yorkshire Ripper. But old loyalties were to override these heady moments at Dewsbury. Oldfield arrived at the police station shortly before the other senior officers. These were bitter-sweet moments for the man whose life had been almost wrecked in the course of the previous five years. He had had his critics, and his insistence on making the affair a personal battle with the Ripper (on the strength of the letters and the tape) had not been to everyone's taste, but few would surely begrudge these few early moments of satisfaction.

The final capitulation came almost suddenly, even unexpectedly, as Sutcliffe's interrogators continued questioning him about Bonfire Night. The hammer and the knife at Sheffield were mentioned. At 2.40 p.m. Sutcliffe sat back on his black plastic and metal chair and said, 'I think you are leading up to the Yorkshire Ripper.' John Boyle asked him, 'What about the Yorkshire Ripper?' And he replied, 'Well, that's me.'

During the following 26 hours, apart from a five-hour break for sleep, the detectives were privy to the first glimpse into the mind of the Yorkshire Ripper and were to be the audience for an amazing saga of horror and destruction of human life, delivered calmly and with hardly any display of emotion. The only moments of apparent agitation came when the police touched on the Joan Harrison killing at Preston, with its overt sexual assault including anal intercourse, in which he vehemently denied any involvement, and the death of 16-year-old Jayne MacDonald.

Sutcliffe seemed to give the impression that he was less upset about the fact that MacDonald had been the first non-prostitute victim that he had killed than that his *modus operandi* had developed a flaw. Meanwhile Sutcliffe was to receive two visitors. George Oldfield briefly introduced himself and, totally without malice, mentioned in passing, 'I'm the one you almost bloody killed as well.' There was no reaction. But Sutcliffe did have one definite request. He wanted to be the one to break the news to Sonia. This he did at 10.30 p.m.

A message was sent to Bradford police station and Mrs Sutcliffe was asked if she would travel to Dewsbury to see her husband. She was accompanied by W.D.C. Crawford-Brown, recently returned to work having recovered from multiple injuries received in a car crash in east Yorkshire. At Dewsbury, Mrs Sutcliffe, in her dark green, hooded top-coat and fawn slacks, was greeted by Mr Oldfield who told her Peter had asked to see her, but didn't say why. As another officer recalls, 'The penny seemed to have dropped; she seemed very calm.' Mrs Sutcliffe was shown into the interview-room and sat across a small table from her husband, whom she hadn't seen since 4 p.m. on Friday. And then it was over. He had told her his terrible, shocking news. Simply and without hesitation, almost like a schoolboy who had been caught out, and who had found it easier to tell the truth than to tell lies. His wife emerged from the interview-room a few minutes later, still very calm, and was to stay at the police station for another 18 hours to be questioned at length, particularly about her and her husband's movements on a large number of nights since July 1975, when Anna Rogulskyj was felled by three hammer blows. Sonia and Peter Sutcliffe were to remain impervious to the quickening pace of events. Sutcliffe gave his statement and Sgt. Smith wrote it down. Det. Insp. Boyle paced around the office as he took Peter Sutcliffe back over his incredible five-year journey.

The crowd of pressmen soon assembled in Dewsbury were told there was to be a press conference before nine o'clock; the West Yorkshire Chief Constable, Ronald Gregory, who was later heavily criticized for the tone of the conference, wanted to end speculation about the arrest, although in many ways the sensational conference fuelled speculation by confirming the fact that the police believed they had caught the Ripper.

When the conference began, with Bob Baxter (the West Yorkshire press spokesman), Ronald Gregory, George Oldfield and Jim Hobson sitting at the head of the room, dapper in lounge suits and smiling as broadly as film stars about to pick up Oscars, there were 80 journalists crammed into the room, which was becoming hot under the television lights. The conference in fact added little to what reporters had already established through their informal channels. The one amazing detail learned was that the suspect was married, which destroyed a lot of the preconceptions built up over the years. What was to make the conference the subject of heated debate at a national level was the extraordinary if understandable elation of the police. (Although at one point Oldfield seemed to be showing concern at the way the Chief Constable was generously answering the questions.)

Policemen in Britain have a way of describing events, sometimes of the most dramatic kind, in an emotionless, deadpan style that is at once infuriating and somehow reassuring. The excited policeman might not inspire confidence. But the Ripper press conference was unique. Reporters felt it was more like an American event, and it was later to be argued that Chief Constable Gregory went too far, expressing his 'absolute delight' at the development and saying that the hunt for the Ripper 'was now being scaled right down'. The overall effect was to suggest that the man – he was not named at the conference, although he was being questioned within yards of the conference-room – was in fact the Yorkshire Ripper. That was an assumption the police were not entitled to make publicly, and may well have contributed to the near-euphoric atmosphere in some areas of the press for the next two days. Strictly established procedures for aiding a suspect's defence by blacking out all but a few facts about him were abandoned by all.

By 4 p.m. that first Monday afternoon the crowd at the side-entrance at Dewsbury Town Hall was almost 2,000 strong and noisy with anticipation at the prospect of seeing the man whom they took to be the Yorkshire Ripper. Some had come prepared, with placards carrying various suggestions about his fate; one youth even held a home-made noose.

In the 24 hours since news of Sutcliffe's arrest had started to emerge the previous Sunday afternoon, the nation's press had converged on Bradford and Dewsbury. London-based representatives of many foreign publications had also hurried north for the anticipated first court appearance of the Yorkshire Ripper. An unseemly scrum of reporters was vetted and allowed into the first-floor magistrate's court, eventually filling every available seat 20 minutes before Sutcliffe's scheduled appearance at 4 p.m.

And then, almost an hour later, at 4.53 p.m., the cacophony from the hysterical crowd in the street heralded the arrival of the police van bearing Sutcliffe. From the public gallery, a balcony at the end of the court commandeered for the press seats, the view out of the high windows onto the street below was startling. As the police van came round the corner of the Town Hall, closely followed by a police car carrying Mrs Sutcliffe and her father, outside-broadcast television lights snapped on and the surging crowd was bathed in brilliant light. Howls of 'Hang the bastard' and 'Killer' percolated through the double glazing.

Almost immediately Mrs Sutcliffe was shown gently by Det. Supt. Frank Morritt, Mr Hobson's special assistant, to a wooden bench immediately in front of the empty dock, where she sat with her father who had come to Dewsbury in *Yorkshire Post* photographer David Parry's car, and who looked on the point of collapse. Suddenly the dock was full of prison officers and plain-clothes detectives. Some surveyed the faces on all four sides of the central dock island, two of the three detectives with suspicious bulges under their jackets. Then the slightly-built man in the blue pullover with its light band at the neck was at the front of the dock, handcuffed to Det. Sgt. Desmond Finbar O'Boyle. Sonia turned and half-rose in her seat, placing her hand briefly on that of her husband immediately behind her. She spoke a low, reassuring sentence, but he seemed to see nothing and feel nothing, staring dully ahead.

The Court Clerk asked him, 'Are you Peter William Sutcliffe, of 6 Garden Lane, Heaton, Bradford?' and after Sutcliffe's affirmative reply continued, 'You are accused that between 16 November and 19 November 1980 you did murder Jacqueline Hill against the peace of our Sovereign Lady the Queen. Further, you are charged that at Mirfield, between 13 November and 2 January, you stole two motor vehicle registration-plates to the total value of 50p, the property of Cyril Bamforth.'

Mr Maurice Shaffner, the County prosecuting solicitor, said that Sutcliffe was not legally represented and that the prosecution were asking that he be remanded in custody

for eight days. He was sure the question of bail would not
arise. A few more words from Mr Shaffner reminding the
press that the affair was now *sub judice,* and the Clerk, Mr
Dean Gardener, asked Sutcliffe if he had any objection to
the remand in custody and whether he wanted reporting
restrictions lifted. Sutcliffe replied 'No' on both counts,
and suddenly it was over. One hundred reporters craned
forward to watch the slim man with the black beard
disappear with a clatter of footsteps down the dock steps.
For a fleeting moment he stumbled and sagged against the
wall, but he quickly recovered and was gone from sight.

Sutcliffe's appearance in Court had been delayed for
almost an hour because he was still giving his statement
late on Monday afternoon, just over 24 hours after first
admitting that he was the Yorkshire Ripper. He compiled a
catalogue so shocking that some officers thought it had to
be accurate; it would have been impossible to have made it
up. He had barely touched upon the reasons, saying
something about a prostitute once having given him a hard
time over some change for a £10 note. But why Jayne
MacDonald, why Josephine Whitaker, why Barbara
Leach? And why Margot Walls, Theresa Sykes and
Upadhya Bandara?

Just after 3 a.m. George Oldfield suggested he should be
allowed to have some sleep. If it ever came to a fight in
Court about the validity of the statement, the 'confession',
it might not look too good if he had been kept up right
through the night.

Later the following morning, Mr Oldfield was told by
Mr Gregory to carry on with his general duties and leave
the job at Dewsbury to the others. The two men's
relationship was to be strained, say colleagues, for some

time afterwards. But on that first Monday in January 1981 Peter Sutcliffe seemed to feel no strain at all. He had never liked the way the press had dubbed the women's killer a 'Ripper', and he wanted to get it right, just as it had happened. It had been five years but he remembered Wilma McCann well – the aggressive way she had spoken to him, telling him he was no good, casting doubts on his manhood. He remembered Emily Jackson's perfume, calling it cheap and strong, and saying a few words to Jayne MacDonald before he killed her. If he had been able to decapitate Jean Jordan, he had thought of hiding her head, perhaps by a motorway somewhere. He had even had to fall on Helen Rytka on the frozen ground because two taxi drivers were parked only 50 yards away and he had to appear as if he was one of the girl's normal customers. As they got out of the car, as the taxi drivers had left, he tried to hit her with the hammer, but missed and hit the door of his car. But he denied having returned to the body or stealing Durex from her handbag.

Josephine Whitaker had become a victim because the red-light areas contained too many policemen. He strangled Margot Walls in an attempt to throw the police off his scent. Theresa Sykes had been wearing a skirt with a slit in it, while Dr Bandara had been wearing tight yellow jeans . . . But all this was to take days to emerge.

That first Monday had been a traumatic day in the lives of many people close to Peter Sutcliffe. His father had to be taken home from work in a state of shock, but recovered sufficiently later in the day to take up an offer from the *Daily Mail,* a newspaper he had read for 25 years, to be transported to the welcome peace and quiet of a hotel in the Dales. He was later to return to his flat in Bingley insisting that he had not accepted money from the *Mail* or anyone else. After he had recovered his composure following those early days he talked about his eldest son.

He said Peter and Sonia's relationship had been one of two very quiet people together. 'I would imagine that most people would think that an extrovert and an introvert would get on very well together; however, these were two very quiet people. Sonia was a very beautiful girl, very soft-spoken, and Peter was very similar. They were very similar in their ways. When she was at college she was very interested in ceramics and she is an absolute marvel with potting clay.'

He said her parents seemed two very intelligent people; her sister was a brilliant pianist. She and Peter were constant companions and didn't get married for such a long time because Sonia had an education to complete and was determined to do so before she committed herself to marriage or anything else. She was a very strong-willed girl despite being so quiet. Peter seemed happy with the relationship.

'We were delighted when they said they were going to get married. There were several of Sonia's relatives from Czechoslavakia who came over for the wedding. Sonia's parents lived only about 400 yards from the Chapel in Clayton. I know they were both determined to work as hard as they could to get their own home, which they eventually did. Since then they have seemed thoroughly wrapped up in the job of making the house into a home, and it's become a beautiful home. I don't think for a moment they were unhappy living with Sonia's parents; it was just the fact that they wanted to be sure they could do what they wanted to do before they went off on their own.

'I couldn't say with any certainty what Sonia's relationship with her parents was. Her mother was a very,

very friendly person, but her father was the type of chap who didn't seem to want to go visiting at all. I think, apart from my wife's funeral, that was the only time Sonia's father set foot through my door. He's not the sort of bloke who likes a lot of company. He's rather a quiet, reserved type of man. Thoroughly nice, and I would say a gentleman in every way. I know her father enjoys a game of chess and while Peter was living there he taught him to play the game. That's an accomplishment that I've never achieved. Peter never said if Sonia's relationship with her father became strained.

'I imagine he was a strict father. He probably had his own methods of keeping things in order in his own home. Some of these continental people are like that I believe at home. Sonia never confided in me.

'I was not surprised when Peter took the job at the cemetery. What's there to be surprised about working in a cemetery? He wanted an outdoor job for a change and that was his opportunity. I don't think it changed or affected him in any way. He perhaps learnt to laugh a bit more by having the company of lads his own age. I don't think Peter was involved in anything irregular at the cemetery. When he went to Clarks he enjoyed driving. He's always enjoyed driving. He passed his driving test at the first go. I think driving was his life and when he got the chance to drive the big stuff he grabbed it with both hands. He was doing what he wanted to do. His and Sonia's life-style was very simple, they didn't go out a lot. They spent an awful lot of time on the house.

'Sonia had at least two miscarriages but this is something that she definitely doesn't want me to talk about. I should think a thing like that happening twice must have had some sort of effect. They never appeared to be different outwardly, but surely it had had some sort of effect. Peter talked quite openly about them, especially when his mother was alive. But they were both very matter-of-fact and didn't make a fuss. They didn't come weeping on our shoulders or anything like that. They took it all in a matter-of-fact way, and left it at that. We were all very sorry for them.'

Mr Sutcliffe said he had been closer to Peter than to any of his other children. 'He was always there in the home. I couldn't get him interested in sport or anything. I've always been interested in sport all my life, played football till I was 44 and if it hadn't been for contracting asthma I should have still been playing cricket even last season. But I could never get him interested in sport, he was just interested in reading, he'd spend hours with a book.

'He was quite normal when he was a kid. He was a slow developer, he must have been getting on for 17, but he was physically like a lad of 15.

'I think his character formed properly between the age of 17 and 22 or 23. He became more outgoing and began to make friends in life. It was as if he had sort of grown up at last and was able to hold his own with other blokes. He became more of the lad he should have been if he'd been a normal-size child. He always had plenty of money in his pocket because he always worked hard. He's only ever had one cigarette in his life and he was so disgusted with it that after a couple of drags he threw it away and has never touched tobacco since.

'When he was in his early twenties he fancied living on his own in a flat. But I think it only lasted about six weeks. Missed the family atmosphere. It was just an experiment on his part, I suppose. I think he missed all of us. His mother was a very loving person and was over-loving with all of them.

'I've heard it said that if the boss at Clarks gave him a

ticking off for being late for work tears would actually roll down his face. But it didn't happen at home. He wasn't used to being shouted at, he never got shouted at at home. He was a very, very good child.

'When the Ripper attacks started in Yorkshire I was just as concerned as the next man for the safety of my daughters who are living in the same area of Bingley as me. I implored them not to go out at night alone. I never discussed the Ripper with Peter.

'On the Sunday night when I first heard a man was helping police with their inquiries, I was very relieved. It had been getting out of hand, the thing had to stop and I was just as relieved as everyone else. I was in an utter state of shock when I found it was Peter. I never suspected Peter might be responsible. No more than any other father would have suspected his own son. If you had known him you would have realised that Peter was probably the last person in the world you would have suspected of having any sort of mental aberrations which would cause him to do these sort of things.

'People will probably think that I'm saying this because I am his father. But he'll still be my son as long as I'm alive. I'm not trying to forgive him for what he's done; I'm just hoping that some day someone will fathom his mind.

'I've no idea what caused him to do these things. It is a hundred per cent certain that there was a side to his character that no one understood. Not even his wife, who was his constant companion. She doesn't understand it. Only he can answer how he lived with himself. I would imagine that it's a great relief to him to be caught. I have examined my own conduct and I can't think at all that it had anything to do with his home life. His home life was as normal as anyone else's.'

Mr Sutcliffe said that when he was first seen by the

police he had told them that he thought an incident a few years earlier when he left home for a few weeks (involving another woman, Mrs Wendy Broughton) could have affected Peter. At about the same time he had started to attack and kill women. 'But now that I know he actually began these attacks as long as 11 years ago, the first chance I get I'm going to retract that statement to the police because I know it no longer has any bearing on the case. I'd no idea that Peter spent a lot of time in the red-light areas of Leeds and Bradford. I just can't understand why he should want to go with prostitutes. Sonia didn't know a thing, she didn't have a clue. Peter never discussed any sexual problems with me. As far as I'm aware his and Sonia's relationship was perfectly normal.

'I don't blame myself, I don't blame my wife, I don't blame the family at all. This is something which is going to have to be sorted out by the medical profession, and we shall just have to accept their findings, whatever they may be. It has been quite hectic since the arrest but there are times I like to be alone so that I can cry myself to sleep at nights. It's a relief, it's something you do just to get your tensions out of yourself, otherwise you finish up not sleeping. It's made me feel extremely old for the first time in my life.'

Sutcliffe's younger brother, 30-year-old Michael, a former amateur boxer with 46 undefeated fights to his credit, who says he has been convicted three times for grievous bodily harm against policemen, candidly admits that he was signed up by a national newspaper, the *Daily Star*. But he was not loath to discuss his brother. 'As far as our family is concerned Peter is faultless, ten times better than me. I would swop places with him, you know. Peter's been so good all his life. He has been so good to everybody who has met him, apart from his victims.'

Mr David Mellor, M.P. for Wandsworth and Putney, stood up in the House of Commons and proclaimed: 'Many MPs of all shades of opinion find the well-publicized junketing which went on in Yorkshire utterly distasteful. Will the Attorney General consult the Home Secretary with a view to setting out guidelines for chief constables on what should be done in future cases?'

The Sutcliffe case had come a long way since the arrest on that icy night in Sheffield less than two weeks previously. The case had reached the Mother of Parliaments and its counterpart in print, the letters columns of *The Times,* virtually from the moment that the police and press had cast aside their customary caution after an arrest and impending charge, and publicized everything about Peter Sutcliffe that they dared, short of stating that he was the Ripper. Although neither side had too many doubts about that, the possibility that the police had arrested the wrong man had to be respected.

Unfortunately, little about contempt of court is available for reference in the legal textbooks. For the most part, editors have to interpret the traditions for themselves. Usually they take the safest and most tight-lipped course; in the case of Peter Sutcliffe, they seemed to feel there was sufficient public interest for it to be valid for them to inform the world that henceforth the streets of the North of England were – or might be – free of the Ripper.

Stories appeared on the Monday morning, ranging from the brave and direct to the obscure. The *Yorkshire Post* named Sutcliffe and published a striking night-time flash photograph by Jack Tordoff of the house in Garden Lane. The *Daily Express* named Sutcliffe as well. Other newspapers were more guarded, but even *The Times,* which thundered on the Wednesday in its leader against the general press reporting, linked the arrest of the unnamed man in Sheffield with the story of the police jubilation over the arrest. The *Guardian,* which also later criticized its less illustrious colleagues, ran photographs of the 13 suspected Ripper victims across the top of its front-page story.

One retired High Court judge made the observation that no paper had actually said 'Peter Sutcliffe is the Yorkshire Ripper' so no real contempt had been committed. Mr Ludovic Kennedy, the eminent writer and broadcaster, stated in a letter to *The Times*: 'I very much doubt whether the reports of the Sutcliffe case that have appeared in the press and television will in any way influence any jury that may in future be empanelled to hear a case against him. Juries are well able to differentiate between what they hear in court and what they may have heard or read in the media months beforehand.'

He went on to point out that, surely, the frequently outrageous statements made in court by prosecuting barristers about crimes that would shortly be explained to the jury, and which are never subsequently proven, are far more harmful to the cause of justice than mere press stories.

The argument was kept alive in *The Times*'s letters column for several days, as well as in Parliament, where the Attorney General, the political overlord of the legal system who later led the prosecution at the Old Bailey, was repeatedly quizzed about the 'Sutcliffe Case' and the 'Yorkshire Murder Case'. Such a high-level debate had the effect of keeping Sutcliffe's name linked with the Ripper case in the minds of those people who read *The Times* and Hansard. After the initial burst of activity in the more popular papers, Sutcliffe's name was not to be seen except in the most rigorously formal framework.

The argument over contempt in the Sutcliffe case was not resolved before the trial. Both the Attorney General's and the Press Council's final decisions on prosecutions or admonitions of editors were still pending. The journalists' trade paper, *UK Press Gazette,* was the strongest critic of its own profession's 'squalid display of unprofessional licence'.

But for all the ins and outs of the case it would surely take a pedant to argue that the press, or for that matter the West Yorkshire Police, did any harm to the public interest, or to Sutcliffe's, by saying or doing what they did in those few heady hours. Not only had it never been suggested that Sutcliffe was the Ripper, but the few things that were published about him, other than in the more scandalous foreign papers which were all banned in Britain for that week, were complimentary in the extreme. The gravest libel made against the man who lived at number six, Garden Lane, was that in some neighbours' eyes he was a bit odd.

When David Mellor referred to junketing in Yorkshire, he was presumably referring chiefly to the police conduct of the Dewsbury press conference, which the magazine of the Police Federation, *Police,* defended a month after the arrest, saying the alternative to such a conference 'would have been equally, perhaps worse, damaging speculation and rumour'.

Some of the real junketing that went on in the days following the arrest, when the press moved into Bradford in force, may shock the fainthearted. It would surprise members of the public who believe that newspapers make stories up to discover the extent to which journalists will go to obtain a piece of truth. The truth may be a banality, it may be boring, predictable, implausible, or even made up by the source that issued it, but if it is spoken, and faithfully taken down in shorthand, it is, as far as a newspaper is concerned, the truth, even if tomorrow further truth is obtained to prove that yesterday's truth was a falsehood, printed in good faith. In the case of Peter Sutcliffe, any truth, any fact from an apparently reliable source, was a valuable gem. Its financial value would vary – from a few pounds for a little fact, to hundreds of thousands offered to members of Sutcliffe's family to tell what they believed to be the truth about him.

In pubs in Bingley, images of Sutcliffe were changing hands for hundreds and, it was said, thousands of pounds. An enterprising freelance photographer found a relative of Sutcliffe's well away from Bradford and bought a series of wedding pictures which were soon to be seen in publications all over the world. An even more enterprising freelance copied one of those wedding pictures from a German magazine, and sold his print to a news agency for £200. Photographs of the colour picture hanging in the Clarks' office soon found their way round the world.

News agencies and newspapers fell out after years of co-operation in the rush for exclusive stories and interviews. Trevor Birdsall was kept in a series of hotels by a Sunday popular anxious to keep him away from their rivals; even the police had to follow him to a Blackpool hotel to arrange for a witness statement to be taken. John Sutcliffe was driven away from his maisonette late on Monday afternoon by the *Daily Mail,* hotly pursued by the *Yorkshire Post* and the local radio station in Bradford; he was taken to a country hotel and interviewed almost dry of facts about Peter.

The foreign press were as keen as the British to go all out for the Sutcliffe story, and had the benefit of no restraints imposed on when, or indeed what, they published. Some foreign reporters clung assiduously to their British journalist contacts and produced laudable accounts of the story. Others came ill-equipped, and did little more than translate what had appeared locally into their own language. Presumably their stories were fresh and interesting over breakfast in Yokohama and Caracas, even if they lacked a great deal of truth. Perhaps the team most ill-equipped for local conditions were the Brazilian television crew who arrived in Leeds. Totally unaware of the strictness of English law, they asked the *Yorkshire Post* if arrangements could be made for them to film in Dewsbury Magistrates' Court when Sutcliffe next appeared.

Sutcliffe's relatives were also victims of his actions in the sense that anyone who cared about him was ultimately to suffer. And certainly the list of sufferers cannot, and does not, end with the names and faces which have become so sadly familiar since 1975. Twenty-five children were left motherless, husbands became widowers, and parents will grieve for the rest of their days.

George Oldfield, Ronald Gregory, Jim Hobson, Dick Holland, Peter Gilrain and others, the anonymous officers the public never hear of, have had their share of heartache and disruption since 1975. Some police marriages have faltered, there have been breakdowns, and even criminal proceedings have been blamed on the Ripper inquiry.

Few people knew that Det. Chief Supt. Dennis Hoban was a diabetic and suffered from asthma, and that two years before he died, while investigating the death of Wilma McCann, he suddenly went blind in one eye. His widow, Mrs Betty Hoban, who lives in Headingley, Leeds, said she tried to persuade her husband to resign when he had completed 30 years' service. But she knew it was useless, and that the weeks without time off, the often unclaimed annual holiday entitlement, would continue. She believes that, ultimately, the strain of the Yorkshire

Ripper inquiry claimed him as a victim also. 'I feel bitter sometimes, I feel as though he should never have got married, because his job meant so much to him. I feel as though, if he hadn't put so much into his work, he might not have died. During the last few years, from the time of the Wilma McCann murder in 1975, until he died in 1978, there was a lot of stress. He had seven major murders to deal with, including the two Ripper killings. The other five were cleared up. He never liked to have any outstanding, and I don't know if that was worrying him.' She is proud of her husband's achievements, but sad about the price he paid.

And then there are the Terence Hawkshaws. Mr Hawkshaw was one of the numerous men who became firm Ripper suspects during the course of the inquiry. A bachelor in his mid-thirties, living with his mother in the village of Drighlington, in the middle of the Ripper triangle of Leeds, Bradford and Huddersfield, he was a prime suspect in 1977. He drove a taxi, a white Ford Cortina with a black roof, and the police started questioning him at all hours of the day after Tina Atkinson's death in April 1977. Maureen Long's attacker drove a white Ford with a black roof three months later, and the police were back at Mr Hawkshaw's door. When Helen Rykta became the Ripper's seventh victim in Huddersfield, the following January, police knocked on his door at 7 a.m. 'They knocked me up and started questioning me. They also took away my clothes. All I had was what I stood up in. I was once taken to the police station at Wakefield and they gave me blood tests and took bits of hair. There were continuous questions; it was a nightmare for me and my mother. When George Oldfield sits behind his desk and tells you he thinks you are the Ripper, it turns your stomach over.'

The nightmare has almost faded for Mr Hawkshaw. But not for so many others – the lovers, the brothers, the mothers. Innocent people leading innocent lives until the Ripper's hammer fell. And one wife, the woman whose fateful decision to allow the dark-eyed young man to sit with her in the pub disco was to produce such unimaginable distress 14 years later. A victim in every sense of the word.

CHAPTER 9

Retrospective

When the Yorkshire Ripper's existence was firmly fixed in the public consciousness – the legend as well as the facts they were allowed by the increasingly harassed police – three issues were uppermost in most minds. Who was the most infamous killer since the original Ripper? Why did he do what he did? And why did it take the police so long to catch him? The latter question may never be answered fully and certainly begs a supplementary query – if there are lessons to be learned, will they be learned?

By chance West Yorkshire was involved within a decade in the two biggest and most complex multiple 'murder' hunts British police had ever been taxed with. The Black Panther, Donald Neilson, had more than his Bradford base in common with Peter Sutcliffe. Despite enormous joint police operations (and in Neilson's case Scotland Yard were called in eventually to run the show) they were both caught almost by accident.

Neilson was picked up by two 'Panda' car officers for routine questioning when he was spotted walking up and down outside a sub-post office in the Midlands. In the car he produced a sawn-off shotgun and was arrested only after a desperate and violent struggle. It was only when razor blades and other implements were found concealed in his clothing that suspicions began to grow that he was more than just another would-be burglar. Might the Yorkshire Ripper have still been a shadowy figure taking lives at random if he also had not made a mistake, fixing false number-plates to his car that night in Sheffield?

It is vitally important that the police's failure to catch their man other than with a large helping of luck should propel them to ask themselves some crucial questions – was it an institutional failure, a breakdown in the actual methods police employ to tackle major crime, or was it a personal failure?

In the 1970s we moved into the area of the abnormal where day-to-day crime was concerned. To cope with terrorism the nationwide anti-terrorist 'special branch detection system' was set up; similarly, there is now a central drugs intelligence system. It appears to be acknowledged that there are specific areas, where broad national interests are involved, where the police force as an institution, probably at the bidding of politicians and civil servants, is prepared to adapt itself to cope with a situation which is unusual. Given the similarity between the Ripper and the Black Panther cases, perhaps the most important question requiring an answer is whether, as an institution, the Police Force ever really takes on board the lessons of the past.

Is its inherent structure such that provincial forces are not equipped to tackle the super-criminal? The similarity with the Black Panther case leads one to believe that by themselves the police, as an institution, prefer to have faith in their general infallibility, and are only prepared to accept that it is the men who make up the institution who display signs of weakness, rather than the institution itself.

Chesterton's aphorism about society being at the mercy of a killer without motive was never more fairly quoted. But is Britain ready to accept the challenge of asking itself whether a National Police Force should be instituted? The West Yorkshire Police could certainly say with some justification that they had to go through the motions of conducting a whole series of separate murder investigations simply because experience had shown them that the real minutiae might throw up the vital clue. Yet there were differences of opinion with, for example, the Lancashire Force over the Joan Harrison case, and Northumbria over the tape and letters.

An overwhelming number of killings are domestic affairs, quickly solved. There are relatively few exceptionally difficult murders, but what special training is there to deal with the abnormal, stubborn crime? Certainly, one hopes, the lessons provided by previous cases, but with the Ripper case there were peculiar and original problems. The police were quite often faced with new difficulties and were unable to benefit from their own or anyone else's experience. On the face of it the clues were plentiful – rare blood group B (sic), the gap in the teeth (sic), tyre tracks, a range of possible vehicles fitting those tracks, ideas as to the various types of weapons used, forensic evidence relating to fine metal particles left behind in some of the wounds, forensic evidence suggesting an engineering connection (traces of some form of milling oil), wellington boot prints, and a description of the attacker given by one or more of the assault victims. These appear to have been the substantive pieces of evidence, but there were other factors relating to the method of attack and, perhaps more importantly, the pattern of Sutcliffe's concealment of his victims. Yet the virtually total reliance on the evidence of the tape and letters perhaps demonstrates most graphically just how little hard or conclusive evidence the police had to work with.

Certainly the senior officers directed themselves to the obvious approaches: the attempts to find the origin of the Jordan £5 note; the red-light surveillance exercises; the search for the man with the Wearside accent – each in its way innovative, but each also fraught with as then unforeseen dangers, the most common being the sheer quantity of leads thrown up: almost 8,000 people who could have received the £5 note in his or her wage packet; five million car numbers producing 21,000 car owners; and the Geordie operation, gigantic by any standards. Yet the latter would have to have been conducted even if there were only a 50 per cent chance that the letters were genuine. Eighteen months' surveillance in red-light districts produced enormous technical difficulties. A whole new programme had to be designed because the language used on the Police National Computer was totally different from that used on the D.V.L.C. computer at Swansea. Checking up on thousands and thousands of drivers proved almost physically impossible. It defeated the police in the end because the computer was throwing up more names and vehicles than they could cope with. And yet Sutcliffe's number turned up at least 50 times, and for different reasons he was seen a number of times by the police before he was arrested.

So were the criteria for eliminating suspects tight enough? The answer must be no. Normally the police would not accept alibi evidence from people who would lie for a suspect; but in the Ripper case the numbers being interviewed were so vast, the time-lag for alibi dates so wide, they had no option other than to accept alibi evidence. If Mrs 'X' said her husband didn't go out on Saturday night could they have realistically challenged what she said? The method of confronting suspects was low-key. Senior officers seemed to be chilled at the prospect of public indignation should the police be seen to be acting too aggressively towards innocent people. There have also been suggestions that when the police accepted handwriting as being a key eliminator, not all examples of handwriting were actually witnessed by an officer in front of a suspect. There was room for deceit. The possibility existed that someone else could have provided handwriting examples. Now, of course, the whole Geordie connection might be regarded as an irrelevance, but it is a fact that police circulars specifically instructed: ' . . . wherever possible to eliminate many persons through enquiries at their present or former place of employment and for samples of cursive handwriting to be obtained.'

Cases of wives writing application forms for jobs, driving licence forms, tax forms and sick notes were manifold. The police response is merely that in this way they could eliminate people easily and without much fuss.

The central thrust of the inquiry might be said to have been passive rather than aggressive – don't be wrong, don't cause waves. To this end the deliberate policy of senior officers was geared to minimum disclosure of information. Examples abounded. Why had the letters still not been published in full at the time of the arrest? Why were the police going to release a censored version of the tape recording before a leak forced their hand? Why were details of boot size held back, and especially the fact that one right boot print showed heavy wearing and twisting in the centre of the sole – possibly attributable to the wearer continually pressing some sort of pedal with his right foot? Sutcliffe's boss, Tom Clark, makes the point that the police who regularly visited his works never really took him into their confidence or gave him the opportunity or the inclination to keep a particular eye on Sutcliffe or any of the other drivers who were questioned.

The letters and the tape had to be given serious consideration – no one would claim otherwise – but should they have dictated the way the inquiry was run in its later stages? Jack Windsor Lewis had noted his doubts about the validity of the tape, hypothesizing that the voice was so distinct that the maker of it, if he lived in West Yorkshire, would be identified almost immediately. If he lived in Castletown, Sunderland, he could not have been the Ripper because he would have been seen and have had a legitimate alibi. Was the advice of the experts only listened to when it fitted in with pre-conceived ideas? 'Experts', of course, tend to see things from their own often narrow standpoint, a luxury rarely afforded investigating police officers.

The 'hoax' letters and tape inexorably tied in the Harrison killing with the Ripper inquiry, east of the Pennines at least, yet concealed the ultimate ironies for the police. Semen traces indicated rare blood group B, as did saliva tests on the third envelope. And indeed Sutcliffe is group B, but a non-secretor. This 'clue' could have trapped him, yet he could not have ejaculated the semen traced in Joan Harrison, nor licked the envelope sent to George Oldfield. Dr Patrick Lincoln, of London University's medical school, an international expert on blood-group typing, states that confusion between a secretor and a non-secretor of any blood group is impossible.

While George Oldfield and Ronald Gregory can now be seen to have been wrong in deciding that the Wearside tape and letter were from the Yorkshire Ripper, it was certainly not the wrong decision at the time. On balance, the references in the letters to Harrison and Millward, the threats to kill again in either Bradford or Liverpool, the traces of oil, made their conclusion irresistible. What must be questioned is the way those conclusions were transmitted to the public; for once the media are not such an easy or convenient target for the police. The Geordie connection was in June 1979 solidly established in the public's mind because the police dictated that it should be.

The Yorkshire Ripper was a Geordie and spoke with a most distinctive accent. There seemed no room for manoeuvre then, and as far as the public, including Sutcliffe's friends and workmates, were concerned, nor was there 18 months later just before his arrest. Apart from Trevor Birdsall, of course. Yet well before then, before the Jacqueline Hill killing, it was apparent that the police were concerned about their prognosis. They would not have been surprised to find that five of the attacks – three killings and two assaults – were not the Ripper's work. Soon after the Hill death George Oldfield said that the biggest question mark of all concerned Joan Harrison, and conceded that his only chance of succeeding lay in his adversary, perhaps through increasing boldness, or even desperation, giving himself away. Prophetic words indeed.

But by then George Oldfield had been, once again, relieved of the day-to-day control of the inquiry. Jim Hobson had been given the task of coping not only with the biggest case any British detective had had to face, but also the so-called Super Squad of outside advisers produced by the Chief Constable to stave off mounting criticism. Before his controversial replacement, Oldfield had referred once again to his struggle with the killer. 'It's a personal thing between him and me,' he told the *Sunday Times*. A familiar quote. Oldfield's sentiments were understandable, particularly at the time the apparent message from the Ripper was received on tape. The central question was whether any force, even one as big as West Yorkshire's, could have captured such a man as the Yorkshire Ripper by detective methods alone.

Was it within the capacity of the team to take the offensive? Could they have tried a stake-out operation with a murder victim and sought press co-operation to keep the whole thing quiet? The body could easily have been removed to protect the sensibilities of relatives. There came a time after Yvonne Pearson's death when this suggestion was put forward. Police reaction was that the press would not co-operate, a predictable and perhaps even wise dismissal; yet as a strategy it did not seem to have been given serious consideration. It works in kidnapping cases, so why not with the Ripper? It is far from being the trivial point it might seem and important when examining how the police inquiry operated. An early conclusion of the Super Squad after it was formed was that the track had been far too narrow. Why did it take until the Hill death before Ronald Gregory moved to forestall growing public opposition, and increasing frustration of course, to the way the inquiry was progressing? There was a general feeling that the move was mainly cosmetic. Such a team could have been at work months, if not two years, before Jacqueline Hill's murder. They would have had no loyalties, and could therefore have examined everything with a completely fresh mind. They would have taken no decisions, thus they would have had no past actions to defend. In the Chief Constable's own words, their task when they were eventually appointed was to look 'critically at police action and to advise'.

We now know that the catalogue of possible Ripper crimes was escalating during the period between the Barbara Leach and Jacqueline Hill killings. We know that during this time the press and consequently the public were starved of information. The Ripper case drifted to the further reaches of the public's mind when it should have been in the forefront. To do this without making the public bored with the whole thing required considerable skill and imagination, yet little was forthcoming. The policy agreed was a publicity clamp-down instead of a blitz. The rationale seemed to be that this might force the Ripper into writing again. But the belief that the Ripper and the writer of the letters was the same man was increasingly being challenged.

Yet, objectively, the overall failure to capture the Ripper sooner was perhaps understandable precisely because of what we know of the way institutions are unable to be critical of themselves. It is not that fact, however, which makes particular criticisms all the more valid where some crucial aspects of the Ripper case are concerned. The £5 note exercise was imaginative and innovative and took the police to the Yorkshire Ripper. Yet it was a sad failure because they then did not recognize their man. Similarly with the red-light checks, and even the engineering connection. Several times the Yorkshire Ripper was interviewed by the police but not isolated. But so were many others seen who at least matched the criteria as well as Sutcliffe.

And yet how many were blood group B, had a gap in their upper front teeth, were regularly recorded in three separate red-light areas, startlingly matched at least one of the photofit pictures, were the right size boot, worked in engineering, and were long-distance lorry drivers? And how many were openly nicknamed the 'Ripper' by their bosses and colleagues?

Thomas Clark, one of those bosses, is objective enough to qualify those remarks by pointing out the benefits of the luxury of hindsight. More than one police officer has expressed the view that the great British public, after the ceremony and symbolism of the Old Bailey, the words and the rationalization, and the sentence – the ultimate gesture of society's fight with the enemy that was Peter Sutcliffe – would be satisfied.

But what about Tom and Mary Priestley, the grandparents of victim number 16, and the stilltranquilized Irene MacDonald, mother of victim number nine? Or an ageing mother called Kathleen Walls, who still clings forlornly to the hope that the neighbours don't know her daughter was victim number 18 of the man they called the Yorkshire Ripper? After all this, surely complacency will not be the epitaph for their loved ones.

EPILOGUE

Better Let Him Sleep?

Until Wednesday 29 April 1981, the principals in the Yorkshire Ripper case seemed agreed. Peter William Sutcliffe was ill, mentally ill, suffering from the relatively rare but clearly definable paranoid schizophrenia; definable but, as yet, incurable, a case for lifelong incarceration.

There was one notable exception. The son of a former deputy chief constable of East Suffolk, Mr Justice Boreham, the judge in No. 1 Court at the Old Bailey, was unhappy with the *fait accompli* that had been presented to him.

The most infamous killer of the century was about to be despatched, just 16 weeks after being caught; five years and six months of immeasurable, harrowing grief, of near-stupefying frustration on the part of both police and public, and it was all to be settled in two, maybe three days.

But the judge recognized the flaws in such an arrangement. Without hesitation he sidestepped all pomp and ceremony and informed a surprised Sir Michael Havers of his decision. It had been Havers, the Attorney General, who had applied to transfer the case to the world's most famous criminal court.

The psychiatrists, both for the defence and the Crown, might have been agreed on their separate diagnoses, but their conclusions were based only on what Sutcliffe himself had told them. What if he were lying? He had been overheard telling his wife during a prison visit that he might only serve 10 years – 10 years instead of 30 – if he could convince people he was mad. Was he simply trying to put his wife at ease? Or was the Yorkshire Ripper, sitting impassively in the dock with his black beard and piercing black eyes, keeping up an evil charade to the end? The queue for the public seats had formed the night before, and 34 citizens perched high in the gallery, staring fiercely at the almost immobile Sutcliffe.

Mr Justice Boreham was adamant. Everyone would return five days later and 12 members of the public would decide whether the Yorkshire Ripper was mad, or guilty of murder. The Americans and some of the Europeans among the press corps could not understand it. If Sutcliffe had admitted killing 13 women, and attempting to murder seven others, what was all the fuss about? But British justice was to be seen to be done. British psychiatry would also be on trial. Peter William Sutcliffe had touched a lot of lives since the start of his strange odyssey, and he had not yet finished.

As cemeteries go, Bingley's is in a prime position, rising steeply at the Catholic end, among the little-changing panorama of that part of Airedale: the Bradford—Keighley road ribboning along the bottom of the valley, the river nearby, and in the distance, the fringes of the moors, the heather and the bracken, with the much-sung-about Ilkley moor beyond. This was the view that must have greeted Peter Sutcliffe that afternoon in 1967, the day he heard the voice of God as he was digging a grave, followed it to the top of the hill, and heard it again, echoing and mumbling, seemingly coming from a cross-shaped headstone bearing words in Polish, words like JEGO and WEHBY and ECHO, words that Sutcliffe regarded as significant, words that told him that this was the voice of Jesus and, as it was to do for the next 14 years, ordering him to kill prostitutes, and even women who seemed to look like prostitutes.

As the years of the inquiry passed, with the death toll

creeping remorselessly upwards and seemingly no end in sight to the awful torment, three questions had been uppermost in people's minds. Firstly, who was the Yorkshire Ripper? A nondescript Bradford lorry driver seemed to many an anti-climax, although his very ordinariness had obviously contributed greatly to the delay in his detection. Secondly, why hadn't the police caught him sooner? And finally, the most tantalising riddle of all: why? Why crack open women's skulls like eggshells, why then violate their bodies so grotesquely? The toll was thirteen women dead and seven more who could have been dead, at least one of the survivors wishing her life had been ended by the man who was the Yorkshire Ripper.

But by the end of the day on Tuesday 5 May the world knew the answer, knew about the voice of God, the mission to kill prostitutes, the experience in the graveyard when the Yorkshire Ripper was only 20, how he had looked across the Aire Valley, feeling exultant and privileged that God had chosen him. The view towards the distant moors was immense, the universe so large, the people so insignificant. Yet Peter William Sutcliffe was different, he had been chosen to carry out the divine mission. But was it true?

Six men and six women at the Old Bailey took six hours to decide it was after listening for 14 days to the evidence in what had been a unique murder 'trial'. The debate, like so many before in the historic court, was intense. But the argument was not whether Peter Sutcliffe had killed the 13 unfortunate women (the work of detectives O'Boyle, Boyle and Smith at Dewsbury over that amazing first weekend of the year had resolved that aspect of the case); it revolved solely around his state of mind. On 29 April everyone but Mr Justice Boreham had seemed sure. The Attorney General and Mr James Chadwin, QC, down from Newcastle to represent Sutcliffe, had been of the same opinion, reassured, no doubt, by the unanimous opinions of the psychiatrists who had probed the mind of the Yorkshire Ripper.

Yet six days later the Attorney General was to take more than four hours to outline the life and times of Peter William Sutcliffe, this time making it clear that the Crown thought the voice in the graveyard, the divine mission, was a lie; a clever attempt by the Yorkshire Ripper finally to come out on top in his bizarre struggle with society. The psychiatrists whom the prosecution had seemed so happy to believe, even those engaged by the Crown, were now to be ruthlessly cross-examined. With the often inspired help of Yorkshire-based Mr Harry Ognall, QC, the Attorney General and the Crown were to give the subjective science of psychiatry as thorough an examination as it is ever likely to experience in a British court; a trial within a trial, which psychiatry lost.

But long before the verdict, the litany of death, with the names that had become so familiar, was to take on a new perspective, from Anna Rogulskyj and Olive Smelt, two of the survivors who were to witness parts of the trial, through to Jacqueline Hill, victim number 20, the last woman to be fatally felled by one of Sutcliffe's numerous ball-pein hammers. Through his original confession to the police at Dewsbury, his subsequent statements to the police, and the numerous meetings with psychiatrists, the Yorkshire Ripper was to present a chilling insight into the mind and thoughts of a mass-killer. But before his dramatic statement was to come another equally extraordinary testimony: that of Trevor Birdsall, the friend who had been with Sutcliffe on the night of what became known in Court as the rock-in-the-sock attack in 1969, and again, in 1975, when they had been drinking in Halifax and Sutcliffe had left him in the car while he broke the skull of Olive Smelt—the friend who eventually contacted the police, by which time however 13 women were dead and the Yorkshire Ripper was only a few weeks away from being caught by other means.

Mr Birdsall, who had to sit on a chair while giving evidence, and who sipped constantly from a glass of water, said he had suspected Sutcliffe of attacking Mrs Smelt after reading about the incident in the local evening newspaper the following day. He hadn't contacted the police and any suspicions he may have harboured as the Yorkshire Ripper affair gained momentum were finally allayed by the Geordie tape in 1979. Mr Birdsall said he realized then that Peter Sutcliffe could not be the Yorkshire Ripper.

The trial was unusual in many ways, not least for the burden that lay upon the defence to prove that Sutcliffe was not guilty of murder, due to his claimed diminished responsibility. He had admitted taking the lives of the 13 dead women, and the Crown's role became almost secondary. Yet in less than a week the Crown had moved from accepting the defence explanation (of paranoid schizophrenia and the resulting voice of God) to an entirely different proposition.

As well as agreeing on the diagnosis of schizophrenia, the three eminent forensic psychiatrists – Dr Hugo Milne, of Bradford; Dr Malcolm McCulloch, of Liverpool; and Dr Terence Kay, of Leeds (originally engaged by the prosecution, but called by the defence) – all also said in evidence that if they were wrong about the paranoid schizophrenia then there was only one likely alternative explanation. The Yorkshire Ripper was a sadist, a man who enjoyed killing women, a cold-blooded murderer, evil rather than mad.

By the end of the trial the Crown were adamant that there had been evidence of sexual sadism in at least six of the attacks, ranging from a slash wound just above the buttocks of Olive Smelt, through Sutcliffe's admitted sexual intercourse with Helen Rytka as she lay dying, to the assault on Josephine Whitaker with a screwdriver. Mr Ognall brought gasps from the packed public gallery when he held up the rusty, 10-inch-long Phillip's screwdriver, sharpened to a wicked point, with which Sutcliffe had stabbed the luckless young clerk 28 times as she walked home from her grandmother's house that April night in 1979. The pathologist's report had shown that on three occasions her attacker had carefully inserted the weapon into her vagina, causing almost no external injury, although her uterus had been punctured. During a fierce cross-examination Mr Ognall took Dr Milne to task about his assertion that there had been no underlying sexual motivation to the killer's acts. The latter did not agree with Mr Ognall's claim that the injuries to Josephine Whitaker's vagina displayed 'the most fiendish cruelty most deliberately done for sexual satisfaction'. But Dr Milne did concede that his original report and diagnosis had been made without studying the depositions and other evidence, including the details of the injuries, and including what Sutcliffe had told the police in his original statement after the arrest, painstakingly dictated over two days to detectives Boyle and Smith at Dewsbury; a statement which had not once mentioned the graveyard incident, voices from God or the divine mission.

Like Dr Milne and Dr Kay, Dr Malcolm McCulloch, medical director of the Park Lane Special Hospital at Liverpool, stuck rigidly to his diagnosis of paranoid schizophrenia. He was so sure about his diagnosis, he revealed that he had reached his conclusion just half an hour after first meeting Sutcliffe in March. But when he told Mr Ognall that he had not seen or considered the Crown evidence until 28 April, the day before the original hearing was due to start, he was accused by the QC of showing 'remarkable calm and apparent indifference'. However, Dr McCulloch was clear in his view: Sutcliffe had fulfilled four of the classic criteria —

the Schneider first-rank symptoms, as they are known in Britain – and was undoubtedly, in his view, a paranoid schizophrenic. He had detected: 1. Bodily hallucinations, sensations of being touched; Sutcliffe had talked of a hand gripping his heart. 2. Influence of thought – either that the subject's thoughts are influenced, or that he can read the thoughts of others. 3. Delusional perception – enforced ideas which are delusions, particularly relevant in Sutcliffe's case, thought 'the doctor. 4. Passivity, where a person believes his actions to be controlled by others (God in the case of Sutcliffe). He, like the other psychiatrists, did not think that Sutcliffe was simulating schizophrenia. Dr Milne even went so far as to say that, if Sutcliffe was simulating, either he was a poor psychiatrist or Sutcliffe was a good actor.

Yet Sutcliffe had had one personal experience of schizophrenia, when his wife suffered a breakdown while studying in London in 1972. Ironically, she had been treated by Dr Milne at his Bradford clinic. She had talked of being the second Christ and had said she had felt pain in the palms of her hands from the Cross. The Crown had wondered if what they regarded as Sutcliffe's lie about the voice of God had been born out of his observations of his wife's experience.

Mrs Sutcliffe had arrived at the Old Bailey for the start of the trial with her mother and was to sit impassively through the prosecution's presentation of its case. During the trial she was said by her husband to be a nag, and obsessive about cleanliness. She also became the centre of a row about cheque-book journalism, triggered off by Jacqueline Hill's mother writing to the Queen and receiving support for her campaign to prevent relatives of the Yorkshire Ripper benefitting financially from his deeds by selling their stories.

But Mrs Sutcliffe was hurriedly taken from the court on the morning of Monday 11 May, the day the defence opened its case. The implication was that she might be called as a witness, and excitement in the public gallery that morning mounted after Mr James Chadwin, QC, defending, asked for a short adjournment. In fact Peter William Sutcliffe was to be the first defence witness. The Yorkshire Ripper had insisted he be called.

Twenty strides and the lean, bearded figure, with his sallow complexion and alert eyes, was in the witness box. For almost two days he was to relate his story in a high, almost unmistakable Bradford voice. Sutcliffe is of high average intelligence (IQ 110), and it shows. He is calm and articulate and the care he takes in his choice of words is quite immaculate.

Sutcliffe recalled without faltering the voice in the cemetery, the divine mission, the protection of God. Even when cross-examined by the Attorney General he was sure of himself, ready with the same response to Sir Michael's most telling thrusts. God had told him to do what on the face of it appeared to be the illogical. He even said that God had prevented the police from catching him; he had been interviewed so many times, he claimed, he had lost count. Occasionally his eyes, unafraid and clear, raked the court, almost challengingly, a glimpse perhaps of the demons that lay beneath the unruffled exterior.

Peter Sutcliffe did not think he was mad. Like the Crown, he thought the doctors had got it wrong. But surely there was something wrong with him? The Yorkshire Ripper stood where the likes of Crippen had gone before and with startling coolness described and debated a calumny of deeds more awful than even that famous place had witnessed. Surely we were observing the distillation of evil. And then he was gone, back to his straight-backed chair, screwed to the floor of the dock.

He rose from that chair for the last time at 4.28 p.m. on Friday 22 May 1981. He had touched it only fleetingly, taking one step back from the front of the dock and lowering himself onto it, only for it to be pulled back instantly by the prison officers at his side.

Six minutes earlier he had been brought from the cells below and had stood rigidly in the dock while the jury foreman, with his bushy ginger beard, delivered their verdict on the Yorkshire Ripper. Thirteen times he was asked, and thirteen times he spoke those simple but dramatic words—'Guilty to murder'. It had taken the six men and six women almost six hours, but finally, by a majority of ten to two on each count, they were agreed.

Peter William Sutcliffe was not mad. He was evil, a sadistic murderer who had taken the lives of 13 north-of-England women not because he heard God telling him to, but to feed a grotesque sexual urge. They thought he was a liar and had fooled the psychiatrists into thinking he was crazy in a last desperate attempt to secure some sort of relative comfort behind the bars of a prison hospital unit, rather than in the bleak cell he would otherwise face.

But Peter Sutcliffe had not slumped back on the chair at 4.28 p.m. numbed with shock. He had simply presumed the end of the delivery of the jury's verdict was the signal for him to take up the position he had occupied for three amazing weeks.

Six minutes it had taken the clerk of the Court and the jury foreman to move slowly and with dignity through the 13 charges which encapsulated five years of the most awful, desperate pain and fear for so many women, parents, relatives, friends and children in Yorkshire and Lancashire. As the verdicts were announced in the absolute quiet of the packed Court, the mother of Barbara Leach, victim number 16, sat upright at the back of the room, her cheeks wet with tears. The mother of Jacqueline Hill, victim number 20, stared grimly at the floor.

But then he was gone. The Yorkshire Ripper, emotionless to the end, jailed for 30 years, in effect the rest of his life; life sentences for the seven charges of attempted murder.

Mr Justice Boreham said that Sutcliffe was a coward and a very dangerous man, but admitted he found it difficult to find the words to describe the brutality and gravity of the offences.

Sutcliffe himself perhaps provided his own epitaph in the last line of a poem he wrote, which the police found in the cab of his lorry after the arrest:

> In this truck is a man
> Whose latent genius if
> Unleashed would rock the
> Nation, whose dynamic energy
> Would overpower those
> Around him. Better let him sleep?

Index

Arangie, Kathleen, 45-6
Ashton, Laurie, 52-3, 165-6
Atkinson, Patricia (Tina), 73-6,
    90, 108, 132, 157
Attorney General, *see* Havers, Sir
    Michael

Bandara, Dr Upadhya, 187-8, 218
Barker, David, 105-6, 125
Barker, Ronald, 104-5, 125
Birdsall, Melissa, 125, 174-5
Birdsall, Trevor, 60, 61, 62, 63, 69,
    89, 125, 174-6, 194-5, 227,
    237, 244-245
Bisby, Anne, 89-90
Boldy, David, 175-6
Booth, Alan, 23, 24
Booth, Barbara, 23-4
Boreham, Mr Justice, 241, 242,
    243, 250
Boyle, Det. Insp. John, 207, 209,
    211, 212, 243, 246
Brookes, Det. Chief Supt.
    Wilfred, 37, 39
Broughton, Wendy, 51, 67, 223
Burton, Peter, 46-7

Chadwin, James, QC, 243, 248
Cheque-book journalism, 247
Clark, Tom, 71, 155, 173, 221,
    235, 239
Clark, William, 71, 155
Clarks (T. & W. H. Clark
    (Holdings) Ltd), 71, 99-100,
    118, 155, 157-8, 166-7, 172-3
Claxton, Marcella, 31-3, 37, 72
Conroy, Gloria, 195
Cooper, Joe, 180-1
Crawford-Brown, Det. Con.
    Jenny, 210, 213

Daily Express, 145, 224
Daily Mail, 218-19, 227
Daily Star, 223
Domaille, Det. Chief Supt. John,
    115

Douglas, Gerry, 159, 161-2
Douglas, Mary, 161, 162
Douglas, Theresa (Tessa), 118,
    159-61, 162, 168

Ellis, Stanley, 135-6, 137-8, 139,
    147-9
Emery, Billy, 49

Finley, Det. Supt. Alf, 193
Fitzgerald, Peter, 65-6

Garside, Mary, 92, 170-2
Garside, Tom, 92, 170-2
Gee, Prof. David, 19, 22, 35, 75-6,
    107, 127, 143, 193
Gilrain, Det. Chief Supt. Peter,
    143-4, 148, 149, 178, 183, 193
Gosden, Tony, 192
Gregory, Chief Constable
    Ronald, 17-18, 78, 115, 145,
    148, 149, 151, 153-4, 183, 204,
    214, 217, 236, 238
Guardian, 225

Hall, Denise, 200, 209
Harrison, Joan, 37-9, 70, 107, 122,
    131, 156, 212, 233, 236, 237
Havers, Sir Michael, 241, 243, 244,
    248
Hawkshaw, Terence, 229-30
Henderson, Robert, 75
Hill, Jacqueline, 58, 190-4, 237,
    238, 244, 247
Hill, John, 167
Hoban, Det. Chief Supt. Dennis,
    18-19, 22, 24-5, 31, 33-4, 71-2,
    228-9
Hobson, Det. Chief Supt. Jim, 34,
    35, 36-7, 39, 81, 87, 98, 139-
    40, 143, 148, 181, 185, 196,
    204, 211, 214, 237
Holland, Det. Supt. Dick, 127,
    128-9, 144-5, 209-10
Holland, Maureen, 57, 62
Holland, Robin, 62-3

Holt, Anna, 97
Housley, Lol, 197
Hussain, Amir, 192
Hydes, P.C. Robert, 7, 201-2, 203

Ibbitson, Jacqueline, 57, 58

Jackson, Emily, 25-31, 70-1, 76, 132, 157, 218
Jackson, Gary, 51
Jackson, Sydney, 26-9, 30, 90
Johnson, Asst. Chief Constable Brian, 135, 138-9
Johnson, Elizabeth, 64-5
Johnstone, John, 167-9
Jones, Carol, 163-5
Jones, Nella, 182
Jordan, Jean, 92-8, 103, 108, 157, 218, 233-4
Judge, Mary, 31

Kay, Dr Terence, 245, 246
Kelly, Susan, 173-4
Kennedy, Ludovic, 225
Kerr, Jean, 160-1
Kerr, Margaret, 64

Leach, Barbara, 140-3, 144, 151, 152, 177-8
Leach, David, 140, 141, 177-8
Leigh, Susan, 64-5
Letters, 'hoax', 107, 121-2, 129-30, 134, 136, 183-4, 196, 235-7
Long, Maureen, 82-4, 88, 91, 104, 149
Lyness, Jim, 177-80

McCann, Gerald, 19, 20, 21
McCann, Wilomena (Wilma), 18-23, 24, 31, 69, 70, 105, 218
McCulloch, Dr Malcolm, 245, 246
MacDonald, Jayne, 78, 80-1, 88, 105, 115, 167-8, 212-13, 218
McTavish, Douglas, 61
Mahoney, Michael, 47-8
Marwood, Ronald, 125

Meijling, Dono, 181, 182
Millward, Vera, 113-14, 115, 121, 131
Milne, Dr Hugo, 245, 246, 247
Moore, Marilyn, 100-3, 114, 149

Neilson, Donald (Black Panther), 25-6, 231, 232
Neville, Commander Jim, 149, 151, 183
Newlands, Betty, 23
Niemeta, Raili, 179-80

O'Boyle, Det. Sgt. Desmond, 206-7, 209, 210, 211, 216, 243
Ognall, Harry, QC, 244, 246
Old Bailey, 241, 243, 247
Oldfield, Asst. Chief Constable, George, 33, 76-8, 82, 83, 84-6, 87, 98, 112-13, 115, 119, 120, 121, 127-31, 132-4, 135, 138, 139, 183-4, 193, 196, 211-12, 213, 214, 217, 229, 236, 237

Pearson, Yvonne, 104, 107-10
Police National Computer, 152-3, 202, 234
Priestley, Tom and Mary, 123, 124, 239

Rahman, Nasim, 72, 90, 91
Rees, Merlyn, 84, 150
Reivers, Olivia, 199-202, 203, 209
Richardson, Irene, 34-6, 40, 71, 103, 114, 115
Ridgeway, Det. Chief Supt. Jack, 96, 97-9, 103-4, 113, 127, 155, 158
Ring, Sgt. Robert, 7, 201-2, 203, 208-9
Robinson, Eric, 52, 53-4
Rogulskyj, Anna Patricia, 9-13, 69, 178-9, 244
Rowntree, Mark Andrew, 24-5
Royle, Alan, 92-3, 96, 97, 98

Ruddick, Alan, 23-4
Rytka, Helen, 110-13, 218, 229
Rytka, Rita, 110-11, 112, 245

Sampson, Paul, 192
Shaw, Dr Stephen, 85-7, 117
Smelt, Olive, 13-16, 69, 179, 194, 244, 245
Smith, Paul, 142, 143
Smith, Det. Sgt. Peter, 210, 211, 213, 243 246
Sugden, Doreen, 55, 56-7
Sugden, Keith, 54-7, 125
Sutcliffe, John, 41-2, 43, 44, 45, 47, 48, 49-50, 60, 66-7, 218-23, 227
Sutcliffe, Kathleen, 42, 43, 47, 48, 66, 67, 117-18
Sutcliffe, Michael, 46, 49, 54, 118, 223-4
Sutcliffe, Peter William:
    arrest, 201; birth, 42; confession, 212, 244; court appearance, 215-17, 242; divine mission, 242, 243, 244, 246, 248; drunken driving charge, 169, 170, 180, 184, 190; and father, 43, 47; first job, 48; and girlfriends, 56, 58, 62, 66, 162, 163; as gravedigger, 50, 51-3, 54, 61; gets HGV licence, 68-9; hears voice of God, 242, 243, 245, 246, 247, 248; intelligence, 248; interviews with police, 100, 118, 152-3, 154, 155-6, 158, 235, 239; interviews with psychiatrists, 244; jobs, 63-4, 65, 68, 69-70, 71; John Sutcliffe on, 219-22; marriage, 66, 67-8; meets Sonia, 58, 60, 162-3; and mother, 43, 44, 46-7, 66, 118; and motorbikes, 47, 48-9; and paranoid schizophrenia, 241, 247; his poem, 250; questioned by police, 206-7, 210-12; at

school, 43, 44-6, 47; sense of humour, 52, 53, 54; sentence, 250; statement, 212-13, 217-18, 244, 246; testimony, 248; trial of, 241-8; trial verdict, 249; unpunctuality, 61, 65, 70

Sutcliffe, Sonia: at Old Bailey, 247; childhood, 59; education, 59, 61, 63; John Sutcliffe describes, 219-20, 223; marriage, 66-8; meets Sutcliffe, 58, 60, 162-3; miscarriages, 89, 169, 171, 175, 200, 220-1; neighbours' descriptions of, 169, 171, 172; nervous breakdown of, 64-5, 166, 247; prison visit, 241; qualifies as teacher, 91; and 6 Garden Lane, 90, 91-2, 118; Sutcliffe confesses to, 213; at Sutcliffe's first court appearance, 216
Sykes, Theresa, 188-90, 211, 218
Szurma, Bodhan, 58-9, 61, 63, 65, 67, 166, 219-20
Szurma, Maria, 58-9, 65, 67, 90, 92, 219-20
Szurma, Marianne, 59, 63, 64

Tape, 'hoax', 131, 132-9, 147, 183-4, 196, 235-7
Times, The, 224, 225

Walls, Marguerite (Margot), 185-7, 218
Whitaker, Josephine, 122-4, 125-9, 132, 157, 218, 246
Whitelaw, William, 149-50, 153, 154
Wilson, Ronald, 67-8
Windsor Lewis, Jack, 136, 138, 139, 147-9, 183, 236

Yorkshire Post, 24, 117, 149, 182, 216, 224, 227, 228
Young, Colleen, 57-8